Best Hikes With
CHILDREN®
in the Catskills & Hudson River Valley

Exploring near the base of Mine Kill Falls at the Mine Kill State Park

Best Hikes With
CHILDREN®
in the Catskills & Hudson River Valley

Cynthia C. Lewis
& Thomas J. Lewis

THE
MOUNTAINEERS

For Daniel and Cecelia Lewis, who accompanied us on our Catskills adventure. Their cheerfulness and boundless energy made the trip much more pleasurable for us, and for our daughters.

We would like to thank our parents, Daniel and Cecelia Lewis and Sharlene and Clayton Copeland, for cheerfully offering their child-care services while we completed the field work for this book. Thanks also to Neil Zimmerman and Daniel Chazin of the New York/New Jersey Trail Conference for reviewing the hikes. We also appreciate the efforts of Donna, Margaret, Marge, Rick, Kyle, Mike, and the other folks at The Mountaineers who have worked so hard on our hiking-guide series.

0 9 8 7 6
6 5 4 3

Published by The Mountaineers
1001 SW Klickitat Way, Seattle, Washington 98134

Published simultaneously in Canada by Douglas & McIntyre, Ltd., 1615 Venables Street, Vancouver, B.C. V5L 2H1

Published simultaneously in Great Britain by Cordee, 3a DeMontfort Street, Leicester, England, LE1 7HD

Manufactured in the United States of America

Edited by Miriam Bulmer
Maps by Debbie Newell
Cover and all other photographs by the authors
Cover design by Elizabeth Watson
Book layout by Bridget Culligan Design
Typography by Graphics West

Library of Congress Cataloging in Publication Data
Lewis, Cynthia Copeland, 1960-
    Best hikes with children in the Catskills & Hudson River Valley /
    Cynthia C. Lewis & Thomas J. Lewis
    p.   cm.
    Includes index.
    ISBN 0-89886-322-8
    1. Hiking—New York (State)—Catskill Mountains—Guidebooks.
2. Hiking—Hudson River Valley (N.Y. and N.J.)—Guidebooks.   3. Family recreation—
New York (State)—Catskill Mountains—Guidebooks.   4. Family recreation—Hudson
River Valley (N.Y. and N.J.)—Guidebooks.   5. Catskill Mountains (N.Y.)—
Guidebooks.   6. Hudson River Valley (N.Y. and N.J.)—Guidebooks.   I. Lewis,
Thomas J. (Thomas Joseph), 1958-   . II. Title.
GV199.42.N652C375 1992
917.47'38—dc20

                                                            92-5135
                                                            CIP

4

Contents

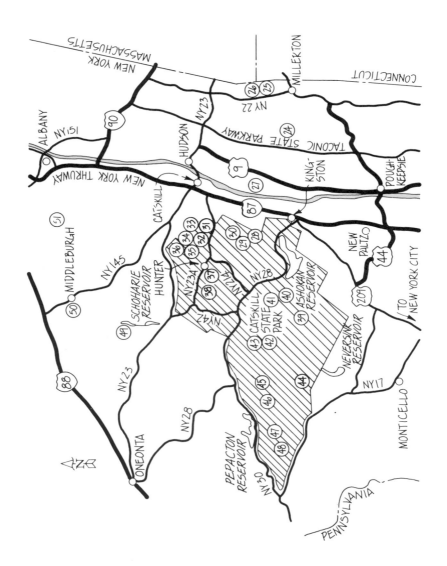

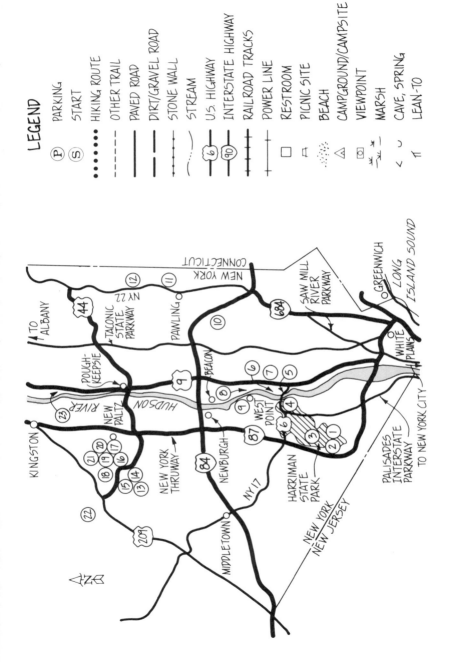

Introduction

You swear you have visited a video arcade for the last time, watched your last Ninja Turtles movie, taken your final ride on a loop-the-loop roller coaster. Meanwhile, the kids are boycotting art museums, flea markets, and anything that takes place on a stage and requires them to wear a necktie and/or dress shoes.

Is this the end of family togetherness?

No. It's time to take up hiking! Did you know that there are more than 800 miles of hiking trails within a one-and-a-half-hour drive of New York City? Healthier than cable TV and cheaper than downhill skiing, hiking is within everyone's capabilities and appeals to toddlers and teenagers, preschoolers and parents. We all love the outdoors, and hiking adds an element of adventure. What will we find around the next bend? A cave; a camping shelter; a waterfall, maybe?

Even though hiking with children requires a good deal more effort than hiking without children, it's worth the extra hassle. Kids notice clouds shaped like hippos and trees that look like witches; they delight in anthills and spider webs. Your daughter will point out everything in the forest that is her favorite color. (She'll also point out everything in the forest that is your favorite color, her cousin's favorite color, and her best friend Rachel's favorite color.) Your son won't remark or observe—he'll squeal, he'll shout, he'll exclaim! Kids react to these adventures the way we'd all like to, if only we didn't feel obligated to act so darned grown up. By taking little folks along, we're able to experience nature with renewed enthusiasm.

HIKING TIPS

Keep in mind the one basic rule for family hiking—it's got to be fun. Gear the trip toward your children's interests, needs, and capabilities. Try to envision the experience through their eyes, and plan accordingly. If the first few trips are memorable, they'll be eager to embark on more family adventures.

Here are a few pointers for hiking with young children.

- **Bring a little buddy.** A friend is a distraction from that blister and a deterrent to whining: nobody wants to look wimpy in front of a school chum.
- **Set a realistic pace.** A child's pace varies tremendously within the course of a walk—from ambling along, examining every stone, leaf, and blade of grass, to racing ahead like the lead runner in the New York City Marathon. By letting the child set the pace (within reason), you convey the message that a hike's success

is not measured in terms of miles covered but rather in the pleasure taken in each step.

• **Choose an appropriate hike.** When in doubt, easier is better than harder, but an athletic twelve-year-old will be bored with a mile-long amble through the woods that is better suited for a preschooler.

• **Give compliments.** Nothing means more to children than their father or mother patting them on the back and telling them they are the best climbers around. Such praise makes sore feet suddenly feel a whole lot better.

• **Make frequent stops.** A trailside boulder, a fallen tree, a breezy peninsula. . . . Children need more frequent rests than adults, but they tend to recover more quickly. Teach them to pace themselves; remind them as they dash out of the car that it will be a long climb to the summit.

• **Offer snacks.** Granola bars; bananas; cheese cubes; a mixture of nuts, chocolate chips, and dried fruits; boxes of raisins— bring along any favorite that will boost energy. Bring plenty of water, too.

• **Play games on the trail.** Suggest things for children to listen and look for: croaking frogs, deer tracks, acorns, birds flying south for the winter. Don't worry about making proper identifications; if you see something interesting just say "Look!" Offer incentives and distractions—"We're halfway there," "The waterfall is just over the hill"—and talk about the day's goals. Have fun—laughter lightens the load.

• **Encourage responsibility.** Children, like the rest of us, tend to meet the level of expectation. An older child given the responsibility of following the hike on the map, keeping an eye out for a loon through the binoculars, or charting directions with the compass will proudly fulfill his or her duties and be less likely to engage in horseplay.

• **Maintain a good attitude.** Misery is contagious, so even if you are anxious because you think it might rain or your pack has somehow doubled its weight in the last half mile, don't complain in front of your kids. A bad attitude will kill a good time much faster than a pair of soggy sneakers.

Stretching

The colder the weather, the more your muscles need stretching before the hike. Kids don't need to warm up as much as their parents do, but it won't hurt them. Stretch your calf muscles and hamstrings by leaning forward against the car or a tree and slowly lowering your heels until they touch the ground. Hold, rest, and repeat. For your quadriceps (front of the thigh), support yourself with one hand while you grab an ankle behind you with the other and pull it toward your buttocks. Hold the position, then repeat on the other side. Repeat these exercises after your hike as well to prevent cramping.

HIKING ETIQUETTE

Sometimes the very qualities that make children so much fun to have along on a hike can present the most problems. Adults recognize that what our ancestors referred to as "dismal wilderness" is our most valuable and threatened resource, but to children the outdoors is a vast playground. While the seven-year-old is gleefully stripping a boulder of its moss blanket in search of worms and beetles, his younger sister is stomping among the wildflowers reciting a spontaneous ode to posies. But by springing to the defense of each cluster of ferns, parents may be concerned that they will turn what should be a relaxed family outing into a running battle. How can parents creatively direct their children's enthusiasm toward nature-friendly pursuits?

Older children can anticipate the consequences of their own actions upon the environment. They will learn respect for the wilderness and its inhabitants from their parents' examples. By recycling, buying biodegradable products, and supporting environmental concerns, parents integrate a conservation ethic into the family's daily life so that "clean hiking" and "clean camping" come naturally to their children. Youngsters so raised understand that as hikers and campers they are becoming, for a time, part of the wilderness; they are not seeking to dominate or ruin it. Willingly, they'll "take nothing but pictures, leave nothing but footprints, and kill nothing but time." Children old enough to distinguish "safe" from potentially harmful trash can be encouraged to pick up the litter of previous hikers as well.

Younger children are more likely than older ones to act recklessly and without concern for the environment and its inhabitants. Offering desirable options rather than simply forbidding certain behavior works best with most children. Instead of picking a wildflower, your daughter can smell it, examine the petals under a magnifying glass, or take a photograph. Binoculars focus attention on soaring birds or far horizons. Such equipment retains its appeal when it is reserved just for special outings. One of the greatest gifts we can give our children is to instill in them a respect for the other living things that share our planet and an understanding of their own importance in determining the future of our natural environment.

Here are some specific ways that hikers can leave the forest without a trace.

- Prepare to take trash out with you by bringing along appropriate bags or containers. Educate your kids: a plastic container takes up to eighty years to decompose, a plastic bag up to twenty years, and a milk carton, five years.

- Stick to the trails. When presented with the choice of stepping on delicate vegetation or rocks, pick the rocks.
- Trails are most vulnerable during "mud season" in March and April; be especially careful then.
- Don't wash in streams or lakes.
- If rest room facilities are not provided, dig a small hole for human waste far from any water source and cover it with soil afterward.
- Conform to the specific regulations of the state park, wildlife refuge, or other recreation area you are visiting.
- Consider joining the hundreds of members of the New York–New Jersey Trail Conference who help pick up trash along the trails on Litter Day, an annual event.

Bushwhacking

To veteran hikers, even wilderness trails can begin to feel civilized. Often, these adventurous souls take to bushwhacking, using topographical maps to locate trailless peaks or leaving a blazed trail to make their own way through the forest. Despite the thrill of going where no one has seemingly gone before, we don't recommend bushwhacking for families. It's easy to get disoriented and tough to keep everyone together. Crashing through the underbrush is likely to scare off any animals or birds in the area; you'll probably see more wildlife if you stay on the trails since many animals follow the trails themselves. You may also inadvertently trample delicate vegetation or disturb a nesting site if you leave the path.

SAFETY

While you cannot altogether eliminate the risks inherent in hiking, you can minimize them by taking proper precautions and by educating yourself and your children. You should carry the supplies necessary (refer to the "Ten Essentials" on page 14) to combat the most frequently encountered problems. Recognize your own limitations and those of your children. Don't attempt to climb Indian Head Mountain (Hike 29) on your first family outing. If you're hiking with very young children, you will probably wind up carrying them, or at least their packs, for some of the way, so choose a hike that is well within your own capabilities.

Getting Lost

Although we have described as accurately as possible the trail conditions and routes, they may be different when you embark on a given hike. Blazes may be painted over, seasonal changes such as erosion or fallen trees might cause a trail to be rerouted, bridges and boardwalks could have collapsed. Change your plans if the trail seems too poorly marked to follow or if the condition of the trail is dangerous.

Prepare for the possibility of getting lost. Leave your itinerary with a friend or relative (or at the very least leave a visible note on the dashboard of the car) and be sure to sign and date the trail register. Carry enough extra food and clothing so that if an overnight is necessary, you are prepared.

Teach your kids to read maps and to pay close attention to trail markers and landmarks. On most marked trails, they should be able to see two blazes (one ahead of them and one behind them) at all times. Most trails are marked with paint blazes on trees or rocks. Cairns—small rock piles—indicate the route above treeline. Double blazes indicate a significant change of direction and triple blazes usually signal the end of the trail. Instruct children to look back frequently to see what the route will look like on the hike out.

You may want to insist on the buddy system or equip everyone with a whistle and establish a whistle code. Three blasts (or three puffs of smoke, three shots, and so forth) is the standard signal for help. Encourage little children to stay put as soon as they realize they are lost. Older children might be able to follow a river downstream or retrace their steps looking for particular landmarks. Above all, emphasize alertness and remaining calm. If you are unable to attempt a return to your car because you are lost or injured or both, make a fire using greens that will smoke and signal anyone looking.

Fire Towers

We have tried to note which fire towers seem dangerous, but you should inspect each one you intend to climb. Many fall quickly into a state of disrepair, some have been sold to private owners, others are in the process of being torn down. No matter what its condition, never use a fire tower for overnight camping.

Hypothermia

If children are particularly engrossed in what they are doing, they may ignore discomfort or an injury. Watch for signs of fatigue, then encourage a rest and food stop. Certain conditions, such as hypothermia, will affect a child sooner than an adult exposed to the same climate. Most cases of hypothermia occur in relatively mild temperatures of between 30 and 50 degrees Fahrenheit, often in windy or wet conditions. If a child seems listless and cranky (early signs of hypothermia), begins stumbling, and certainly once he or she complains of being cold, begins uncontrollable shivering, or exhibits impaired speech, add another layer of warm clothes or change the child into dry clothes, wrap the child in a sleeping bag, and offer a warm drink or soup.

Weather

Be conscious of weather conditions and do not hesitate to rechart your course because of a potential storm. Even the least challenging trail can pose a hazard in foul weather. And some of the toughest routes are nearly impossible to navigate in a blizzard or severe thunderstorm. The only thing worse than getting caught in bad weather while hiking is getting caught in bad weather while hiking with your children.

Remember: the higher the elevation, the colder, windier, and wetter it is likely to be. The tallest peaks in the Catskills region receive about 35 percent more precipitation than the Hudson River Valley. And the weather in New York City is no indication of the conditions in the mountains. The system that drops light rain in Manhattan may let loose a blizzard on top of Hunter Mountain.

Wildlife

The areas covered by this guide are known for their abundance of wildlife. We saw deer on nearly every hike, and smaller creatures such as porcupines, chipmunks, and rabbits frequently. Most encounters with wildlife are delightful surprises. When a hiking family meets a bear for the first time, however, it can be frightening. Between 800 and 900 bears live in the Catskills region, so if you camp and hike for an extended period, it's likely that you'll meet up with one. (We came upon five in a two-week period.)

There is actually little cause for worry. Unless you are situated between a mother bear and her cubs, any bears you encounter will likely lumber away as soon as they smell, see, or hear you. (Our five bears ran away from us much faster than we ran away from them.) Only when a bear refuses to flee after you've yelled or blown a whistle should you assume that it may be dangerous. In this case, back away slowly.

Campers can make bear encounters less likely by keeping food out of the animal's reach. String a rope at least 15 feet off the ground between two trees and hang bagged food from the rope, 6 feet away from any tree trunk. Never leave food in your tent or on the ground nearby.

EQUIPMENT

The "Ten Essentials"

The Mountaineers recommends ten items that should be taken on every hike, whether a day trip or an overnight. When children are involved and you are particularly intent upon making the trip as trouble-free as possible, these "Ten Essentials" may avert disaster.

1. Extra clothing. It may shower, the temperature may drop, or wading may be too tempting to pass up. Be sure to include rain gear, extra shoes and socks (especially a pair of shoes that can be used for wading when bare feet might mean sliced toes), a warm sweater, and hat and mittens.

2. Extra food. Too much is better than not enough. Carry sufficient water in canteens or fanny packs in case there is no suitable source on the trail.

3. Sunglasses. Look for a pair that screens UV rays. A wide-brimmed hat or visor also works to shade your eyes.

4. Knife. Chances are you'll never need it, but if you do and it's with the string and masking tape in the top drawer to the left of the refrigerator, you'll be sorry.

5. Fire starter—candle or chemical fuel. If you must build a fire, these are indispensable.

6. First-aid kit. Don't forget to include moleskin for blisters, baking soda to apply to stings, and any special medication your child might need if he or she is allergic to bee stings or other insect bites.

7. Matches in a waterproof container. You can buy these in a store that carries hiking and camping gear.

8. Flashlight. Before you begin your hike, check the batteries (and bring along extras).

9. Map. Don't assume you can just "feel" your way to the summit.

10. Compass. You don't need anything fancy—for under $10, you can find a sturdy, accurate compass at an outdoor equipment or sporting goods store. Teach your children how to use it, too.

In addition to the "Ten Essentials," a few other items can come in mighty handy, especially when young children are along.

Until you've hiked or camped during black fly season (mid-May through June), it's hard to understand how immensely annoying a swarm of these little buggers can be. Insect repellent doesn't deter all of them, but it helps. (Be sure the repellent you have is appropriate for children.) In addition to this protection, dress children in lightweight, long-sleeved shirts and long pants. A cap may come in handy as well.

Mosquitoes flourish in low, wet areas like swamps and seem to congregate around little children who haven't perfected their swatting techniques. A head cover made of mosquito netting (with elastic to gather it at the neck or waist) may be a hike saver. If you're surrounded and defenseless, try tucking a fern into the back of your shirt collar (my father-in-law swears by this technique) and give the kids fern "flags" to wave around.

Toilet paper may come in handy; a yard or two per person is usually enough for a dayhike. And don't forget to protect children from the sun. Kids can get sunburned even in wintertime, and their skin will burn faster at higher altitudes.

Binoculars, a camera, a magnifying glass, and a bag for collecting treasures are fun to have along and might keep children from trying to push each other into the brook.

In some parks, a fee is charged for entry or parking. These fees are generally minimal (between $1 and $5) and some, such as those for Audubon properties, do not apply to members. Be aware that fees increase and a place that only charged in-season or didn't charge at all when we did our research may have changed its policy. It's best to come prepared with some cash.

Leave your poodle, portable radio, and the kids' toys at home.

Footgear

In selecting footwear, make comfort the number-one priority. You do not want to find out two miles from the car that Mikey's boots (which were a tad small in the store but were half price) have turned his toes purple. Buying shoes that are too small, in fact, is probably the most common mistake new hikers make. Many stores specializing in outdoor equipment have steep ramps that you can stand on to simulate a downhill hike. If your toes press against the tip of the boot when you are standing on the ramp, try a larger size. Be sure to bring the liners and socks that you plan to wear on hikes for a more accurate fit. (In most cases, the sales people in sporting goods stores are very helpful and will be able to guide you to an appropriate pair of boots.)

You probably want lightweight, ankle-high, leather, or fabric-and-leather boots. Be sure they have sturdy soles and provide good ankle support and adequate resistance to moisture. In a few cases, sneakers

Brothers relax on the grassy bank of Rudd Pond.

or running shoes will be adequate, but on most trails, hiking boots are preferable. Especially if you will be doing a lot of hiking, invest in a good pair that will hold up to rugged terrain. (Be sure to wear new boots at home for several days before hitting the trails.)

In the wintertime, insulated boots are a must and in the spring or after a rainstorm, opt for waterproof boots. Snowshoes or cross-country skis can also be used for winter hikes on fairly level terrain, although I do not recommend winter hiking for children since it's not nearly as enjoyable for most kids as hiking in spring, summer, or fall.

Clothing

As with footgear, comfort is top priority. Think layers—they can be added or taken off as the temperature allows. Often, if you are visiting a ravine or heading to a summit, factors such as wind and temperature change noticeably. With layers, the moment you begin to feel warm you can remove an article of clothing to avoid becoming wet. In bug season, long sleeves and long pants are best. Jeans, a perennial favorite among kids, aren't necessarily the most comfortable walking pants. When wet they are very heavy and cold, seem to take forever to dry, and unless well-worn can be stiff as cardboard. A better bet might be sweatpants or lightweight slacks or tights. Be sure not to wear clothing that is too loose, since it will snag on branches and brush.

If you plan to hike in cool weather, consider synthetic thermal long underwear. Cotton tends to retain moisture, whereas polypropylene keeps it away from your skin. You don't want to perspire on your climb and then become chilled once you stop for a rest or head back to the car. Socks should be medium-weight and wool (even in warm weather); try the ragg-knit type found in most shoe or sporting goods stores. Wear a thin, silken liner under the socks. (Thick over thin will usually prevent blisters.) A hat will help keep the sun out of your eyes and the black flies out of your hair, and your head will be somewhat protected if a rain shower takes you by surprise.

A hooded rain poncho that can be folded up into a small pack is essential for every member of the family. Bring windbreakers if you're heading to a breezy summit. A few bandanas are not critical, but may prove handy for a multitude of annoyances such as runny noses, dirty hands and faces, cuts, and sunburned necks.

Packs

Older children will probably want to carry their own packs, while the little ones will want to move unencumbered. Child-size packs can be purchased at stores carrying hiking and camping supplies; be aware, though, that they can quickly become too small. Unless you have a number of other little hikers who will be using it, you may want to fill an adult pack with a light load instead. Kids like to carry their own liquids and snacks.

Adults should carry as light a load as possible in case a child needs or wants to be carried. Backpacks should have a lightweight but sturdy frame, fit comfortably, and have a waist belt to distribute the load.

Fanny packs (small pouches that strap around the waist) have become a popular accessory, especially with kids, and can be used to carry snacks, cameras, sunglasses, and other smaller items. One for each member of the group may hold all you'll need on a short dayhike.

Child-related Equipment

Infants can be carried easily in front packs. We took our oldest daughter on a mountain hike when she was just three weeks old. The walking rhythm and closeness to a parent is comforting to the littlest tykes. Older babies and toddlers do well in backpacks, where they can enjoy gazing around from a high vantage point. Look for a backpack that also has a large pouch for carrying other hiking essentials. (To keep backpacked toddlers amused, try filling a bottle with juice and several ice cubes—it's a drink and rattle in one!)

We have also used a carrier resembling a hip sling that will accommodate children up to four years old. Ours folds into a wallet-sized pouch and can be put on when the three-year-old has had enough walking for the day. Look for ideas in outdoor stores, toy stores, and stores specializing in baby furniture and supplies. Ask hiking friends what they have found useful and, whenever possible, try before you buy.

Overnight Equipment

You will need additional equipment if you plan to spend the night on the trail. Sleeping bags, foam pads, a small stove and cooking utensils, plus a tent or hammocks, are obviously needed. Generally, folks who work at stores stocking outdoor supplies will be more than willing to help you outfit your family for an overnighter. Trailside shelters, tent platforms, or lean-tos are available on some hikes. Learn everything about the accommodations (including whether you need to reserve or rent space) before your trip.

FOOD

If you are staying overnight, you may want to buy freeze-dried food, although the kids might prefer more familiar nourishment. While a food's nutritional value, weight, and ease of preparation should take precedence over taste, kids—even hungry ones—may turn up their noses at something that just doesn't taste right. You can try one-pot meals, such as chili or beef stew, or bring foods that require no cooking at all. Cooking equipment is cumbersome and it usually takes more time than you expect to prepare and cook the meal.

Dayhikers need easy-to-carry, high-energy snack foods. Forget about three filling meals; eat light snacks as often as you are hungry. The time of year will affect your choices: you won't want to be peeling an orange with fingers frozen by the cold—you're better off with meatballs. Nonsquishable fruit is good—try dried fruit, raisins, papaya sticks, and banana chips. Fig bars, cheese cubes, granola, and nuts are also hiking favorites. Let the kids help you mix chocolate chips, peanuts, raisins, and other "gorp" ingredients: it's cheaper than buying the ready-made trail mix. My kids like granola bars, store-bought or homemade. Often, we buy a loaf of our favorite bakery bread and a hunk of mild cheese that will appeal to the kids, and then hard boil some eggs to take with us. Let your family's taste buds and your good judgment determine what you bring.

Hikers need to drink frequently and the best way to ensure a safe water supply is to bring it along. The plastic water bottles used by bicyclists are easily packed. It's never a good idea to drink water from an unknown source, even in the wilderness. If you must, boil it for 20 minutes, use a commercial water filter, or treat it with an iodine-based disinfectant or halazone compounds to remove the *Giardia lamblia* parasite, which can cause symptoms ranging from cramps to diarrhea and vomiting.

CAMPING

Vandalism and overuse of trails has led to strict regulations regarding backpack camping. Where we've identified an agency or individual for you to contact for more information, refer to the "Addresses" section in the back of this book.

On New York's public forest lands, camping is prohibited within 150 feet of any road, trail, spring, stream, pond, or other body of water except at camping areas designated by the state. In the Catskill Park, camping is not permitted above the 3500-foot mark, except in an emergency or between December 21 and March 21. Overnight camping is permitted in state forests outside the Catskill Park. Of course, all garbage must be removed from state land.

A (free) camping permit is required for stays of more than three days; obtain one from the forest ranger in whose area the planned trip first enters onto state land. Groups of ten or more must obtain a group camping permit.

In most Wildlife Management Areas, camping is not permitted.

THE HIKING SEASONS

Although we indicate in each hike's information block the months when a trail is considered hikable (see "How to Use This Book," page 21), you can select an optimum time by being aware of certain seasonal hazards and pleasures.

Spring is the best time of the year to visit cascades, waterfalls, or any natural area where a heavy flow of water will add more drama and interest. But watch out for river crossings in the spring—August's tiny stream is often May's roaring, swollen river. Waterproof boots may be necessary since the ground is bound to be soggy. Step with care; trails are particularly susceptible to damage in the spring.

Mud season is as well known to folks in the Northeast as hurricane season is to those in the tropics. Many mountain access roads are dirt, and may be tough to navigate (or closed) in early and mid-spring.

Because March and April snowstorms are frequently the fiercest of the year in the north, we have often recommended May as the earliest hiking month. Even during the first few weeks in May, you're best off exploring drier trails at lower elevations. The pleasant weather in the lowlands often does not reflect harsh summit conditions.

Look for wildflowers that make an appearance in May: Dutchman's breeches, Canada violet, purple trillium, and trout lily are among those you will spot. Visit places where you'll be able to witness the bird migration.

One final springtime reminder: black flies and mosquitoes work overtime in May and June.

Summer is a terrific time to hike to cool ravines, breezy mountaintops, or lakeside parks with swimming or cookout facilities. (As summer progresses, the woods become drier, so be careful with campfires.) It's also the best time to camp, as the evenings will not be too chilly for kids. Of course, most folks recognize this and popular spots will be crowded. Whenever possible, hike midweek and avoid holiday weekends. Summer's longer days allow hikers to remain on the trail until well into the evening. Weekend hikers can get an early start to beat the crowds or head for more remote locations.

Winterlike conditions can descend upon the higher elevations even in midsummer, so be prepared with extra clothing.

Autumn in this region draws visitors from all over the country. This is the premier hiking season, offering hikers pleasant temperatures and colorful views. Look for spots from which to admire the blushing hills as well as the annual hawk migration, a spectacular sight.

Mid-November ushers in hunting season, so in most cases we have suggested that you hike through October (although small game hunting is permitted in October). If you elect to share the woods with the hunters, be sure to dress every member of your family in brightly colored clothing, including the characteristic orange hats worn by hunters, and make plenty of noise. Late fall can also bring unexpected snowstorms. As is the case in springtime, valley weather conditions do not reflect the conditions on top of the mountains.

Winter snowshoeing or skiing expeditions along the mountain trails are recommended for only the hardiest and most experienced hiking families. We have included a limited number of year-round hikes, most of them on flat terrain at lower elevations. Many access roads are closed in the winter (lengthening the hike considerably in some cases), and finding trail markers can be difficult. Often, snow and ice make the route dangerous. If you do embark on a winter hike, stick to easy, familiar trails, following a leader experienced in such outings. Expect the trip to take at least twice as long as the time we've allotted, and be conscious of the limited daylight hours.

Weather is likely to undergo abrupt and hazardous changes in the winter, especially in the mountains. The exposure and the wind-chill factor demand that kids be dressed as warmly and covered as completely as possible.

HOW TO USE THIS BOOK

This book covers the Hudson Valley and Catskills region of New York. The guide is divided into two broad geographical sections, with area maps that show the locations of the hikes.

Read the trip description thoroughly before selecting a hike. Each entry includes enough information for you to make an appropriate choice.

Name: The name of the mountain, lake, or park as it appears on most road maps.

Number: Use this to locate the hike on the map.

Type: There are two possible choices for each entry. A "dayhike" means that this hike can easily be completed in a day or part of a day for most families. There is no camping shelter or cabin along the route. "Dayhike or overnight" refers to trails on which there are designated campsites, lean-tos, or shelters. The overnight location is evident on the trail map. This indication does not necessarily mean that the hike is too long or difficult to be completed in an afternoon.

Difficulty: Hikes are rated for children on a scale of one to three hiking boots (easy, moderate, or difficult). Ratings are approximate, taking into consideration the length of the trip, elevation gains, and trail conditions. It's best to gain practice as a family on the easier trails, but don't reject a "difficult" hike before noting the turnaround point or reading about an optional shortcut.

Distance: This is the loop or round-trip hiking distance. If a side trip to a waterfall or view is included in the text and on the map, it is included in the total distance. An alternate route described within parentheses—whether it increases or decreases the total distance—is not factored into the total.

Hiking Time: This is an estimate based on hiking length, elevation gains, and trail conditions. Actual time will vary somewhat from family to family. Short rest stops are factored in—longer lunch stops are not.

High point/elevation gain: The first number given reflects the height above sea level of the highest point on the trail. The second number indicates the total number of vertical feet gained during the course of the hike. When analyzing a hike, the latter notation is more significant than the high point in determining difficulty.

Hikable: The months listed are when the trails are hikable. Hiking earlier or later may mean that you'll encounter icy terrain or potentially dangerous storms. See "The Hiking Seasons" on page 19 to get a better idea of appropriate hiking months.

Maps: We list New York/New Jersey Trail Conference maps by number. These maps, available from the New York/New Jersey Trail Conference (see "Addresses," page 217), provide the most current trail information. In some cases, the name of the topographic map published by the United States Geological Survey (USGS) is also included.

Many outdoor and office supply stores stock these maps, which are a good supplement to those in our guide because they include contour lines, which indicate elevations and terrain features. Be aware, however, that a trail may have changed since the map was printed (some USGS maps are quite old), so don't follow them exclusively.

Each entry is divided into three general sections: a summary or history of the hike and region, driving and parking instructions, and a complete description of the hike. The route is described for your hike in; any potential difficulties you may encounter on the return trip are addressed at the end of each entry. The symbols within the text, in the margins, and on the maps indicate turnaround points, views, campsites, picnic spots, and caution points. (See "Key to Symbols," page 29.)

Happy hiking!

AREAS COVERED BY THIS GUIDE
Bear Mountain–Harriman State Parks

Named for the railroad builder Edward H. Harriman, whose idea it was to set aside land in the Hudson Highlands for public enjoyment, Harriman Park was formally established in 1910 when Harriman's widow donated 10,000 acres to the state. Today, the combined Bear Mountain and Harriman state parks' 54,000 acres make up over 75 percent of the Palisades Interstate Park, extending from Newburgh to the George Washington Bridge.

Major William Welch, general manager and chief engineer of the Palisades Interstate Park from 1910 to 1940, created an extensive road system and numerous man-made bodies of water during his term. (Lake Welch, the park's newest artificial lake, was named for him.)

Most hikers prefer to explore the less developed areas of the park, following woods roads used by long-ago ironworkers. Between 1730 and the early 1900s, more than twenty iron mines operated here. At its peak, during the Civil War years, the iron industry ruled the area, supporting a sizable population. As the industry declined at the turn of the century, the workers moved away, leaving behind abandoned shafts, pits, and

Grandmother and granddaughter stroll along a Lake Minnewaska carriageway (Hike 15).

dumps, as well as decaying homesteads and crumbling foundations. Today hikers enjoy visiting these historic sites.

About 200 miles of blazed trails wander through the park, permitting visitors to choose from a wide range of hiking routes. Experienced hikers can opt to climb to the summits of the Timp, West Mountain (Hike 4), or Almost Perpendicular (Hike 2), while those who prefer flatter terrain may decide to weave among the rhododendron bushes near Pine Meadow Lake (Hike 1) or follow an old road to a forgotten mining village. From the New York Port Authority Bus Terminal, hikers can take public transportation to Bear Mountain–Harriman state parks.

Hudson Highlands

The Hudson Highlands brood over the Hudson River, flanking both the eastern and western rims of its rugged gorge from Newburgh to Peekskill. On the west bank, much of the land falls within the boundary of the Palisades Interstate Park; on the eastern side, it is part of the Taconic State Park. As dramatic as the sheer Hudson Highlands cliffs appear today (some stand 1600 feet over the river), they were many times higher before the great Ice Age glaciers wore down the peaks and filled the channel.

History comes alive in these hills, situated just 30 miles from New York City. During the Revolutionary War, the militia successfully defended Forts Montgomery and Clinton near Anthony's Nose (Hike 5), West Point, and Fort Hill and Defiance Hill (Hike 7), farther east. At one point during the war, a chain was stretched from West Point to Constitution Island, where the river narrows, to prevent enemy troops from advancing. Anthony's Nose is also the site of the old Manitou Copper Mine, which began operations in 1767.

The Hudson River Conservation Society began working to preserve the Storm King–Breakneck section of the Hudson River Valley in the early twentieth century, and by 1938 had convinced the owners of 177 acres on Breakneck Ridge to deed the property to the New York State Conservation Department. Thirty years later, the State Council of Parks began planning a program of scenic reservations in the Highlands area. Since that time, nearly 3800 acres have been obtained as part of Hudson Highlands State Park, including the Constitution Marsh property (Hike 8) now managed by the National Audubon Society.

The Taconic State Park and Recreation Commission controls the property on the river's eastern side, and the New York/New Jersey Trail Conference blazes and maintains the hiking trails.

This relatively wild, geographically rich area is unique in its proximity to a large city. New Yorkers are fortunate to have such prime hiking territory within a one-hour drive from Manhattan.

Hudson River

The Hudson River, an estuary, begins in the Adirondack Mountains of eastern New York and meanders generally southward for 315 miles to its mouth near New York City. The volume of fresh water generated in the Adirondacks, enhanced by tributaries and rainwater, pushes back the salt front from the Atlantic Ocean, halting it near Poughkeepsie. Thus, the water at Tivoli Bays (Hike 27) is fresh, while the water at Constitution Marsh (Hike 8) is discernibly salty.

More persistent than the salt front, the ocean tides extend northward to Troy, where the river's southernmost dam is situated, affecting the level of the water from 3 to 4 feet.

Poison ivy flourishes along the river's edge due to optimum soil conditions, humidity, and temperature. Teach your kids how to identify poison ivy, and have them wear long pants as an added measure of protection.

Shawangunk Mountains

The Shawangunk Mountain ridge, a distant piece of the Blue Ridge Range, stretches from the New York–New Jersey border northeastward to the Hudson River Valley near Kingston. Rising more than 2000 feet above sea level, this ridge has been drawing tourists for more than a century, ever since it became accessible by railroad from the Hudson River and New York City. Seasoned hikers can take on rugged mountain trails or the rocky cliffs of Bonticou Crag (Hike 21), while less experienced families can visit Lake Minnewaska (Hike 15) and follow the wide, level carriage roads that lead past lovely overlooks.

Two hundred miles of hikable trails and paths cross the Shawangunks, within the boundaries of both the Mohonk Preserve and Minnewaska State Park. The area is immaculately maintained, with rustic benches and gazebos punctuating the routes that visit the ghosts of grand turn-of-the-century hotels.

Rock climbers flock to the "Gunks" from all over the Northeast. The narrow ridge that falls away sheer to the valleys on either side is the result of differential erosion in which softer shale layers are worn down more quickly than the rest of the conglomerate. This makes the Shawangunks strikingly different from any other nearby range, and makes the cliffs ideal for climbing.

The Mohonk escarpments of Bonticou Crag, Sky Top (Hike 17), and Eagle Cliff highlight the ridge's low northern tip. As the ridge moves southward, it gains height and width. Five mountain lakes rimmed with jagged cliffs dot the range: Mohonk (1250 feet), Minnewaska (1650 feet), Awosting (1875 feet), Haseco or Mud Pond (1850 feet), and Maratanza (2250 feet).

Humans inhabited the Shawangunks as long ago as 6200 B.C., although their impact was not critical until the coal and tanning industries led to the destruction of the area's hemlock forests. The barrel hoop industry followed, further reducing the hemlock population.

Fires, fueled by the rotting hemlock trunks that littered the forest floor, significantly altered the landscape as well. Blueberry bushes, mountain laurel, and pitch pines flourished in the fire-scarred soil. Today, the forests are made up of red cedar, birch, white pine, and oak and maple varieties. As you hike, watch for signs of the deer and porcupines that thrive here.

Mohonk Area

The Mohonk estate stretches from Bonticou Crag to Millbrook Mountain, a distance of about 8 miles. Choices include short, easy strolls along wide paths near the Mohonk Mountain House and challenging hikes over rugged terrain in the more remote areas. From the short trip to Copes Lookout (Hike 18) to the wild excursion through the Labyrinth (Hike 19), this area offers a tremendous variety of hiking options.

The land holdings acquired during the nineteenth and twentieth centuries by the Smiley family have been divided into two separate properties: Mohonk Lake Resort includes the Mohonk Mountain House and its 2500-acre grounds; the Mohonk Preserve encompasses an undeveloped parcel of 5000 acres, accessed by carriage roads and hiking trails. An inexpensive permit is required to hike on either property.

In the years since 1869, when Albert K. Smiley bought the original 300 acres that included Mohonk Lake, more than 200 miles of scenic hiking trails and horse and carriage paths have been cut. The Smileys were pioneers in land conservation and construction of roads. Today, hikers benefit from their efforts and vision.

Minnewaska Area

The former Minnewaska Estate of 10,000 acres is now the Minnewaska State Park. A system of hiking trails and carriage paths crosses the park, which is situated primarily on the 2000-foot-high Shawangunk Mountain ridge, extending southward to Millbrook Mountain (Hike 14), a well-known viewpoint for hawk watching.

Lake Awosting (Hike 13) is the largest of the Shawangunk lakes and a popular hiking destination. From this pristine lake, most of the park's other points of interest are accessible.

The Catskills

The Catskills lie just north of the well-known metropolitan hiking areas and west of the central Hudson Valley. Although there is a good deal of development along the major roads, with motels, resorts, theme parks, and boardinghouses fighting for road frontage, the more remote parts of the Catskills are prime hiking territory. At least thirty-four peaks exceed the 3500-foot mark and nearly a hundred loom over 3000 feet. From barren ridges and summit clearings, the views of the Hudson Valley and New England mountain ranges are dramatic. Although a third of the highest peaks are accessible only to bushwhackers, hundreds of miles of trails lead through wilderness areas and over mountaintops. Families of all ability levels will find suitable hikes.

Geologists consider these "mountains" to be a massive plateau, one that was molded into peaks through millions of years of erosion and weathering. The bedrock configuration created in some instances asymmetrical ridges with one steep slope and one gently rising slope. The Escarpment (Hike 34), an example of this phenomenon, allows hikers to travel near the sheer edge of a ridge with unparalleled views over the valley and adjacent hills.

Because of disputes over land ownership during the 1600s and 1700s, the Catskills area remained relatively undeveloped for many years. The Industrial Revolution brought the hemlock-hungry tanning industry into the region, however, invading the wilderness and dramatically altering the natural landscape. Quarrying, logging, and farming also contributed to the destruction of the forests.

Some people did come to the area to enjoy, rather than destroy, the wilderness. During the nineteenth century, grand hotels were erected on many of the mountain summits. While most of these fell into disrepair over time, New Yorkers continued to flock to the Catskills to escape the hectic pace and crowded conditions of the city. Smaller hotels and boardinghouses opened to accommodate the steady flow of vacationers that continues today.

Southern Taconics

The Southern Taconic Highland stretches from New York's Harlem Valley to the Housatonic Valley of Connecticut and Massachusetts. The Southern Taconics are a klippe, a gigantic slice of rock that slid many miles from its original location about 440 million years ago.

The property is remote and undeveloped, with a network of trails that takes in waterfalls and ravines, wilderness lakes and views that extend to Mount Greylock northward and to the Catskill Mountains to the west. Much of the New York section of the highland falls within the boundaries of the Taconic State Park.

Like most in the region, the forests of the Southern Taconics are second or third growth, nourishing lush colonies of mountain laurel that bloom in June and July. Most of the land was cleared during the 1800s to provide charcoal for the booming iron industry. We have included several hikes that take in the lovely lakes of this region, including trips to Riga Lake (Hike 26), Rudd Pond (Hike 25), and Thompson Pond (Hike 24).

The Long Path

In the 1930s, a member of the Mohawk Valley Hiking Club of Schenectady suggested cutting a trail that would link New York City with the Adirondack Mountains. Little progress was made for nearly twenty years. Finally, in the 1950s, the acquisition of property for the Palisades Interstate Parkway made the project seem more feasible. It wasn't until 1981, however, that the New York/New Jersey Trail Conference, operating under a grant, developed the trail as it is today. Two hundred of the projected 400 miles have been blazed, with the path beginning on the New Jersey side of the George Washington Bridge and currently ending in the northern Catskills. Plans to continue the trail across the Mohawk Valley and into the Adirondacks await the completion of successful negotiations with landowners.

The turquoise-blazed Long Path offers hiking families challenging routes with superb views, since it tends to follow high mountain ridges. Hikes to Vernooy Kill Falls (Hike 22), Acra Point (Hike 36), and Boulder Rock (Hike 33), among others, follow sections of the Long Path.

The Appalachian Trail

The longest continuously blazed footpath in the world, the Appalachian Trail (AT) was originally proposed in 1921 as a way to preserve the wilderness and make it accessible to East Coast city dwellers. The AT was initially conceived as a path that would follow the backbone of the Appalachian Mountains, connecting existing trails.

The first section of trail, which began at the Bear Mountain Bridge (the lowest point along the AT's 2000 miles), was completed in the early 1920s. Under the umbrella of the Appalachian Trail Conference (formed in 1925), numerous hiking clubs worked on portions of the trail until its completion in 1937. To protect the trail from development, Congress passed the National Trails Systems Act in 1968, and designated the AT as a national scenic trail.

You will encounter sections of the AT as you hike to Anthony's Nose (Hike 5), West Mountain (Hike 4), and through Pawling Nature Preserve (Hike 11).

A NOTE ABOUT SAFETY

Safety is an important concern in all outdoor activities. No guidebook can alert you to every hazard or anticipate the limitations of every reader. Therefore, the descriptions of roads, trails, routes, and natural features in this book are not representations that a particular place or excursion will be safe for your party. When you follow any of the routes described in this book, you assume responsibility for your own safety. Under normal conditions, such excursions require the usual attention to traffic, road and trail conditions, weather, terrain, the capabilities of your party, and other factors. Keeping informed on current conditions and exercising common sense are the keys to a safe, enjoyable outing.

The Mountaineers

KEY TO SYMBOLS

 Dayhikes. These are hikes that can be completed in a single day. While most trips allow camping, few require it.

 Backpack trips. These are hikes whose length or difficulty makes camping out either necessary or recommended for most families.

 Easy trails. These are relatively short, smooth, gentle trails suitable for small children or first-time hikers.

 Moderate trails. Most of these are 2 to 4 miles total distance and feature more than 500 feet of elevation gain. The trail may be rough and uneven. Hikers should wear lug-soled boots and be sure to carry the Ten Essentials (see "Safety" in the introduction).

 Difficult trails. These are often rough, with considerable elevation gain or distance to travel. They are suitable for older or experienced children. Lug-soled boots and the Ten Essentials are standard equipment.

 Hikable. The best times of year to hike each trail are indicated by the following symbols: flower—spring; sun—summer; leaf—fall; snowflake—winter.

 Driving directions. These paragraphs tell you how to get to the trailheads.

 Turnarounds. These are places, mostly along moderate trails, where families can cut their hike short yet still have a satisfying outing. Turnarounds usually offer picnic opportunities, view, or special natural attractions.

 Cautions. These mark potential hazards—cliffs, stream crossing, and the like—where close supervision of children is strongly recommended.

1. Pine Meadow Lake

Type: Dayhike
Difficulty: Moderate for children
Distance: 4.0 miles, loop
Hiking time: 2.5 hours
High point/elevation gain: 1260 feet, 620 feet
Hikable: March–November
Map: NY/NJ Trail Conference Map 3

It's not always easy to maintain your kids' interest in family hiking: cable television's seventy-odd channels, the latest rap recordings, and the newest video games provide stiff competition. That's why every hike in this book is loaded with neat "kid features."

On this route, which encompasses Pine Meadow Lake and Diamond Mountain, children can search for frogs in a swamp, skip stones on the calm water of a lake, play "King of the Mountain" on mammoth boulders, and pretend to be giants on a safe, sheltered summit. Brief ascents and descents, as well as numerous trail junctions, keep the kids focused between the various points of interest.

Beat that, Nintendo!

 From New York City, take the Thruway North to Exit 15. Follow NY Route 17 North approximately 4.5 miles. Just past the village of Sloatsburg, turn right onto Seven Lakes Drive at a sign indicating the entrance to Harriman State Park. Continue for about 4.3 miles, passing by Lake Sebago on the left, and turn left into a driveway (the second driveway to the left after you cross the dam at the outlet to Lake Sebago), which leads to a parking area for boat launching, hiking, and fishing. (Swimming is not permitted in this area.)

Walk back along the driveway to Seven Lakes Drive and cross the road. Look for the Seven Hills trailhead (marked with a "7"), blazed in blue-centered white circles. Head southward on this footpath, marching uphill for 0.3 mile through spacious woods. (Make sure kids know the rule: whiners must walk backward for 30 paces!) Loose rocks litter the way as you gain altitude; kids may need some help to keep from slipping. The trail widens and crests, then embarks on a gentle descent. Look for clusters of blueberry bushes along the way.

At 0.6 mile, meet a woods road (Woodtown Road) at an intersection marked with double blazes. Turn left (east), and cross a trickling seasonal stream on a row of rock slabs. Can you spot any beebalm (also called Oswego tea) sprouting along the bank? This wildflower appears

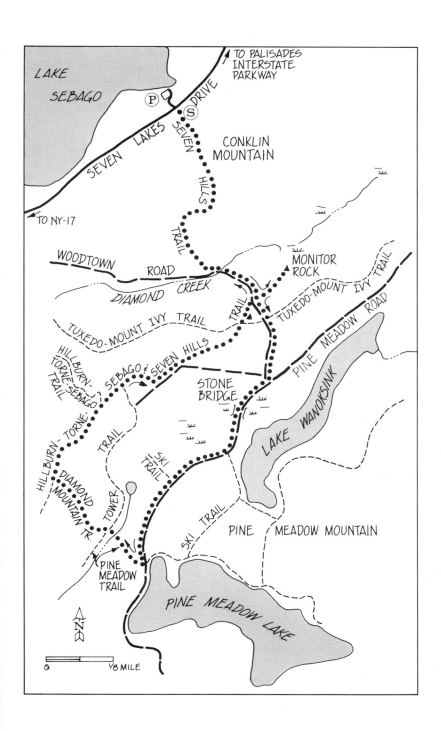

in late summer, growing along streams like this one. At 0.7 mile from the start, the white-on-blue-blazed trail turns right off Woodtown Road as you follow a white-blazed side trail left toward Monitor Rock. Push through blueberry and laurel bushes for 0.1 mile to crest a block of ledge offering seasonal views and crowned by two impressive glacial boulders. Can anyone scramble up one of these?

Return to Woodtown Road and turn left, soon crossing the Tuxedo–Mount Ivy Trail, blazed with red dashes on white. Now descending gradually, continue on Woodtown Road for 0.25 mile to a junction with gravel Pine Meadow Road. Turn right (southwest) onto Pine Meadow Road. On the left, a swamp encroaches on the road; shortly, you cross the swamp outlet over a stone bridge. If the kids need a rest, let them sit near the swamp and just observe for a few minutes. What kinds of insects scoot across the water or hover above it? What sounds do they hear? Can they describe various smells?

At 1.35 miles from the start, avoid a cross-country ski trail that turns left (south); continue straight (southwest) on Pine Meadow Road near the swampy bank of Lake Wanoksink. At 1.8 miles, head straight across the white-on-red-blazed Pine Meadow Trail to arrive at the northwestern shore of pristine Pine Meadow Lake. Spread out a picnic lunch on the sunny, sloping ledge that slides into the water. Adults can take in the sun while the kids explore the water's edge. Swimming is not permitted, but there are no rules against stone-skipping contests, frog "hunting," or water bug collecting. Do you see any turtles basking in the sun on the rocks near the edge of the lake? Of all of the turtles native to the area,

Exploring the rocky shoreline of Pine Meadow Lake

the snapping turtle is the largest. Its shell is between 8 and 18 inches long, but it is not large enough to shelter the large limbs, head, and tail of the snapper. Thus, powerful jaws allow this turtle to defend itself against predators.

To begin the return trip, turn left (northwest) onto the Pine Meadow Trail (another trail blazed with red squares on white). Drop modestly down a rugged path, crossing a seasonal stream. Quickly, at a junction, continue straight (northwest) on the white-blazed Diamond Mountain Trail as the yellow-blazed Tower Trail splits right and the Pine Meadow Trail turns left (southwest). Begin an ascent up the southern slope of Diamond Mountain. Similar to the ascent at the start of the hike, this climb is steady and rugged.

At 2.1 miles, the trail opens onto a grassy plateau that nourishes a few scrub oaks. Instruct the kids to keep a careful watch for blazes, often splashed on rocks rather than trees. As you cross the broad, open summit of Diamond Mountain, cropped panoramic views take in Lake Sebago. There's no need to worry about curious kids: this is a child-friendly summit with no sudden drop-offs, no sheer cliffs, no dilapidated fire towers.

Cresting, the Diamond Mountain Trail ends at an intersection with the Seven Hills and Hillburn-Torne-Sebago trails. Turn right (northeast) to follow the combined white/white-on-blue trail. Track across exposed ledge on level ground. If the kids are startled by a snake darting in front of them, remind them that most snakes you'll encounter on any hike in the Northeast are common garter snakes. Because they live primarily on an earthworm diet, garter snakes have flourished despite human intrusion and development. If you hike in midsummer, you might spot baby garter snakes; females give birth to between twelve and seventy-two live offspring in July and August.

Almost 2.5 miles from the start, the combined trail splits: the white Hillburn-Torne-Sebago Trail departs left as you follow the blue-on-white Seven Hills Trail straight. To the left, Lake Sebago shimmers far below. In another 0.1 mile, the yellow-blazed Tower Trail merges from the right (east). Stay straight here also, following the blue-on-white Seven Hills Trail.

Beyond this junction, drop gently on ledge as an even better view of Lake Sebago emerges. The trail snakes through patches of blueberries, searching for the easiest route off the mountain. Briefly join a woods road before double blazes guide you northeastward, back into the woods, as the woods road departs right. At the base of ledge, you meet the trail marked with red dashes on white. As this trail bears right, bear left over more ledge, through lush colonies of laurel. Let the kids run ahead with instructions to wait for you beside the huge, cracked erratic boulder known as the "cracked diamond." (We thought it looked like a giant mouth. What do you think?) At 3.25 miles, turn left onto Woodtown Road and retrace the initial 0.7 mile, following the blue-on-white blazes of the Seven Hills Trail back to your car.

2. Almost Perpendicular

Type: Dayhike
Difficulty: Moderate for children
Distance: 1.6 miles, round trip
Hiking time: 1.5 hours
High point/elevation gain: 900 feet, 400 feet
Hikable: March–November
Map: NY/NJ Trail Conference Map 3

Almost Perpendicular is almost too good to be true! This south-facing ledge on Daters Mountain, which we judged to be the "Best Overlook in Harriman State Park," is less than a mile from the trailhead. Its dramatic views will appeal to little people as well as big people. While the kids may not be interested in identifying distant peaks or hills, they will feel like giants as they watch the Matchbox-size cars racing along the highway below. And it won't be hard to keep them on the wide, grassy expanse set back from the edge.

On the return trip, have the kids lead the way. Allow enough time for wrong turns and let the leaders discover their own mistakes. It's the only way to learn.

 From New York City, take the Thruway North to Exit 15. Follow NY Route 17 North approximately 4.5 miles. Just past the village of Sloatsburg, turn right onto Seven Lakes Drive at a sign indicating the entrance to Harriman State Park. Continue on Seven Lakes Drive for about 0.7 mile, passing under the thruway. Where a sign indicates that you are entering Harriman State Park, turn left, then turn right at a T-intersection onto Johnstontown Road. Drive 1.3 miles to the end of Johnstontown Road and park at the cul-de-sac.

About 100 feet southwest of the cul-de-sac on Johnsontown Road, follow a wide gravel road that tunnels through the woods on the right (northwest) past a huge erratic boulder. The Blue Disc Trail, indicated by white blazes with blue centers, narrows to exclude vehicular traffic as it passes a natural-gas pumping station on the right within the first 0.1 mile. (Tell the kids to pay close attention to landmarks such as this and to trail junctions because they will lead on the hike out. Such an exercise teaches critical outdoor skills and focuses kids' attention on their surroundings.) Begin a short, moderate ascent and hunt for textures: look for something smooth, something fuzzy, something rough, and something prickly.

At 0.15 mile, a grassy path continues straight (north) as you bear left (west), still on a gravel road following blue-on-white blazes. Avoid

"What made these holes, Dad?"

unmarked side trails splitting left and right. At 0.45 mile, the road forks: follow the right (northwest) branch. In 75 feet, the white-blazed Kakait Trail angles in from the right; in another 125 feet, this white trail departs left (south). (Are the kids paying attention?) As you stay true to the two-colored blazing, look right, through the spacious oak forest, to see a boulder slide, evidence of nearby cliffs.

The road narrows to a path and embarks on a moderate ascent at the 0.5-mile mark. Now have a scavenger hunt for sounds. Can you hear distant highway noise? The chattering of red squirrels? The tapping of a woodpecker? What else? When you reach the base of the boulder slide, navigating the jumble of stones will be a challenge for little legs. At 0.65 mile from the start, the slope steepens and double blazes indicate a northeastward bend. Follow the footholds worn by previous hikers who trudged up this stiff incline.

By 0.7 mile, the trail has leveled. Cross a seasonal stream and curl left to follow its bank briefly. Soon, the trail twists right and resumes a steep climb between ledge outcroppings. Look ahead to see blue sky; shortly, you will crest the exposed ridge. Here, leave the main trail (which veers left) and turn right (east), soon reaching Almost Perpendicular.

What a tremendous overlook! The ledges step down to precipitous cliffs, so encourage children to stay well back from the edge and remain where the broad summit is open and grass-covered. Dramatic southwest-

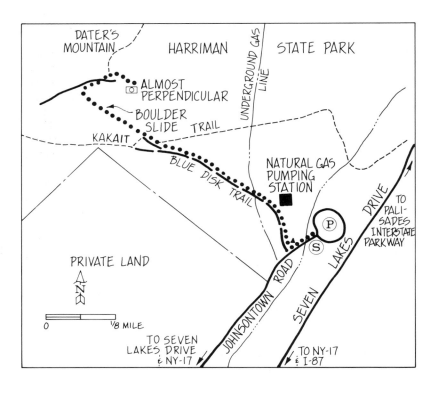

ern and eastern views take in Ramapo Torne, the New York Thruway, and the Ramapo Mountains of New York and New Jersey. Enjoy the views, unpack the picnic lunch, chat with other hikers, fly a kite! When you're ready, return to your car the way you came. (Remember: Let the kids lead on the way back.)

---

3. Pine Swamp Mine

Type:	Dayhike
Difficulty:	Easy to moderate for children
Distance:	3.1 miles, loop
Hiking time:	2.5 hours
High point/elevation gain:	1180 feet, 300 feet
Hikable:	March–November
Map:	NY/NJ Trail Conference Maps 3 and 4

Within the last three centuries, more than twenty iron mines were opened and worked in the Hudson Highlands and the area now known as Bear Mountain and Harriman state parks. The iron they produced was shipped to England during the early 1700s to be turned into tools, nails, cooking utensils, and other common articles. In this period of taxation without representation, duties were collected on both trips. King George III's iron manufacturing policy (along with his stamp and tea taxes, of course) was highly unpopular with the colonists, leading, eventually, to the Revolutionary War.

Today, the open mine shafts and mammoth pits are fascinating to visit. Pine Swamp Mine, your goal on this trip, is the largest remaining mine with a slanting chamber that is open for exploration. The mine workers had homes nearby that they were forced to abandon when the mines closed; some foundations are still apparent along the Dunning Trail. The occasional apple tree or lilac bush is a living reminder of the families who once inhabited the area.

This loop hike is well suited for inexperienced hiking families or for folks whose desire for an unusual adventure surpasses their endurance levels.

From New York City, take the Thruway North to Exit 15. Follow NY Route 17 North approximately 10.5 miles. At a traffic light, bear left where a sign indicates a turn for Harriman State Park. Go up a ramp and, at the top, make a right on Orange County 106. Continue for 4.2

miles to the Kanawauke Circle. Go around the circle and turn onto Seven Lakes Drive North. Proceed for 0.75 mile and, at a sign for "FISHING ACCESS," turn left into a driveway. Continue down the driveway to a large parking area at Lake Skannatati, and leave your car here.

From the northern end of the parking area, duck into airy, rock-strewn woods on the Arden-Surebridge (ASB) Trail, marked by red triangles inside white rectangles. (Do you have any preschoolers learning shapes and colors? Put them in charge of finding the sharp, frequent blazes.) Pass near the northern end of Lake Skannatati and angle right, away from the water, heading northwestward. One-tenth mile from the start, the trail climbs up a moderate slope toward a ledge and rock area. As you track through slabs of ledge and mounds of glacial boulders, you'll pass kid-size caves on either side. Since everyone knows that kids and caves go together like cookies and milk, plan to pause here to let the little ones do some investigating.

After a short uphill scramble, the trail begins to hook left, cresting a grassy plateau that nourishes a few oak trees. Can you find a double acorn? As you continue, watch for blueberry bushes edging the trail, and do some picking if the berries are ripe. At an intersection 0.35 mile from the start, bear left (west), still following the familiar red-and-white blazes, as the Red Cross Trail departs right (northeast). Beyond the intersection, the woods open up, allowing you to view Lake Skannatati on the left. As you wander through the pleasant woodlands, choose categories (birds, tree stumps, toadstools . . .) and see how many of each you can find.

Scale a section of ledge and then drop gently down the other side. If the kids are getting restless, play "Name that Tune": take turns singing the first few notes of familiar melodies while the others guess the title. The trail trends northward as it descends, then swings back to resume a westerly course at 0.5 mile. From a sag rimmed with hemlocks, look left to see the mucky edge of Pine Swamp.

Laurel crowds the trail at 0.75 mile as you roll over gentle hills through more hemlock forest. Approaching the swamp, the spongy trail crosses a seasonal stream and snakes up a slope to crest a knoll. After a moderate to steep descent, bear left at double blazes to dodge an area littered with boulders. As you pass a large glacial erratic boulder (who will be king of this "mountain"?), point out the rust-colored earth to the kids as you climb the slope. What mineral causes the discoloration? (It's the iron.)

When the trail meets an old woods road that heads right (northeast) and left (west), turn left, still following the red-and-white-triangle blazing. Almost immediately, cross a seasonal brook on stones. Who took the fewest number of steps to get across?

At 1.2 miles, just beyond another stream crossing, turn left (south) onto the yellow-blazed Dunning Trail, a woods road, as the ASB Trail continues straight. As you pass through stands of hemlock and white

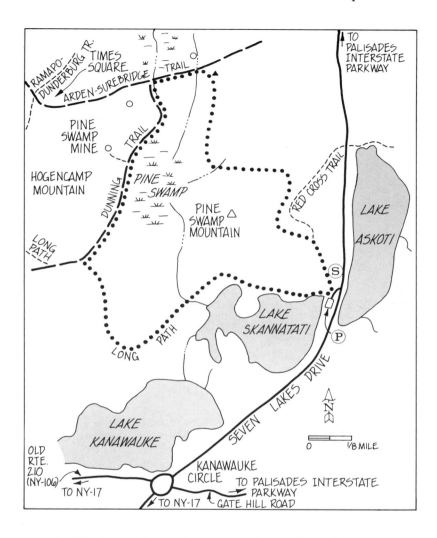

pine, find the largest hemlock cone and the smallest white pine cone. Which is bigger? Hemlock needles are flat; can you name the only other tree with flat needles? (The fir tree.)

Pine Swamp washes toward the road on the left. One-tenth mile from the last intersection, as the edge of the swamp meets the path, look to the right up a steep slope for unblazed side trails. Take a trail, any trail: all lead in 0.1 mile to Pine Swamp Mine on the east side of Hogencamp Mountain. Encourage the kids to stay with you as you enter the mine, a tremendous man-made cavern. It's relatively safe to explore, since the

On a sweltering summer's day, hikers plod through open woodlands near Lake Skannatati.

floor slopes upward, but keep kids away from the cavity at the base, which is full of water. (The abandoned mines are 10 feet to 6000 feet deep. The Forest of Dean Mine, worked from 1754 to 1931, was the deepest—and most productive—mine, although no one can locate it today. The entrance was sealed off long ago and it is believed to be buried on land owned by the U.S. Military Academy.)

Back on the Dunning Trail, ask the kids to list the animal sounds they hear: frogs conversing in the swamp, squirrels scampering through layers of leaves, birds piping overhead. What animals can you see? As we walked along the road, we met two lovely fawns. (Your chances of seeing a deer are greater if you move quietly.) Do you see any signs of deer? Look carefully along the ground for tracks. Examine the double-tear-shaped hoof marks: if the toes are together, the deer was walking when it made the print; if the toes are separated, the deer was running. Look for deer droppings (small cylindrical pellets), and signs that twigs were torn from low thickets. In early fall, check young trees for antler rubbings; deer rub their mature antlers to remove a velvety covering.

Departing the swamp, the trail rises gradually and, 1.85 miles from the start, meets the rugged, turquoise-blazed Long Path. Turn left (southeast), stepping down a grassy, rock-covered slope. As you descend, pass through dense thickets of mountain laurel, sometimes referred to as "laurel slicks" or "laurel hells." This shrub, native in the Northeast, is quite common, and grows in low clusters when young, attaining heights up to 13 feet. Can you find the shortest and tallest bushes within this "slick"?

Two and one-half miles from the start, the trail snakes past impressive ledge outcroppings and then crosses an active stream on stones. To the right, you can see Lake Skannatati. Appoint a young hike leader here to guide the group on the upcoming descent. Tumble down the soggy slope, hopping from one stone to the next behind your leader. The trail pitches and heaves over rugged ground, angling closer to the lake. One-half mile from the stream crossing, after skirting the northern rim of the lake, you reach the parking area and your car.

Note: The park closes at dark. Swimming is permitted only at protected beaches and pools; boating is by permit only. Camping, picnicking, and fires are confined to designated areas.

4. West Mountain

Type: Dayhike
Difficulty: Challenging for children
Distance: 4.6 miles, loop
Hiking time: 5.5 hours
High point/elevation gain: 1250 feet, 800 feet
Hikable: March–November
Map: NY/NJ Trail Conference Map 4

When everyone's boots are broken in and you feel up to tackling a real mountain, spend a day exploring West Mountain in the northeastern region of Bear Mountain and Harriman state parks. After a solid climb, you'll be treated to expansive views from West's lengthy, exposed ridge-top summit. And since the ridge is safe for little hikers, with no sheer drop-offs, parents can relax and enjoy the panoramas.

Harriman State Park is named for Edward R. Harriman, a nineteenth-century financier and railroad magnate who wanted to establish a state park in the region. In 1910, his widow, concerned about plans to build

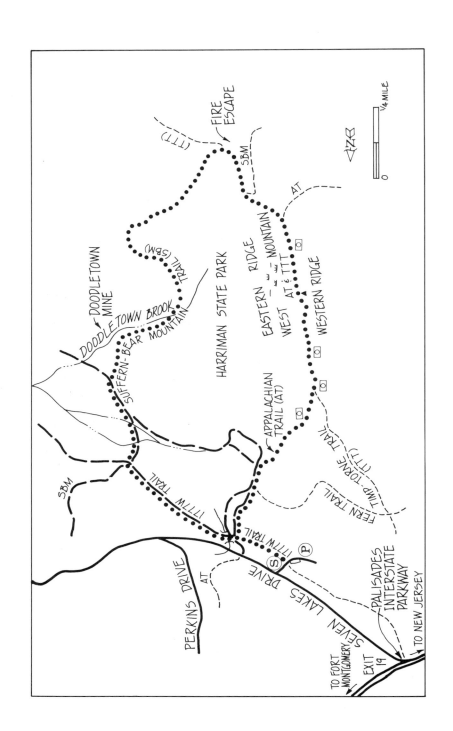

a prison near Bear Mountain, donated 10,000 acres of land for a park—with the understanding that the state would take its outlaws elsewhere, of course. The park has since expanded to cover 52,000 acres.

From New York City, go over the George Washington Bridge and take the Palisades Interstate Parkway North to Exit 19. Drive 0.5 mile south on Seven Lakes Drive and turn right into a narrow, paved driveway. In about 0.1 mile, the driveway ends at a substantial parking area.

Look for the meager trailhead on the eastern side of the parking area. Follow the white diamond blazes of the 1777W Trail, marked "1777," up a moderate, wooded slope, heading southeastward. The trail is fringed with mountain laurel and blueberry bushes. At a junction, turn left (east), guided by the white 1777W blazes, as an unblazed path continues straight. Drop off the ridge and meet a wide woods road near Seven Lakes Drive. Turn right (south), now following the white rectangular blazes of the Appalachian Trail (AT).

Quickly you reach a major intersection with hiking trails, skiing trails, and woods roads radiating in all directions. Turn right (south) to follow the white AT blazes on an old road, departing the 1777W Trail. Initially, the trail parallels a southeast-bound ski trail; after a brief ascent, it bears left to join the ski trail. Shortly, continue straight as the Fawn Trail joins from the right. Ask the kids for help in finding upcoming blazes—they are hard to spot in this open forest.

At 0.65 mile, double blazes indicate a significant change in direction: turn right (southwest) with the AT as the ski trail heads southeastward. March upward on a rocky trail, crisscrossed by roots, that leads through pockets of mountain laurel. As you climb the airy, rock-strewn eastern slope of West Mountain, the grade steepens. Distract the kids by singing songs, playing memory games, or telling silly riddles. Look behind you at the Bear Mountain summit and lookout tower and the Hudson River.

At 0.9 mile from the start, reach the West Mountain summit plateau, an extensive, grassy ridge with outstanding views of the Hudson River Valley and Bear Mountain. The trail, struggling to be seen under layers of wild grasses, curls southward and flirts with the ridge's eastern edge. As you take in the wonderful northern and eastern views, try to find Anthony's Nose (Hike 5). (Remember, Anthony's lying down!) March along the eastern flank of the mountain for 0.1 mile before veering right (south), and slipping into a col. Embark on a short, steep climb up a river of boulders, but follow the AT blazes left (east) partway up, avoiding the roughest section.

One-tenth mile from the eastern ridge, the AT crests on the western ridge of the mountain, after being joined from the right by the blue-blazed Timp-Torne (TT) Trail. Bear left (south) to follow the combined TT and Appalachian trails, taking in great views to the east and west. Stop for a snack and an extended look at the panoramas on one of the rock outcroppings. Watch the cars glide along the snaking Palisades

Interstate Parkway far below.

As you continue southward, the combined trail defines the contour of the ridge, first dipping slightly, then ascending. One and one-tenth miles from the start, leave the exposed western rim and return to the ridge's sparsely wooded center. March down this midsection for 0.2 mile, until suddenly you face a formidable piece of ledge. The blazes lead over the exposed top, although a 30-foot drop-off on the right makes this a little treacherous for youngsters. Offer assistance or, to save a little one's pride, ask him or her to take your hand and help you across. Beyond the ledge, the trail slides between more hunks of ledge, sweeps right, and reaches the base of the massive ledge you just crossed. The igneous

Let the kids run ahead and wait for you atop a "resting rock."

rock that crowns the summit of this mountain is typical of the Highlands region, and is known for its ability to resist erosion.

Trending southwestward once more, the trail returns to the edge of the western ridge at 1.4 miles, treating hikers to more lovely views of the rolling countryside. Can you find signs of an old burn here? If you're hiking in August, you'll appreciate the stiff breeze that sweeps along this ridge. Do any of the kids know what makes a breeze? Let everyone take a guess before you give the answer: a change in temperature. Air expands and rises as it heats up and cooler air rushes in to take its place, causing the movement of air that we call wind.

Who will be the first to spot the small erratic boulder perched on the edge of the ridge, 1.5 miles from the start? Scale a final hill to reach the height of the land and follow the combined TT and Appalachian trails for another 0.2 mile, enjoying more commanding views. Pass around the binoculars to watch kettles of hawks riding the thermal updrafts. Explain to the kids that one way thermals are created is by wind sweeping across a valley and being diverted upward by a mountain. The rising air cushions the hawks, allowing them to glide without effort and conserve energy, which is especially important during migration seasons. In fact, hawks seek migratory routes punctuated by geographical features (such as valleys and mountains) that are likely to produce thermals.

At 1.8 miles, turn left (southeast) at a junction to follow the blue-blazed TT Trail, guided by a sign to the West Mountain shelter; the white-blazed AT continues straight (southwest). Soon, continue straight as the yellow-blazed Suffern–Bear Mountain (SBM) Trail joins from the right. Delightful views persist until the combined trail drops into a sag choked with laurel and blueberry bushes.

Depart the TT Trail at 2.25 miles; its blue blazes lead right (southeast) as you turn left (northeast), now guided solely by the yellow markings of the SBM Trail. After curling eastward, the trail drops beside a rock slide at 2.4 miles, then scrambles uphill about 0.2 mile later. In another 0.3 mile, you plummet down a rugged hillside, the pitch easing as you descend. At 3.2 miles, cross Doodletown Brook on stones. Follow yellow blazes along the northern bank of the stream for 0.3 mile.

As it cuts left (north), away from the brook, the trail widens into a woods road and soon intersects a red-blazed ski trail. Turn left (northwest) as the SBM Trail joins the ski trail. In another 0.15 mile, watch carefully for the yellow blazes as the SBM Trail veers right, away from the ski trail, and inches up a short rocky ridge, then rolls over uneven terrain. After crossing a pair of streams, turn left (north) onto the wide, gravel 1777W Trail (diamond blazes, remember?), 4 miles from the start. Here, the SBM Trail and a cross-country ski trail depart right (east).

At 4.3 miles, cross a footbridge over a stream and in another 0.2 mile meet the AT. Cut straight across the intersection, on a familiar section of the 1777W Trail, and follow it for 0.3 mile to your car.

5. Anthony's Nose

Type: Dayhike
Difficulty: Moderate for children
Distance: 2.2 miles, round trip
Hiking time: 1.5 hours
High point/elevation gain: 900 feet, 700 feet
Hikable: March–December
Map: NY/NJ Trail Conference Map 1

In twenty minutes, you and your kids could watch two-thirds of a sitcom, lose $7 or $8 at a video arcade, or be halfway to Anthony's Nose. It's up to you. This being a hiking guide, we'll elaborate on the third option. You follow the famous Appalachian Trail for the first 0.5 mile, and then a gently rising woods road brings you to the tip of the big guy's nose. Here, the kids will have a giant's perspective on two impressive sights, one natural and one man-made: Bear Mountain and the bridge of the same name that spans the Hudson River. Bring binoculars to survey the countryside, extra shoes for wading in the frog pond, and containers for collecting blueberries at the summit (if you hike in midsummer).

The choice is yours, of course. Watching a rerun of "Three's Company" does sound tempting. . . .

 From New York City, take the Thruway North to Exit 9 in Tarrytown. Follow US 9 North to Peekskill and turn left onto the combined US 6 and US 202 just north of Peekskill, as US 9 continues straight (north). Follow US 6 and US 202 to the Bear Mountain Bridge, but do not cross the bridge. From the junction of US 6, US 202, and NY 9D on the east side of the Bear Mountain Bridge, follow NY 9D north. Watch for the Putnam County line and a sign with a hiker symbol 0.2 mile from the bridge. Drive another 0.1 mile and park in a small turnout on the right side of the road. (No parking on the roadway from midnight to 7 A.M.)

Carefully backtrack on NY 9D for 0.1 mile to the trailhead, indicated by the sign with the hiker symbol and the white blazes of the Appalachian Trail (AT) on a telephone pole. Head northward up a wooded slope. Quickly, the rocky path bends left (north). On the right, a rock slide tumbles down the hillside toward you; on the left, a side path descends to the road. The kids can search along the trail for sturdy walking sticks to assist them on the climb.

At 0.2 mile, a trail sign announces that Viewpoint Trail is 0.4 mile away and Hemlock Springs campsite is another mile beyond that. As you

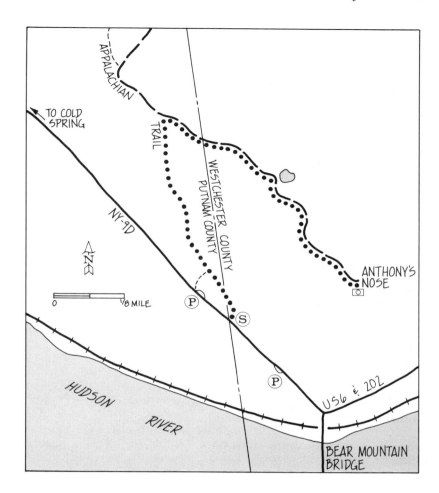

mount stone steps, you pass interesting ledge formations on the left. How many tiny caves can you find? What types of animals might live in these caves? The rugged trail levels momentarily and then scrambles up another natural rock stairway through groves of mature hemlocks. Hemlocks, which are capable of surviving under the shaded canopy of the forest, thrive—like these have—once they are exposed to more direct sunlight.

The trail meets a woods road 0.5 mile from the start. As the white-blazed AT turns left (northeast), you turn right (southwest) and follow the wide road that leads in 0.6 mile to Anthony's Nose. The road rises gently and, 0.25 mile from the junction, passes a tiny frog pond on the left. What types of water creatures can the kids find? Remind turtle

The view from Anthony's Nose across the Bear Mountain Bridge to Bear Mountain

hunters that a turtle's shell is not its house, as many people assume, but is actually part of the turtle itself. Be careful when you handle one. Where do you think turtles (and frogs) hide during the winter months? (Under the mud at the bottom of the pond!)

The sometimes-grassy road winds leisurely through the woods, giving no indication of the approaching ridge. Look at the different types of trees that make up this forest. Get silly: if you were a tree, what kind would you be? Why? Get serious: how do deciduous trees benefit by shedding their leaves each fall? (Once the leaves have fallen off, the tree's interior is sealed off from the frost and snow. Also, less snow accumulates on bare branches, thus fewer branches break off.) Whoever answered that question correctly can take over as hike leader!

At 1 mile, the trail crests, then switches up a gentle slope to reach Anthony's Nose, a broad, exposed area that nourishes a few stunted oak and birch trees. The ledges drop in tiers toward the lovely western view, and are safe for children to *carefully* explore. Look across the Hudson River and the Bear Mountain Bridge to formidable Bear Mountain, and pass around the binoculars. Who can spot the observation tower on top? Does anyone hear the lonely whistle of a train? In late June and early July, pick from the abundant low-bush blueberries.

Return to your car the way you came.

6. Lost Pond at Manitoga Preserve

Type:	Dayhike
Difficulty:	Easy for children
Distance:	1.8 miles, loop
Hiking time:	1.5 hours
High point/elevation gain:	470 feet, 250 feet
Hikable:	March–December
Map:	NY/NJ Trail Conference Map 1

Lost Pond is not as elusive as it sounds. In fact, even a preschooler can follow the picture markers that lead the way (a deer track, a pine branch, and rippling water for the Deer Run, White Pine, and Lost Pond trails respectively). After 1 mile of easy walking (punctuated by rocky climbs, brook crossings, and trail junctions), you find the wild pond, cradled by ledge and chock-full of turtles, frogs, and fish. This pleasant, 1.8-mile trip is even more appealing because it's a loop: you don't cover the same territory twice.

Manitoga (an Algonquin word meaning "Place of the Great Spirit") is an 80-acre forest garden that was created fifty years ago by the industrial designer Russell Wright. He transformed a barren, heavily quarried property into a lovely, wild garden crossed by brooks and curving paths, enhanced by open meadows, ravines, and sheltered overlooks. Bring binoculars, a guidebook, and a wooden bird caller and introduce the kids to bird-watching. Ask the naturalist/caretaker for tips on what species to look for and where you're likely to spot them.

From New York City, take the Thruway North to Exit 9 in Tarrytown. Follow US 9 North to Peekskill and turn left onto combined US 6 and US 202 just north of Peekskill, as US 9 continues straight (north). Follow US 6 and US 202 to the Bear Mountain Bridge, but do not cross the bridge. From the junction of US 6, US 202, and NY 9D on the east side of the Bear Mountain Bridge, follow NY 9D north. In 2.5 miles, turn right onto the access road to the Manitoga "Man with Nature" Center. In 0.1 mile, park near the information board.

Before the hike, stop at the guide house to pay the small per-person entrance fee. Heading back toward the parking lot, turn left (southeast), following signs for the Deer Run, White Pine, and Lost Pond trails. (Each of these trails eventually splits from the others to loop through the preserve, covering distances between 0.8 and 1.8 miles.) Borrow a walking stick from the collection on the left and hike to the edge of Mary's Meadow, where you'll find portable restrooms.

Signing in and gathering information at Manitoga Preserve's Guide House before embarking on a hike

Cut southeastward across the meadow toward the trailhead at the edge of the woods. Follow the combined trails on a manicured path under a high ceiling of hemlock and fir boughs. Colonists stripped the bark from hemlock trees (which is very high in tannin) to use in skin tanning; Native Americans valued the hemlock's astringent properties, and made hemlock tea to apply to wounds to arrest bleeding and to drink as a cure for severe diarrhea. Kids, can you guess what vitamin you absorb by chewing on hemlock needles? (Vitamin C.)

Wind through an area littered with small boulders. Climb a wooded hill along a switchback and crest, cutting through thickets of mountain laurel as you hike eastward. At 0.15 mile, the trail dodges huge boulders dumped by the receding glaciers more than 10,000 years ago. How many of these can the kids scale? As the trail curls northeastward, avoid a cutoff trail that splits right.

Can you hear a distant water sound? The path approaches a cascading brook and crosses to the other side on a wide footbridge. Have a splashing contest; drop acorns, pebbles, pine cones, and twigs from the bridge to see what will make the best splash. Beyond the bridge, the path bends left, briefly hugging the bank of the stream, then curls right. One-quarter mile from the start, bear left (north) to follow a short side trail to Osio Lookout as the multiblazed trail turns right (east). On the edge of a gently sloping ridge, three mammoth boulders gaze westward at the cropped Hudson River view.

Return to the intersection and turn left (east), snaking through a shallow gully near the left bank of the stream. Play "How Is It Like Me?" Pick anything you see—a tree, a mushroom, a squirrel—and ask the kids what that object has in common with them. Does it need water to live? Have a family? Make any noise? Hop from one stepping stone to the next, reaching a junction at 0.35 mile. As the Deer Run Trail turns right (south), continue straight (east) on the combined Lost Pond and White Pine trails. (If you follow Deer Run for a short distance, you reach a spot where the stream water collects in a wading pool.) Follow more stepping stones and recross the stream 0.1 mile from the Deer Run split. Shortly, the White Pine Trail parts right (south) as you follow the Lost Pond Trail straight (northeast) on a moderate uphill slope. At 0.6 mile, the path curls to track southward under a hemlock canopy. Remember Christmas by rolling a few needles between your fingers and sniffing. Here, you are sweeping near the border of the Hudson Highlands State Park.

At 0.8 mile, a sign points left (south) to the Osborn Loop Trail as you follow the Lost Pond Trail right (southwest). Cross a stream on a course of flat rocks and embark on another ascent. Climb amidst oaks and clusters of mountain laurel. (Who can find the most perfect acorn?) One mile into the hike is unassuming Lost Pond. Wild, mossy banks plunge into the clear water of this tiny basin, a wonderful place for searching out frogs and salamanders. Let the kids wander to the far side of the pond, where a jumble of boulders borders the shoreline. Plan to take an extended energy break here; the kids will surely want some time to explore.

At the western edge of the pond, the Lost Pond Trail turns right (west) as the Osborn Loop Trail follows a straight course, eventually connecting with the Appalachian Trail (AT). Continue to follow the Lost Pond Trail, dropping quickly in a series of switchbacks. Let the kids take the lead, stopping to wait for you at the 1.2-mile mark near a tree that clings stubbornly to barren ledge, growing horizontal to the ground.

Turn left (west), guided by a sign for a second Osio Lookout, as the

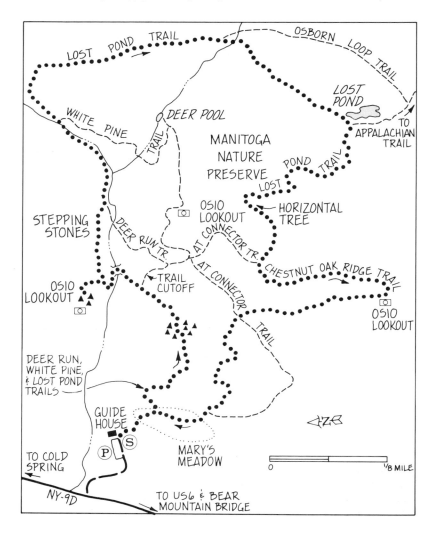

combined AT Connector and Lost Pond Trail splits right (north). Follow acorn symbols along the relatively new Chestnut Oak Ridge Loop, curling southward through thickets of laurel and blueberry bushes. Just under 1.5 miles from the start, you reach the sheltered lookout, with fine views of the Hudson Highlands—much more dramatic than those from the first Osio Lookout. A log bench provides a good excuse for giving your feet a rest.

Heading northward from the lookout, pass patches of moss as you descend to a four-way intersection. Head straight (north) across the intersection on the "Return Trail," blazed with the familiar symbols for the Deer Run, White Pine, and Lost Pond trails. The path winds gently toward Mary's Meadow, snaking through a chaos of boulders and then plunging down a wooded hillside on stone steps. From the southern end of the meadow, head diagonally right (north) across the field to reach your car. Don't forget to return your walking stick!

Note: The preserve is open every day. Guided tours are available. (See "Addresses" for more information.)

7. Denning Hill

Type:	Dayhike
Difficulty:	Moderate for children
Distance:	4.4 miles, round trip
Hiking time:	3.5 hours
High point/elevation gain:	900 feet, 475 feet
Hikable:	March–November
Map:	NY/NJ Trail Conference Map 1

If your family likes to combine hiking with history lessons, you'll enjoy this visit to Little Fort and Denning hills in the Hudson Highlands. During the Revolutionary War, British troops marching northward from Peekskill sent 2000 Continentals racing for the safety of nearby fortified hills, including Fort, Little Fort, and Fort Defiance. The trail leaves from Old West Point Road, which once led to Benedict Arnold's headquarters at Garrison. British spy Major John Andre was taken from North Salem to Garrison along this road, following his capture and Arnold's flight.

Most of this hike follows the popular Appalachian Trail (AT), although this section of the 2140-mile trail isn't particularly well known. Chances are good that any hikers you meet are on their way to Katahdin, Maine, where the AT ends. Because there aren't many locals who hike this trail, the trailhead is a little inconspicuous. But it's worth searching for, especially if you enjoy solitude, because many of the other trails in this area are heavily traveled.

From New York City, take the Thruway North to Exit 9 in Tarrytown. Follow US 9 North to Peekskill. Just north of Peekskill, stay on US 9, heading north, as the combined US 6 and US 202 fork left. Drive approximately 4 more miles to the junction of US 9 and NY 403. Remaining on US 9, drive another 0.6 mile and turn right (west) onto Old West Point Road, following a sign to Mother Lurana House. Drive less than 0.5 mile and park on the right shoulder of the road near a four-way intersection.

Study our map before you begin searching for the trailhead. Look for the gravel road that leads left into the woods, just past the four-way intersection. Sidestep the chained gate and begin an easterly descent,

A cautious deer, a common creature in this region, pauses at the meadow's edge.

guided by the white blazes of the Appalachian Trail (AT). At 0.1 mile, turn left (northeast) onto a wide footpath at double white blazes splashed on a huge tree. The trail rises into an overgrown field choked with berry bushes, then winds through mixed woods, still climbing gently. Head through a break in an enduring stone wall. Can each child find something blue, something yellow, and something red?

One-quarter mile into the hike, the blazes lead through a shallow ravine. Can you spot any New York asters? These wildflowers thrive in wet conditions. Soon, the trail embarks on a steady climb up the southern side of Little Fort Hill. At 0.5 mile, look for an orange marker shaped like a cross at the junction with a side trail. Follow the right-hand side trail (marked with frequent orange crosses) uphill for 0.1 mile to a tiny prayer shrine with local views, a lovely spot for an initial rest stop.

Back on the AT, continue heading northeastward. Blooming mountain laurel adorns the trail in late spring and early summer. Drop off Little Fort Hill and squeeze through another stone wall at 0.7 mile. Whitetail deer are quite common in this area; you're likely to spot one if you instruct the kids to whisper and walk quietly. The old orchards that you are passing through are a favorable habitat for the deer, which tend to gather on the edge of clearings. In fact, the deer population is larger today than it was when the settlers first moved into this area, due in part to the current lack of predators.

Who can find signs of an old burn at the 0.8-mile mark? (Biologists learn a great deal about patterns of plant growth by studying an area that has been burned. In fact, carefully managed fires are sometimes used to enhance the environment, for example, by perpetuating open meadows and encouraging the propagation of species that flourish in fire-scarred soil.) The trail climbs once more to reach an airy knoll, 1 mile from the start. Drop back into the cool woods heading north; let the kids run ahead, with instructions to wait for you at the junction with an old woods road. When you are reunited, turn right (east) onto the road and cut between two ridges.

Climbing gradually and angling toward the ridge on the right, the trail reaches another junction. A blue-blazed trail heads left (north), while the AT continues straight (east). Head left for great views, straight for good views, or take in both by continuing to follow the AT for now. (If the kids are wearing out, skip the next paragraph and follow the description of the blue-blazed trail.)

The AT, now a narrow foot trail, continues to thread through a gully between the two ridges. As the path approaches the left side of a shady ravine, hop over a fast-moving stream. Beyond the gorge, climb the steep western slope of a ridge on Denning Hill, giving little hikers lots of encouragement. At 1.9 miles, crest the ridge top (at 900 feet, the highest in this cluster of hills); here, the trail divides. Follow the white-blazed AT right (southwest) through a grassy meadow. Look for signs of deer:

droppings or tracks, twigs and buds that have been chewed off, matted grass where they might have slept or rested. Track through clusters of blueberry bushes to reach a rocky outcropping with a fine view toward the Hudson River and New York City. Pause here to admire the vistas, but save your picnic lunch for the next overlook.

Retrace your steps to the intersection with the blue-blazed trail. Turn right onto the blue trail and soon begin a moderate ascent northward, cutting up this ridge, to a grassy, exposed ridge top that affords spectacular views north to the Hudson River, framed by the lofty hills of the Hudson Highlands (notably Storm King, Hike 9) on the left bank and Beacon Hills on the right. Now you can unpack your picnic lunch. Not only are these the best views of the trip, but this spot is perfectly safe for little explorers.

Return to your car the way you came.

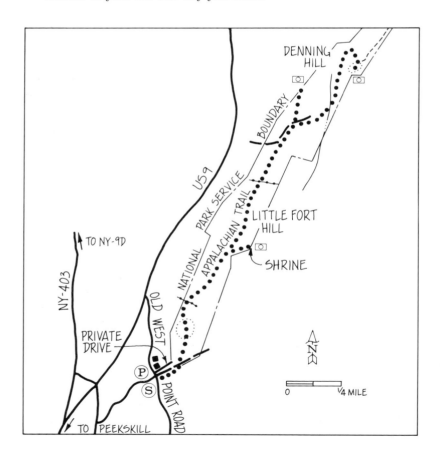

8. Constitution Marsh Sanctuary

Type:	Dayhike
Difficulty:	Easy for children
Distance:	2 miles, round trip
Hiking time:	1.5 hours
High point/elevation gain:	140 feet, 140 feet
Hikable:	Year-round
Map:	USGS West Point

In his day, Henry Hudson was not a favorite with the Indians. Their mistrust of him (and his entourage) seems justified, since he had a habit of killing Native Americans in large numbers. During a voyage on what is today the Hudson River, a group of Hudson's sailors went ashore near Glenham. Unlucky Jacobus Van Horen was captured by vengeful Indians, who presented him to their chief and discussed plans for his demise. For the chief's daughter, however, it was love at first sight, and she begged the braves to release Van Horen. His life was spared, and he was presented to the enamored Princess Manteo.

Alas, their marriage, set for one year later, never took place. While swimming beneath a waterfall one day with his betrothed, Van Horen noticed a European ship sailing up the Hudson River. He raced along the brook toward the riverbank and was spotted and soon rescued by the sailors. Later, Indians found the body of the princess in the brook below the falls. Did her future husband murder her so that he could escape? Or did the distraught princess climb to the top of the falls after his departure and leap to her death? We will never know. But the legend has been told and retold for generations, and is the source of the names of the brook and waterfall: Indian Brook and Indian Brook Falls.

The route we've chosen takes in the brook and waterfall, as well as an Audubon property with a nature trail, an Indian cave shelter, and an active marsh accessed by a boardwalk. The hike's best feature, though, is its length: all of this neat stuff is crammed into 2 easy miles.

From New York City, take the Thruway North to Tarrytown; here, take Exit 9 to US 9 North. Drive approximately 30 miles to McKeel Corners and turn left (west) onto NY 301. In about 3 miles, in Cold Spring, head south on NY 9D. In 1.4 miles, turn right onto unmarked, gravel Indian Brook Road. Drive 0.5 mile to a fork and park near the sign for Constitution Marsh.

From the parking area, follow the gravel woods road that heads southwest. Pass through a gate and drop gradually along the road that leads in 0.25 mile to the Audubon Nature Center and Museum. The private property on the right side of the road is bordered by a stone wall; to the left, Indian Brook cascades through a deep gorge. If you hike in the spring, you may witness snapping turtles depositing eggs on the hillside that plummets toward the brook; if you visit late in the summer, look for the newly hatched baby turtles plodding toward the marsh.

Just inside the gate is a box containing leaflets that describe the numbered stations along the Tree Trail, which coincides with the entrance road until station 25, when it turns and loops through the woods. One of the species you'll encounter on your way to the Audubon buildings is the mockernut hickory (station 2, on the left side of the road), which is used for furniture, flooring, and baseball bats, and is also valued as firewood for smoking hams and bacon. At station 4, also on the left, is a sugar maple, well known for its sap, which is boiled down to make maple syrup. A butternut tree thrives at station 10 (on the right side of the road), producing characteristic large, edible nuts, the husks of which are used to make dyes. And look for the familiar eastern hemlock, scarred with cavities chiseled by active woodpeckers, on the left at station 13.

A foot trail leaves the western side of the Audubon buildings, drops briefly through the woods following signs saying "TO MARSH," and splits. The left (south) fork leads to the boardwalk and the right (north) branch wanders toward the Indian shelter. Turn left for now (you'll visit the Indian shelter later) and follow the narrow, blue-blazed trail as it squeezes between a lush cattail marsh on the left and a dry, rocky slope on the right. The trail curls to the right at the tip of the peninsula and climbs steeply up the rocky hillside, where a thick rope strung along the ledge aids hikers.

At the top of this rugged ridge, crowded with pitch pine, a bench beckons hikers to rest and gaze at the nearby marsh and river, and at the distant layers of mountains stretching westward. When you're ready, plunge down the northern side of this rough knoll. One-quarter mile from the nature center, a boardwalk leads through Constitution Marsh. Railings guard against accidental tumbles into the water, although kids inclined to climb under or over the rails should be watched.

The boardwalk extends nearly 100 yards into the marsh, concluding at a bird-observation platform. The view from the platform across the open marsh is stunning, taking in the mountains of the Hudson Highlands with Storm King (Hike 9) looming to the south and Blue Hill rising on the northern horizon. Also look for muskrat lodges and feeding platforms tucked among the cattails.

Because the Hudson River is an estuary, its water level fluctuates with the tides. The boardwalk may be close to the surface of the water or far above it. At low tide, shorebirds, gulls, egrets, and herons stalk the exposed mud flats. Indeed, the marsh is teeming with many species of birds, especially during the spring and fall migrations. Late-summer

The lengthy boardwalk jutting into Constitution Marsh, with the Hudson Highlands on the horizon

hikers visiting as dusk approaches sometimes witness tens of thousands of swallows descending on the marsh at once. Some ornithologists believe that the birds gather here each year in preparation for a mass migration.

This 270-acre freshwater tidal marsh nourishes an enormous network of plant and animal life. Red-winged blackbirds, which use the cattail fibers to build their nests, are noisy neighbors to marsh wrens, which devise intricate homes from dead cattail leaves. Bald eagles soar over the marsh, usually in the winter months. Shrimp and blue crabs move silently among the marsh plants. Smell the ocean, hear the clang of distant buoy bells, feel the crisp breeze that moves among the cattails.

A visit to this serene, seemingly undisturbed cove offers parents a chance to share with their kids a disturbing chapter in the state's environmental history. A battery factory, built in 1952 by the U.S. Army Corps of Engineers in Cold Spring, discharged highly toxic cadmium, nickel, and cobalt into nearby Foundry Cove for twenty-seven years, creating one of the country's most dangerous hazardous waste sites. These dangerous heavy metals, soaked up by the muck at the bottom of the marsh, were absorbed first by the cattails, and then by every animal that fed on any part of the cattails. Once an ecosystem has been so greatly distorted, it is extremely difficult to return it to its natural state.

Return to the junction near the Audubon buildings, where the left branch of the path leads in 0.1 mile to the Indian shelter. Let the kids run ahead to investigate the great overhanging glacial erratic boulder that split to form a narrow cave. Small groups or families sought shelter here as recently as 400 years ago (and as far back as 5000 years). The floor was deeper then, and the cave was enclosed by walls of bark. The former inhabitants of this shelter drew water from a nearby spring, used local clay deposits for pot making, fished in the Hudson River, and hunted near its banks.

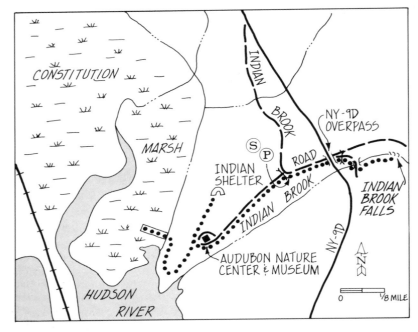

From the Indian shelter, return to your car the way you came. But don't stop here! Since you've walked only a little more than 1 mile, pass your car, heading northeastward on gravel Indian Brook Road. In 0.15 mile, you walk under the NY 9D bridge and see massive stone pillars bracing a rusty iron gate on the right side of the road. Sidestep the left pillar and follow the old carriage road blocked by the gate. Quickly, the road curls right and crosses Indian Brook on a stone bridge.

After you cross the bridge, turn left, departing the carriage road to head northeastward on a narrow foot trail. Follow the southern bank of the brook under a hemlock ceiling. Notice how dark it is beneath these trees. How many plants are growing on the damp, shaded forest floor under the giant hemlocks? The trail cut into the steep ridge is level, though rugged. When the brook isn't swollen, kids will find it easier to hike along the water's edge. One-tenth mile from the bridge, 0.35 mile from your car, is delightful Indian Brook Falls. The kids can play in the sand and wade in the pool beneath the falls, the very same pool that Jacobus and the princess were swimming in when he spotted the ship.

Return to your car along Indian Brook Road. Aren't you glad you didn't miss the falls?

Note: The trails at Constitution Marsh Sanctuary, a National Audubon Society property, are open from 8 a.m. to 6 p.m. Pets are not allowed.

9. Storm King

Type:	Dayhike
Difficulty:	Moderate for children
Distance:	2.5 miles, round trip
Hiking time:	2.5 hours
High point/elevation gain:	1350 feet, 400 feet
Hikable:	March–November
Map:	NY/NJ Trail Conference Map 7

Storm King rises regally from the western bank of the Hudson River, south of Newburgh. The Stillman Trail, which climbs over Butter Hill to Storm King's summit, has suffered from its proximity to the city. The first quarter mile is a disturbing testament to human disrespect and interference: garbage litters the parking area and trailhead, graffiti covers the ledges, traffic and construction noise drone incessantly. Nevertheless, civilization at its worst is soon overtaken by nature at its best. Dark caves dot the wooded slopes, scrambles up boulder-strewn hillsides lead to open ledges with splendid views over the Hudson River, generous blueberry bushes engulf the trail. Far away, the crowded roadways snake toward the city and boats jockey for space on the busy river, but you are above it all, in the clouds, hearing only the wind and smelling only the trees.

It's disheartening to hike with the results of carelessness and disregard for the environment, even though the damage is limited to a relatively short section of trail. But climbing past the results of teenage pranks and parties sends a powerful message to kids—especially older kids, for whom this hike is intended—saying more to them in silence than an adult can say with a year's worth of warnings. And there's no doubt that the rewards of this route far outweigh the drawbacks.

From New York City, cross the George Washington Bridge and take the Palisades Interstate Parkway north to its end at the Bear Mountain Circle. Continue north on US 9W for 8.5 miles to substantial off-road parking on the right.

From the parking area, walk westward between the highway barricade and the edge of the woods. Watch for Stillman Trail's yellow markers leading northwest into the woods. Stay with the yellow blazes, avoiding the side trails that quickly split left and right. Within the first 0.1 mile, the path embarks on a steep, rugged ascent up Butter Hill. Urge the kids to imitate rabbits. (Since rabbits have longer hind legs than forelegs, they run faster uphill than downhill.) Play "Chase the Rabbit": assign one child to chase the others, the "rabbits," and tell the kids how real rabbits escape. (They crisscross their tracks and take giant leaps to confuse animals following their scent. They also stamp the ground with their hind feet to warn one another of danger.)

The trail quickly opens onto exposed ledge. Can you spot your car in the parking area below? Gazing to the southeast, you can see the Hudson River twisting toward Anthony's Nose (Hike 5). At 0.2 mile, scramble up a steep slab of ledge to reach a loftier plateau with expanding southerly views. From this overlook, the trail cuts left to wind between stone pillars and old cellar holes, and reenters the woods. At 0.35 mile, a blue-blazed trail heads left (west) as you bear right (northeast), continuing to follow the yellow-blazed Stillman Trail. Send the kids ahead to find a massive trail-side boulder that has settled to create a small cave. After leading hikers through a hodgepodge of boulders, the trail climbs to another exposed area. Thankfully, you've left the crowds, the litter, and the traffic behind now, and the forest feels peaceful and wild.

Curling right (east), the path climbs with conviction up the rocky ridge, trudging through an area choked with mountain laurel. Although you are forced to take a lot of steps as the trail snakes around the ledge, you are avoiding the steepest grade. After passing briefly through forest illuminated by birch trees, the trail arrives above the southeastern cliffs of Butter Hill. Instruct the kids to follow the blazes carefully, since they guide hikers away from the precipitous edge. Now look down at your car in the parking lot—it looks like a Matchbox version! The kids will

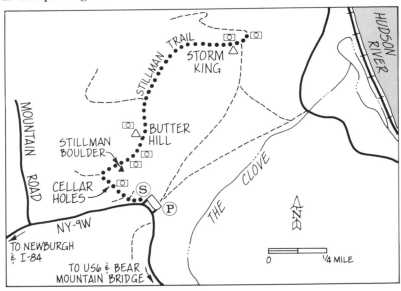

appreciate this graphic confirmation of how many vertical feet they have climbed. (Three hundred feet, to this point.) Quickly, the trail cuts left (north) away from the cliffs.

Track through the woods for 0.1 mile before reaching the official summit of Butter Hill, 0.5 mile from the start. Let the kids take turns as king or queen of the mountain, standing on the U.S. Geological Survey marker that identifies the high point. (We once saw a wild turkey here.) What evidence can you find of an old burn all along the Stillman Trail? (Notice the new growth and charred remains—such as the blackened, hollow tree trunks.) From this rock outcropping, views extend northward from nearby Schunemunk Mountain to the distant Catskills. Look eastward to see Beacon Mountain and south toward Bear Mountain and the Bear Mountain Bridge.

Drop off the hill heading northward, still following the yellow-blazed Stillman Trail, and descend through stunted oaks, mountain laurel, and low-bush blueberries. (Pause to pick if you're hiking midsummer.) Two-tenths mile from Butter Hill, avoid a side trail that departs left (west), and stay straight on the Stillman Trail. Struggle over protruding ledge and then climb. Soon, the trail trends downward and bottoms out in a sag before embarking on another ascent between two rock outcroppings at the 1-mile mark.

As you follow a northeasterly course, cropped views emerge of the Hudson River to the north. If the kids are struggling, tell them to look left through the trees. Can they see the blue sky? Behind the trees, the land slopes down: you are getting close to the eastern end of this ridge and Storm King. Listen for the sound of the freight trains that run along the shoreline of the Hudson. Now, heading eastward, work your way up more ledge to reach a grassy plateau with excellent views north up the river.

Drop through thickets of laurel into a wide gorge. In the belly of the gorge, avoid a trail that splits right (south) and continue to follow the yellow blazes of the Stillman Trail. One-tenth mile from the last overlook (and 1.25 miles from the start), the trail crests Storm King, a summit softened by patches of grass. Parents can relax while kids explore the broad, child-safe ridge top with wonderful views up and down the Hudson River. Count boats and islands. Listen for the lonely whistles of the trains. Can you see Constitution Marsh (Hike 8) protruding into the river to the southeast?

Storm King was originally considered part of Butter Hill, but received its current name from a writer who lived at the foot of the mountain. He felt that Storm King was more romantic and more appropriate for this part of the hill. What would you have named it?

As the Stillman Trail continues eastward and descends, reverse direction to return to Butter Hill and then to your car.

10. Ninham Mountain

Type: Dayhike
Difficulty: Easy to moderate for children
Distance: 1.5 miles, round trip
Hiking time: 1 hour
High point/elevation gain: 300 feet, 150 feet
Hikable: March–November
Map: USGS Lake Carmel

So much to see for so little effort! This quick trip up a gravel road to the summit of Ninham Mountain rewards hikers with panoramic views that take in nearby Pine Pond and West Branch Reservoir, Bull Hill and South Beacon Mountain, the Shawangunks and Catskills to the west and the faraway skyscrapers of New York City on the southern horizon. The kids can lead the way, carrying the binoculars and the picnic basket.

 From New York City, take I-95 North to Exit 12. Continue on I-287 West to Exit 9, and follow I-684 North to I-84 West. Take Exit 15 off I-84 to head west on NY 311. In 0.9 mile, at the intersection with NY 52 in Kent Corners, turn left onto NY 52, heading south. Drive 3.1 miles on NY 52 and turn right (at a traffic light in Carmel) onto NY 301. Head west on NY 301 for 1.3 miles to the intersection with Gypsy Trail Road; turn right. Follow Gypsy Trail Road for 2.2 miles to Ninham Mountain Road on the left. (Watch for the sign: "NINHAM MOUNTAIN MULTIPLE USE AREA.") Drive 0.5 mile on Ninham Mountain Road to a small parking area near a metal gate.

Two gravel roads lead from the parking area beyond locked gates. While the adults pull out backpacks and boots, the kids can explore the banks of a small frog pond that lies near Coles Mills Road, just inside the left-hand gate. When your group is reassembled, follow the maintained gravel road that heads straight (north) toward the summit of Ninham Mountain. Climb on a gradual to moderate ascent, playing a game of "Forest Bingo": who will be the first to spot a mushroom, a pine cone, a bird's nest, an animal track?

On your way to the top, look for signs of earlier settlers. Enduring stone walls wander through the woods, stone foundations border old cellar holes, overgrown pastures nurture forgotten apple trees. This area was farmed by the Smalley family many years ago. In fact, Ninham Mountain was once known as Smalley's Hill. At 0.2 mile, the road straightens out, fringed in the summer with daisies. Ask the kids why flowers look and smell so nice. What are the flowers trying to attract?

Camping on Ninham Mountain for Field Day festivities

Three-quarters of a mile from the start, you reach the grassy summit. On the left sits a fire warden's cabin. When we hiked this mountain near the end of June, the summit was littered with tents and canopies. Amateur radio operators had gathered for "Field Day" and were transmitting messages as part of a nationwide effort to prepare for a time when normal communication systems may be unable to operate. With prior permission from the state's Department of Environmental Conservation (DEC), you can camp at the summit as these folks did.

Beyond the cabin is a fire tower, built in the 1930s by the Civilian Conservation Corps (CCC). It looms over the mountain like a skyscraper, with 110 steps to take hikers to the top. From there (even from the twenty-fifth step), the sweeping views take in the Hudson Highlands, Catskill Mountains, and, yes, the New York skyline. Even the kids will be impressed—especially when the forceful wind vibrates the tower.

Return to your car the way you came.

11. Pawling Nature Preserve

Type: Dayhike
Difficulty: Easy for children
Distance: 1.8 miles, loop
Hiking time: 1.5 hours
High point/elevation gain: 1050 feet, 200 feet
Hikable: March–November
Map: USGS Pawling

It's not panoramic views that excite most kids, but boardwalks and bridges, cascading brooks, and chance encounters with wildlife. Within the Pawling Nature Preserve that blankets Hammersley Ridge, we found a short, easy route encompassing a variety of natural habitats: a hemlock ravine, woodland swamp accessed by a boardwalk, and once-farmed fields that have been reclaimed by the forest. Although some of these trails are quite popular with local hikers, the preserve still feels remote and unexplored, perhaps because its 1000 acres are bordered by 2000 acres of undeveloped, private property. Indeed, many endangered species of animals (as well as more common creatures) thrive within the preserve, making it likely that kids will spot a real live woodpecker, porcupine, deer, or—gulp—bear along the trail.

 From New York City, take I-95 North to Exit 12. Continue on I-287 West to Exit 9, and take I-684 North. Depart I-684 at Exit 20 in Brewster and follow NY 22 North approximately 12 miles to the junction with NY 55 in Pawling. Continue north on the combined NY 55 and NY 22 for about 2.5 miles and turn right (east) onto Dutchess County 68 (Hurds Corners Road). Drive 0.2 mile and bear right (still Dutchess County 68) onto North Quaker Hill Road. In 1.4 miles from NY 22, turn left (north) onto Quaker Lake Road, which turns to gravel in 0.6 mile. Turn left into the parking area for Pawling Nature Preserve 1.5 miles from Dutchess County 68.

From the northern side of the parking lot, follow the wide yellow-blazed trail that ducks into the woods, heading northwest. Quickly, the trail rises to the top of a gorge wall. A side trail leads right, tracking along the edge of the ravine, with views of the dark water cascading through this narrow, rocky canyon. Point out the predominance of hemlocks, reflecting this species' preference for shady, damp conditions.

Back on the Yellow Trail, walk to the western end of the rugged gorge. As you watch Duell Brook plunge into the ravine, imagine how this tireless stream of water carved the 25-foot-deep chasm over thousands of years. Don't allow the kids to venture too far from the path, because the boulders lining the gorge floor are moist, moss-covered, and slippery. How many different types of ferns can you count? (There are at least six, including bladder fern, walking fern, and fragile fern.)

From the edge of the gorge, the Yellow Trail curls left (west), following the bank of Duell Brook to a springy footbridge 0.1 mile from the start. Turn right and cross the bridge, and gaze into the water at the mica chips sparkling in the pebbly shallows. (Notice the Red Trail splitting right, east, here; you will return on this trail.) Continue straight (northwest) on the Yellow Trail, now ascending gradually. The trail curls westward and, at 0.3 mile, sidesteps an imposing rock overhang that forms a broad cave. Make this your first rest stop, allowing time for the kids to duck under the ledge ceiling and pretend to be the Indians who took refuge here thousands of years ago. Hunt for arrowheads. Look closely at the layered rock; it is mica schist and is part of a major schist formation that extends southward to Manhattan.

Follow sharp yellow blazes along terrain that heaves and swells for 0.2 mile, rolling through hemlock and spruce groves, mixed hardwoods, and patches of mountain laurel. Who can tell spruce trees from hem-

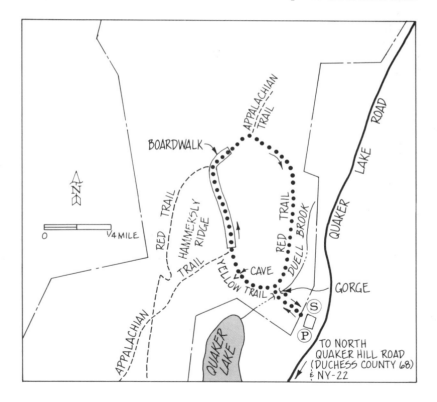

Explore a cave at the Pawling Nature Preserve.

locks? (Spruces have sharp, square needles and hemlocks have flat, short needles.) At an apparent junction, bear right (north) following yellow blazes, as the side trail quickly dissipates. At 0.5 mile, the Yellow Trail meets the renowned, white-blazed Appalachian Trail (AT). Turn right, stepping onto an extensive boardwalk that spans a swampy area.

Can you see signs that this was once an open meadow, cleared and farmed by the Quakers in the late eighteenth century? Some clues lie in the species of trees that dominate this area. The gray birches were the first trees to grow in the open field, thriving in the hot, dry conditions. In the moist environment under their branches, oaks and sugar maples took root and outgrew the gray birches, eliminating the sunlight they require and causing them to die out. You may also notice barberry shrubs, which were often planted along field borders in colonial times.

Near the end of a section of boardwalk, a red-blazed trail joins from the left. The boardwalk ends abruptly, within a tunnel of overhanging vines. Follow the Red Trail as it exits right (east), leaving the AT behind. Kids may have a hard time avoiding prickly undergrowth on this section of trail in the summertime. They can take turns riding piggyback. The trail curls right and begins descending the eastern side of Hammersly Ridge.

Many songbird species, such as the hermit thrush and winter wren, inhabit the preserve. Can the kids imitate or recognize any of the bird-calls they are hearing? Did you know that birds have accents just like people do? Even though a bird's ability to sing is instinctive (as opposed to learned), a bird living in one part of the world sounds different from the same kind of bird living in another part, just like an Atlanta native speaks differently than a person who grew up in Boston.

At 1.3 miles, balance on a log to cross a seasonal stream. Look for animals tracks in the muddy banks; animals known to inhabit the preserve include deer, wild turkeys, coyotes, bobcats, and beavers. Embraced by low-bush blueberries and mountain laurel, the ribbonlike Red Trail snakes along rolling terrain. See if you can spot a wintergreen plant, a small evergreen that looks a little like a dwarfed mountain laurel. Gently tear off the end of a leaf and let the kids take a sniff.

At 1.5 miles, the overgrown trail comes to a hemlock grove, where it leaves the intrusive underbrush and becomes much easier to follow. In another 0.1 mile, a lookout on the left provides pretty views to the adjoining ridge. Drop down a wooded hillside, cross more seasonal streams, and return to the Yellow Trail 1.7 miles from the start. Turn left onto the Yellow Trail and follow the blazes across the familiar footbridge. Pass the hemlock gorge and soon return to your car.

Note: This Nature Conservancy property is open to the public from sunrise to sunset. Fires, alcoholic beverages, and motor vehicles are prohibited.

12. Schaghticoke Mountain

Type: Dayhike
Difficulty: Difficult for children
Distance: 6 miles, round trip
Hiking time: 5 hours
High point/elevation gain: 1300 feet, 1000 feet
Hikable: April–November
Map: USGS Dover Plains

This is a hike for kids who don't mind shoveling down a little cauli-flower in order to finish the meal with chocolate cake and ice cream. You'll begin with a challenging climb that will test your repertoire of distraction techniques. ("Who knows how to count backwards from 100 . . . in French?") The path then rolls over miles of gentle terrain punctuated by five terrific overlooks. This trip encompasses land in two states, which kids think is very cool. ("Now I'm in Connecticut!" . . . one giant step . . . "Now I'm in New York!" . . . one giant step backward . . . "Now I'm in Connecticut again!")

The route is well-marked with the sharp and reliable white blazes of the Appalachian Trail (AT), the well-known path that winds over the backbone of the Appalachian Mountain range for 2140 miles from Georgia to Maine. The first section of the trail was blazed in 1922 and the final stretch in 1938; in 1968, Congress proclaimed the AT a National Scenic Trail, to be kept as a hiking path forever. Thanks to the efforts of volunteers affiliated with the Appalachian Trail Conference and with local clubs, the trail is regularly maintained and reblazed.

From New York City, take I-95 North to Exit 12. Continue on I-287 West to Exit 9, and take I-684 North. Depart I-684 at Exit 20 in Brewster and follow NY 22 North approximately 12 miles to the junction with NY 55 in Pawling. Continue north on the combined NY 55 and NY 22. In 8 miles, turn right (east) on NY 55 as NY 22 continues straight. In about 2 miles, turn left onto Dutchess County 22 ("DOGTAIL CORNERS ROAD"). Drive 1.4 miles on Dutchess County 22 to a four-way intersection ("DOGTAIL CORNERS"). Turn right, still on Dogtail Corners Road (Dutchess County 22). In 0.6 mile, enter Connecticut; the road is now named Bulls Bridge Road. In 1.0 mile, turn left onto Schaghticoke Road. In 0.3 mile (following the white blazes of the Appalachian Trail), park on the shoulder where the trail dives into the woods.

Begin on the white-blazed Appalachian Trail (AT), initially running parallel to the road; hop a stonewall at 0.1 mile. Soon, you'll veer away from the road, heading toward the mountain. The trail passes through

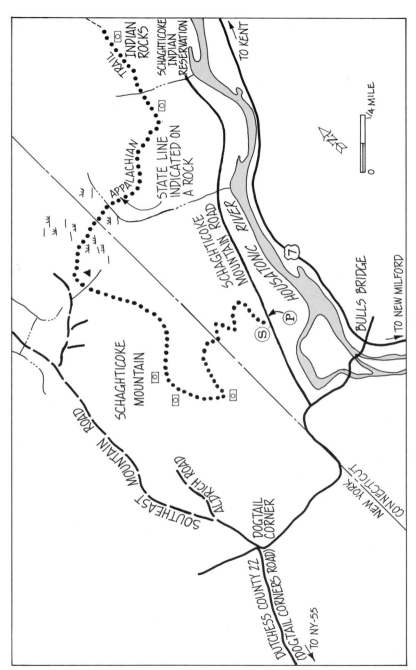

SCHAGHTICOKE MOUNTAIN

another stonewall and sidesteps the AT sign-in station. Leap over a brook and embark on a steeper ascent. To distract the kids, have them keep count of the number of switchbacks (often marked by double white blazes). Does anyone hear the drilling of woodpeckers?

As the trail climbs steeply from the 0.5- to the 0.8-mile mark, snaking around ledges and heaps of boulders, have the kids watch the ground for deer droppings. This may help keep their thoughts away from their tiring legs. Soon, level and downward-trending ground bring a short reprieve. A final few switchbacks lead you to a slab of exposed rock at the 1-mile mark with dramatic southerly views over Connecticut's Housatonic River Valley. Allow the children a well-earned rest period here. Let them know that most of the significant climbing is behind you!

When the kids are ready, continue to follow the AT as it cuts over the top of Schaghticoke Mountain from the eastern to the western side of the ridge. Two-tenths of a mile from your rest stop, enjoy your first westerly overlook across the rolling hills of upstate New York. Drop to another open rock face with more views to the west.

Now the trail plunges into a thickly wooded section of the ridge, then follows gently descending ground for 0.5 mile. Though this section is rather uneventful by kid standards, it passes quickly. Cross a small stream and assign a child to watch for another set of double white blazes indicating a right turn. Here the trail widens into a generous path where you join an older section of the AT. (This trail has been rerouted within

Hikers on the Appalachian Trail

the last few years to avoid encroachment on some private land.) In another 0.1 mile, the blazes lead down granite "steps." Trending downward toward a marsh, the trail marches between rows of ferns.

Two and a half miles from the start, cross a pleasant stream on stones. The water runs quietly under the branches of hemlocks, tirelessly dodging moss-covered rocks. Toss a few stones into the pool on the left. Is there any sound more satisfying to a youngster's ears than the kerplunk of a rock breaking the surface of the water? Can you imitate the noise a big stone makes? How about a pebble?

At 2.8 miles the trail struggles out of the wetlands through an area thick with ground cover, winding under an oak canopy. Who can find a "double" acorn? Who can find one with its "hat" still on? As you pass more frequently over baldface, the forest begins to open up. The first child to step from New York into Connecticut (according to the state line indicated on a rock in the middle of the trail) wins a piggyback ride for 20 paces!

Soon the trail reaches the eastern tip of the Schaghticoke Mountain ridge, where it bends northward. The path sweeps close to the edge of the steeply sloping ridge, eventually reaching an overlook with eastward views into the Housatonic Valley. The Housatonic River runs dark and silent far below you. Though the drop-off is not sheer, it is significant, so keep little hikers close by.

Double white blazes mark the end of your 3.0-mile journey (the AT does continue) and the final overlook at Indian Rocks. Here, within the bounds of the Schaghticoke Indian Reservation, ledge outcroppings dive down the hillside in tiers toward the Housatonic River. As you enjoy a picnic lunch or a snack, watch cloud shadows racing silently across the distant, anonymous hills to the east and south. When you are ready, return to your car the way you came.

Note: For more information about camping on Appalachian Trail lands, call (212) 986-1430.

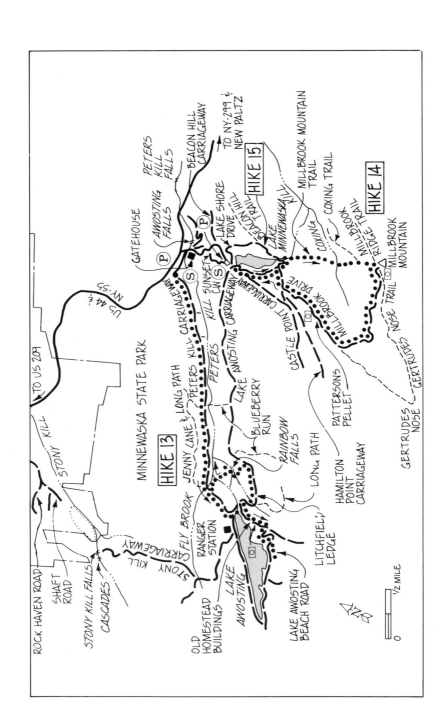

ROCK HAVEN ROAD

SHAFT ROAD

STONY KILL FALLS

CASCADES

STONY KILL

TO US 209

MINNEWASKA STATE PARK

HIKE 13

STONY KILL CARRIAGEWAY

FLY BROOK

JENNY LANE & LONG PATH

PETERS KILL CARRIAGEWAY

OLD HOMESTEAD BUILDINGS

RANGER STATION

LAKE AWOSTING

LAKE AWOSTING BEACH ROAD

LITCHFIELD LEDGE

BLUEBERRY RUN

RAINBOW FALLS

LONG PATH

PATTERSONS PELLET

HAMILTON POINT CARRIAGEWAY

GERTRUDES NOSE

GERTRUDES NOSE TRAIL

US 44 & NY-55

GATEHOUSE

AWOSTING FALLS

PETERS KILL FALLS

BEACON HILL CARRIAGEWAY

TO NY-299 & NEW PALTZ

HIKE 15

LAKE SHORE DRIVE

LAKE MINNEWASKA

BEACON HILL

MILLBROOK MOUNTAIN TRAIL

COXING

COXING TRAIL

MILLBROOK RIDGE TRAIL

HIKE 14

MILLBROOK MOUNTAIN

LAKE AWOSTING CARRIAGEWAY

PETERS KILL SUNSET

CASTLE POINT CARRIAGEWAY

MILLBROOK DRIVE

P

P

S

S

N

0   ½ MILE

13. Lake Awosting and Rainbow Falls

Type:	Dayhike
Difficulty:	Challenging for children
Distance:	7 miles, round trip
Hiking time:	6 hours
High point/elevation gain:	1900 feet, 340 feet
Hikable:	March–November
Map:	NY/NJ Trail Conference Map 9

Are you tired of hopping over rows of sweaty bathers to get to your tiny square of beach? Fed up with dodging volleyballs and Frisbees? Had your fill of blasting boom boxes and buzzing speedboats? On the remote, undeveloped shores of Lake Awosting, you can find solitude and some of the best swimming you can imagine. Relax on the smooth, sloping ledge that sinks to the edge of the water while the kids splash about. Be sure to wear bathing suits under your clothes—there's no bathhouse in this wilderness. After your swim, hike to Rainbow Falls, where the kids can count the rainbows shimmering in the misty spray and dare one another to put an arm, a leg, or a head under the splashing water.

Although this is a long hike, the terrain is relatively level and the wide path that takes you most of the way is free of roots and rocks. Perfect for kids who may not be experienced hikers, but who have good endurance levels and love the water.

Follow the driving directions for Lake Minnewaska (Hike 15). From the entrance to Minnewaska State Park, continue on the combined US 44 West and NY 55 for another 0.4 mile. Turn left into a large gravel parking area and park at the southwestern end near a gate blocking the entrance to a carriageway.

Head southwest on the Peters Kill Carriageway, a level gravel road that you follow for 2 miles to remote Lake Awosting. Although this is the shortest and easiest route to the lake, and quite a pleasant stroll, be prepared to offer diversions to kids who might lose interest. Initially, ask the kids to compare the leaves of the mountain laurel bushes on the left with the fern fronds on the right. Do they feel the same or different? The laurel leaves feel waxy, don't they? Since the laurel bushes don't drop their leaves in autumn, but keep them throughout the year, this coating is necessary to protect the leaves from the effects of freezing temperatures. In fact, these leaves are poisonous to deer and other animals, so even during the winter, when food is scarce, laurel bushes don't tempt wildlife.

Maintain a steady pace, but take time for the kids to investigate trailside curiosities. Compare scents. Which plant smells sweetest? Do the different smells remind you of particular times and places? Between the 0.5- and 1-mile marks, avoid foot trails branching left into the woods heading to Peters Kill ("Kill" is from the Dutch *kil*, meaning "creek"). Sometimes it's fun to play a thinking game. Suggest an outlandish scenario and ponder possible results. What if snow were pink? Animals who use their color for camouflage in snow like snowshoe hares and polar bears might become extinct. It might melt into pink puddles. What if all cars were blue? It would be hard to find yours in a full parking lot, but it would be easy to match the color if it needed repainting. What if everyone had the same first name? What if no tree was taller than 6 feet?

If your group would appreciate a brief detour, follow an obvious side trail (the unmarked Blueberry Run) on the left at 1.5 miles. In 100 yards, you'll reach the edge of Peters Kill. The kids can explore the banks, look for animal tracks, and play water games. Does a stick swim faster than a child can run? Do acorns float? How about clusters of pine needles? What leaf makes the best boat?

Back on the carriageway, begin an easy, though steady, ascent, avoiding a side trail that departs right (north) just beyond Blueberry Run. Can you distinguish between a hemlock and a white pine? (Hemlocks have flat, short needles and white pines have long, thin needles that grow in clusters of five.) Look for colors as you hike. The woods might seem to be shades of green and brown, but can you find a red berry? A blue blossom? A white mushroom? Now look for shapes. A hole in a tree might look like a circle, a leaf may be shaped like an oval, a rock might resemble a triangle.

At 2.2 miles, the Peters Kill Carriageway joins one branch of the blue-blazed Long Path; the other branch departs right (north). The combined carriageway and Long Path soon bends left (south), crossing a large culvert carrying Fly Brook, a tributary of Peters Kill. Less than 0.1 mile from its entrance, the Long Path departs left (east). Stay straight and take special note of the intersection; you will emerge here after following the Long Path from Rainbow Falls. Who can point out a pitch pine? These short, rather scruffy evergreens tend to grow on dry, barren ledges. Look for the characteristic immature first-year cones as well as developed cones with sharp points on the edges of each scale.

Over the next 0.2 mile, the trail climbs moderately, crests, then follows a twisting route downhill to arrive at the northeast tip of Lake Awosting. Bear left (east) as the trail forks near the water (the right branch leads to the ranger station) and crosses a causeway at the outlet to the lake (where Peters Kill originates). The kids may be tempted to dive in; remind them that swimming is not permitted here. (In another 0.75 mile, you'll reach the swimming area.)

Climb a wooded slope heading eastward, away from the lake. Turn right at a junction onto the Lake Awosting Carriageway, following a sign

The view from the base of Rainbow Falls

that directs hikers to Castle Point and Lake Awosting Beach Road. Rising gently on this more sheltered carriageway, you pass an abandoned homestead on the right, with a barn and house falling into disrepair. Take turns telling stories about haunted houses. Soon, a very short side trail leads right to precipitous ledges and a lovely overlook of the lake. Keep the kids beside you as you enjoy the view.

At 3.2 miles (0.45 mile from the last intersection), turn right (west) onto the Lake Awosting Beach Road as the Lake Awosting Carriageway continues straight. Snake down a wooded slope for 0.3 mile to reach the Lake Awosting shoreline. Follow the trail for another 0.1 mile to the beach. From a distance, it looks as if the expansive beach is covered with white sand. As you get closer, you'll realize that the "sandy beach" is a massive slab of white granite! Finally, it's time to peel off your hiking garb and plunge into the clear water.

When you're ready to continue the hike, return to the junction of the Peters Kill and Lake Awosting carriageways. Follow the Lake Awosting Carriageway, guided by a sign to Lake Minnewaska. Quickly the path curls eastward. Two-tenths mile beyond the intersection, a stream flows under your path through a culvert and the Long Path joins from the right. Now the combined Lake Awosting Carriageway and Long Path sweeps northeastward.

Over the next 0.4 mile, the cliffs of Litchfield Ledge that loom over the right side of the trail grow more lofty and impressive. Near the end of the ledge, follow the blue-blazed Long Path as it splits left (west), leaving the Lake Awosting Carriageway behind. The trail drops down a steep slope and bottoms out on spongy terrain under high hemlocks. What types of plants and trees flourish in damp conditions like these? How many different varieties of ferns and mosses can you identify?

Hop over a stream that trickles through this gorge, known as Huntington Ravine. Shortly, climb out of the ravine, heading for distant water sounds. A final surge up a rock slide brings you to Rainbow Falls, where a delightful veil of water dives 40 feet. Behind the mist, rainbows shimmer. As the trail leads right (northeast) over stepping stones across the base, you'll be sprinkled with the spray.

From the bottom of Rainbow Falls, the trail tumbles back into Huntington Ravine and follows the stream, winding among boulders and hemlocks. Watch for double blazing, indicating a left turn as the trail bends away from the stream and begins a rugged ascent along ledge to the top of the ridge above the falls. After cresting the top of Rainbow Falls, the Long Path begins a gentle descent through laurel, pitch pine, and blueberry bushes. Two-tenths mile from the falls, cross Peters Kill on stones and climb gradually for less than 0.1 mile to the junction with Peters Kill Carriageway. Turn right onto the carriageway and begin the final 2.2-mile march back to your car.

Note: In season, the park opens at 9 A.M. and closes at 7 P.M. on weekdays, 8 P.M. on weekends. Trails close at 6 P.M. on weekdays, 7 P.M. on weekends. Dogs must be leashed.

14. Millbrook Mountain

Type: Dayhike
Difficulty: Moderate for children
Distance: 4.7 miles, loop
Hiking time: 4.5 hours
High point/elevation gain: 1765 feet, 700 feet
Hikable: April–November
Map: NY/NJ Trail Conference Map 9

Does the description of Lake Minnewaska sound too tame for your adventurous group? If so, follow the Minnewaska loop for the first 0.8 mile, then leave the mellow carriage path for wilder terrain and more demanding hiking. You can enjoy water views on the initial and final legs of the hike, and in between you'll have breathtaking views from Millbrook Mountain's summit and explore some of the more remote corners of Minnewaska State Park.

Follow the driving directions for Lake Minnewaska (Hike 15), then hike the route described to the lake's southern tip, where it crosses Coxing Kill. From here, leave Lake Shore Drive to follow the red-blazed

A porcupine bumbles along the Millbrook Mountain Trail.

Millbrook Mountain Trail on the right (south). The rugged foot trail plunges recklessly through woods dominated by mountain laurel and hemlocks. In stark contrast to the tame carriageway, the narrow trail drops over a jumble of boulders, heading south, and quickly crosses Coxing Kill.

One-tenth mile from Lake Shore Drive, the Millbrook Mountain Trail slices across a steep hillside on level terrain. Beyond the ridge, lush patches of moss carpet the trail, cushioning your steps. Why does moss seem to grow so well here? (Moss is one of the few plants that can survive these shady, acidic conditions. It began as a sea plant and it still requires constant moisture. In fact, it needs water to reproduce!) Award a granola bar to the child who is first to reach the neat kid-size cave on the left.

At 1 mile, the trail sweeps across exposed ledge and tracks through an area thick with wild blueberry bushes. If you are hiking in midsummer, stop to fill a bucket. In another 0.2 mile, push aside the laurel that invades the trail and dive down the bank of a cool ravine that carries a tributary of Coxing Kill. As you head straight, crossing the brook on stones, urge the kids to step onto the small island in the middle as they make their way across. (This is the safest and easiest route.) On the other side of the creek, the trail climbs the southern bank through a rough, seasonal streambed. As more slabs of ledge intrude underfoot, blueberry bushes reach across the path and pitch pines cluster in the woods.

As the blue-blazed Coxing Trail joins from the left (north) 0.7 mile from Lake Shore Drive, stay straight on the red-blazed trail. Peek over your shoulder for spectacular northeastern views of the Trapp Ledges. At 1.7 miles, the trail opens onto a gently sloping ledge outcropping where triple red blazes indicate the end of Millbrook Mountain Trail. As the blue-blazed Millbrook Ridge Trail joins from the left, turn right to join another red-blazed trail, the Gertrudes Nose Trail. Hike less than 100 yards (with the kids close by) to reach the top of Millbrook Mountain,

at the edge of a magnificent escarpment. The easterly views, reaching deep into the Hudson River Valley, are unequaled.

From the edge of the precipitous escarpment, head westward, leaving the Gertrudes Nose Trail to join a yellow-blazed carriage path known as Millbrook Drive. The carriage path is characteristically wide and smooth, passing through groves of pitch pine and stunted oaks. Initially, views to the right encompass distant mountains. As you follow this lengthy stretch of carriage path, ward off midhike fussiness with a game of "Simon Says": "Simon says, 'Hop like a bunny!' Simon says, 'Wave a leaf in the air like a flag!' Now gallop like a horse! You're out!" One mile from the Millbrook Mountain summit, remain on Millbrook Drive as it bends right (north); the Gertrudes Nose Trail joins from the left (south).

As the ground falls away on the left side of the trail, begin a trek along the southern wall of the Palmaghatt Ravine, an impressive V-shaped gorge rimmed with sheer cliffs. Within the ravine, you'll notice stands of giant hemlocks. Somehow these trees escaped the loggers' axes. Look for trailside tree stumps and count the rings. As you embark on a gradual climb, the drop-off increases, although the trail stays between 10 and 20 feet from the edge. Soon the ravine narrows, the carriageway approaches the edge of the cliff, and you pass Pattersons Pellet. This formidable glacial boulder rests on the edge of the cliff, so advise the kids to investigate it with caution.

Shortly beyond Pattersons Pellet, Millbrook Drive meets the yellow-blazed Hamilton Point Carriageway. At this T-intersection, turn right (east) and follow the Hamilton Point Carriageway for 0.25 mile. At the junction with red-blazed Lake Shore Drive, turn left and return to your car along the shore of Lake Minnewaska.

Note: In season, trails close weekdays at 6 P.M., weekends at 7 P.M. The park opens at 9 A.M. and closes at 7 P.M. on weekdays, 8 P.M. on weekends. Dogs must be leashed.

15. Lake Minnewaska

Type: Dayhike
Difficulty: Easy for children
Distance: 1.6 miles, loop
Hiking time: 1 hour
High point/elevation gain: 1765 feet, 200 feet
Hikable: March–December
Map: NY/NJ Trail Conference Map 9A

If Henny Youngman knew about hiking in Minnewaska State Park, he would tell you "Take this hike—please." (Ta-dum.) The civilized carriageways around Lake Minnewaska are part of a 50-mile road system developed over a century ago by area hotel owners who wanted their guests to be able to access scenic spots in horse-drawn vehicles. Today's hikers will appreciate those long-ago land barons for providing a way to take in lovely vistas without stumbling over roots or pushing aside prickly underbrush. And what vistas! The peaceful water views are enhanced by dramatic cliffs that rise from Minnewaska's rugged shoreline.

Don't forget to bring your bathing suits; the hike begins and ends near the lake's only official swimming area and you may want to take a dip. But be warned: the water in this deep, spring-fed lake is chilly (read "like ice"), even on the steamiest August day.

From New York City, take the Thruway North to Exit 18 in New Paltz.

Follow NY 299 west for approximately 7.5 miles to its conclusion at the intersection with US 44 West and NY 55. Turn right onto combined US 44 and NY 55, and drive approximately 4.5 miles to the entrance of Minnewaska State Park on the left. Enter the park and pay a moderate day-use fee at the gatehouse. Drive about 1 mile to the parking lot at the end of the park road.

From the western side of the parking lot, head south on Sunset Path, passing the picnic area. Soon, turn right onto red-blazed Lake Shore Drive, the carriage path you will follow around the lake. Drop briefly toward a lifeguard-supervised swimming area (the only spot on Lake Minnewaska where swimming is permitted). Beyond the beach area, continue to follow Lake Shore Drive as it follows the shoreline. Warn the kids that mountain bikes frequently zip along these roadways.

Thick clusters of mountain laurel edge the carriage road, embracing mixed woods dotted with boulders. Who can find a white pine? (Here's a hint: this tree has the largest cones of any pine tree found in the Northeast. If that doesn't help, count the needles—white pine needles grow in bunches of five.) Compare hemlock cones with white pine cones. What are some differences between them? One-tenth mile from the start, the green-blazed Awosting Lake Carriageway joins from the right; continue straight, still following red blazes.

As side trails split left and right, remain on the main carriage road. At a major intersection 0.25 mile from the start, the blue-blazed Castle Point Carriageway bears right (west) to Kempton Ledge. Continue straight (south) on Lake Shore Drive. One-half mile from the start, as the yellow-blazed Hamilton Point Carriageway departs right (west) toward Gertrudes Nose, stay straight once more to remain on Lake Shore Drive. Just beyond Hamilton Point Carriageway, Lake Shore Drive switches down a slope; let the kids run ahead with instructions to wait for you at a rustic bench on the right. Shortly, as the trail sweeps from south to north, you'll have grand eastern views across the Shawangunks.

An easy descent follows the switchback; quickly, you reach the shoreline of this spectacular lake. Toss pebbles into the water. Who can throw the farthest? As you cross Coxing Kill at the southern tip of the lake, the Millbrook Mountain Trail branches right (south) into the woods. Follow Lake Shore Drive as it curls left (north) to continue a counter-clockwise sweep around Lake Minnewaska. Avoid minor trails that lead left from the carriageway. Revive weary little hikers with a game: imitate bird calls, with prizes for the best chickadee, bobwhite, or crow. (Or try to sound like a pileated woodpecker or tufted titmouse, two birds you're likely to see in the state park.) First prize: a five-minute piggyback ride!

One-tenth mile from the river crossing, avoid unmarked Pine Cliff Path, which departs right. As you crest a gentle grade, Lake Shore Drive forks. Take the left branch, which leads shortly to an expansive, mani-cured picnic area. The kids may be ready for a rest (or they may want

Resting on a rustic bench along Lake Shore Drive

to toss a Frisbee, fly a kite, or just wrestle on the grass). Follow the path along the edge of the field and take in the lake views.

From the northwestern side of the picnic area, the path shortly rejoins the principal branch of Lake Shore Drive. Follow the red blazes northward as a number of paths and roadways diverge left and right. (Let the kids know you are just 0.25 mile from your car.) As you hike under a rustic footbridge (known as Dry Bridge), the kids may want to leave the trail to investigate how to reach the bridge and the gazebo that perches nearby. After passing the park office (it has a soda machine, if you're desperately thirsty), Lake Shore Drive leads to the paved entrance road. Turn left and return to your car (or head to the beach for a—*BRRRRR!*—swim).

Note: The park opens at 9 A.M. and closes at 7 P.M. on weekdays, 8 P.M. on weekends. The trails close weekdays at 6 P.M., weekends at 7 P.M. Dogs must be leashed.

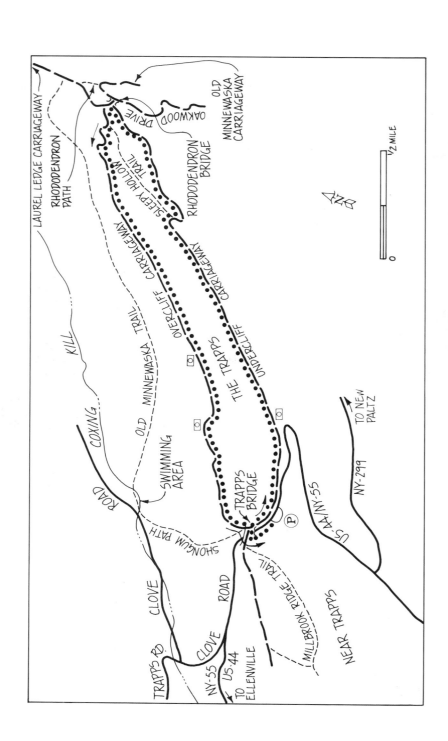

LAUREL LEDGE CARRIAGEWAY

RHODODENDRON PATH

OAKWOOD DRIVE

OLD MINNEWASKA CARRIAGEWAY

RHODODENDRON BRIDGE

SLEEPY HOLLOW TRAIL

OVERCLIFF CARRIAGEWAY

OLD MINNEWASKA TRAIL

KILL

COXING

THE TRAPPS

UNDERCLIFF CARRIAGEWAY

SWIMMING AREA

TRAPPS BRIDGE

SHONGUM PATH

TO NEW PALTZ

NY-299

US-44/NY-55

P

NEAR TRAPPS

MILLBROOK RIDGE TRAIL

CLOVE ROAD

CLOVE ROAD

TRAPPS RD.

NY-55

US-44

TO ELLENVILLE

½ MILE

0

N

16. The Trapps

Type: Dayhike
Difficulty: Moderate for children
Distance: 4.8 miles, loop
Hiking time: 4 hours
High point/elevation gain: 1100 feet, 200 feet
Hikable: March–December
Map: NY/NJ Trail Conference Map 10

If you consider rock climbing a fine spectator sport, you won't want to miss this trip within the Mohonk Preserve that highlights the dramatic Trapps. Along a 1-mile stretch, you can witness athletes inching up sheer walls as high as 300 feet. But for its length, the level loop around these cliffs would be classified as a stroll rather than a hike: the smooth, wide carriageways make walking so easy!

Because the most tiring aspects of hiking for kids are climbing and negotiating rugged terrain, this docile route is within the limits of almost any youngster, even one who may not have successfully completed other long hikes.

From New York City, take the Thruway North to Exit 18 in New Paltz. Follow NY 299 west for approximately 7.5 miles to its conclusion at US 44 West and NY 55. Turn right onto combined US 44 and NY 55, drive about 1.4 miles, and turn left into a parking area (crowded on summer weekends) just before the overpass known as Trapps Bridge.

From the parking area, head northwest, climbing along the shoulder of US 44/NY 55. Just as you are about to march under the Trapps Bridge, turn left, joining a woods road that quickly leads onto this overpass. After crossing the bridge, turn right onto the wide, gravel Undercliff Carriageway and begin the loop that encircles the Trapps. Almost immediately, you can look to the south and see your car and, beyond that, the bucolic valley far below. Looking westward, you view a section of the impressive ridge upon which you are hiking, known as "Near Trapps."

Expect the first mile to be slow because the path runs along the base of the Trapps cliffs. The kids will no doubt gaze up at the swarms of rock climbers clinging to the sheer walls. Skilled climbers from all over the Northeast (and beyond) flock to these impressive cliffs to perfect their techniques and mingle with other climbers. These proficient athletes follow strict guidelines and procedures. This is not a sport to be attempted by reckless novices; a number of untrained climbers have been killed trying to scale these ledges.

Eventually, the trail swings away from the dramatic scarp, dodging a massive boulder slide. Numerous side trails split left, leading back to the base of the Trapps. If the kids are begging for another look at the climbers, follow any one of these green-blazed paths. As you continue on the Undercliff Carriageway, tell your young hike leader to announce when the huge, overhanging ledge comes into view. Can everyone find his or her own cave in this area of boulder piles and outcroppings?

At 1.5 miles, the carriageway ducks under another impressive overhang. As it moves away from the ridge, the trail curls right, then bends left, passing through a cool ravine. Enjoy final glimpses of the lofty ledges above and to the left.

Avoid the Sleepy Hollow Trail that splits left at 1.9 miles. In another 0.4 mile, continue straight on the Undercliff Carriageway as another carriageway splits right (southeast) toward Rhododendron Bridge. Bear left (northwest) soon after, now on the Overcliff Carriageway, as the Laurel Ledge Carriageway splits right. At this junction, a sign marks your progress: you have come 3.7 kilometers (or 2.3 miles) from the Trapps Bridge on the Undercliff Carriageway. Another sign announces that this same bridge is 3.8 kilometers away via the Overcliff Carriageway, your return path. Point out to the kids that you're close to the halfway mark!

The Overcliff Carriageway, running parallel to the Undercliff Carriageway, quickly sweeps to the left (southwest) to establish a southwesterly trend. Avoid the other end of the Sleepy Hollow Trail, splitting left. After snaking around a series of curves for 0.25 mile, the path embarks on a fairly straight course toward Trapps Bridge. Three-tenths mile from the Sleepy Hollow junction, northern views emerge, taking in much of the Catskill Range.

How does the foliage on this side of the ridge differ from the plant growth on the other side? Do the gnarled pitch pines and scrub oaks appear stunted on this exposed rim? Over the next mile, the trail crosses fairly level ground, tracking in and out of woods decorated with mountain laurel. Lovely northern views persist along this ridge. Are the kids beginning to feel the miles? Suggest that instead of just walking, they lumber like elephants, leap like frogs, stalk like tigers, or dash like gazelles.

Nearly 2 miles along the Overcliff Carriageway, your direct route to the bridge is interrupted by a string of twists and turns on flat terrain. As you pass substantial ledge outcroppings on the left, tell the kids to run ahead and wait for you at the accessible kid's cave near the end of the exposed rock. More views of the Catskills follow before you sidestep a boulder slide on the left.

Recross the Trapps Bridge, 4.8 miles from the start, and return to your car.

Note: The preserve charges a relatively high per-person or per-family rate for day use. Fees are collected by a patroling ranger or can be paid at any pay station.

A climber scales the Trapps.

17. North Lookout to Sky Top

Type: Dayhike
Difficulty: Moderate to challenging for
children
Distance: 6 miles, round trip
Hiking time: 5 hours
High point/elevation gain: 1542 feet, 550 feet
Hikable: March–December
Map: NY/NJ Trail Conference Map 10A

Lofty gazebos highlight this trip in the Mohonk Mountain House property that concludes triumphantly at the tower on Sky Top. The views are superb, and not only because of their scope. Parents can enjoy these panoramas anxiety-free because the sturdy gazebos keep youngsters corralled, away from the edge of the cliffs.

To maintain the kids' interest along the way, put the older ones in charge of following the map and keeping a lookout for the many turns and junctions; the younger ones can be given the task of announcing upcoming gazebos and keeping a count. Although it's a 6-mile trek, extended rest stops at each lookout will rejuvenate the kids and keep them moving right up to the final gazebo. Bring binoculars to gaze toward the New York City skyscrapers, the climbers clinging to the Trapp Ledges, and the historic Mohonk Mountain House (a privately owned hotel).

 From New York City, take the Thruway North to Exit 18 in New Paltz. Drive 2 miles west on NY 299 and turn right onto Ulster County 7 (Springtown Road) at a sign for "MOHONK MOUNTAIN HOUSE, 4." Shortly, turn left (northeast) onto Ulster County 6 (Mountain Rest Road). Drive approximately 4 miles on Mountain Rest Road to the entrance of the Mohonk Mountain House, at Mountain Rest. Turn left and pay a moderate to high day-use fee at the entrance gatehouse. Park in the lot adjacent to the gatehouse.

From the gatehouse, follow the worn path that runs along the right-hand (north) side of paved Huguenot Drive. In 0.25 mile, turn right onto gravel Whitney Carriageway at a sign that reads: "TO NORTH LOOKOUT ROAD." Two-tenths mile from Huguenot Drive, head straight across North Lookout Road. (Refer to our map to see the shortcut you're taking.) Soon, climb a flight of steps that leads to another section of North Lookout Road and turn right (north). As the road sweeps westward, you pass interesting ledges on the left. From a rustic gazebo on the right, take in the hike's first dramatic views into the Catskills. These frequent gazebos

Take in views of the Sawangunks from a gazebo along the Sky Top Carriageway.

offer safe places from which to enjoy the vistas as well as mark the group's progress. Children can switch off as hike leader as you pass one, or they can run ahead to a lookout and wait for the group to reassemble. The last lookout along this stretch is known as North Lookout.

At about 1 mile, turn left (east) onto Hemlock Lane. March through a hemlock forest (what else!) to a gazebo with views to the south. One-quarter mile from the intersection with North Lookout Road, Hemlock Lane merges with the paved "in" road. Turn left and walk about 100 yards, cross the road, and enter the woods on the right, still on Hemlock Lane. Take turns guessing how many miles of paths and carriageways wind through the Mohonk Mountain House property. Whoever guesses 50 miles (or gets closest) wins a piggyback ride for 50 paces.

After a brief climb, a railing on the left guards hikers from a steep drop-off. Shortly, at an intersection, turn right (north) onto Huguenot Drive (now a carriageway) and climb gradually through deciduous woods garnished with laurel and peppered with pitch pines and hemlocks. Gently rub a hemlock cone and then a pitch pine cone. Which one pricked you?

After passing Whitney Path on the right, Huguenot Drive bends southwestward and meets the Sky Top Carriageway. Turn left (southeast) onto the carriageway as Huguenot Drive continues southwestward toward

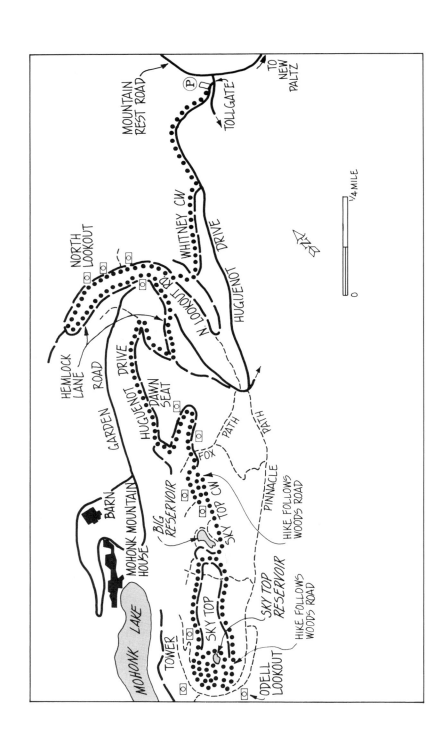

Mohonk Mountain House. Pass a gazebo known as Dawn Seat offering pretty easterly views. The carriageway curves sharply southeastward, then takes you past a lookout with views of the Mohonk Mountain House. The lodge's Victorian guests walked these paths a century ago, and exclaimed over the very same views!

Beyond the gazebo, pass Fox Path (a direct route to the Mountain Rest area), then look for the third gazebo on Sky Top Road, boasting even better views of the Mohonk Mountain House. Beyond the lookout, avoid Pinkster Path, which descends to the right. (How are your young hike leaders doing? Don't interfere. Allow them to find the way, even if it means you have to backtrack a few times.) Sky Top Road switches left, then right, and sweeps past a fourth gazebo. In another 0.1 mile, you can see Big Reservoir, a pretty pond choked with lily pads. The plush flowers that crown these pads blossom for most of the summer. Unlike other water-loving plants such as the rigid cattail, lilies have hollow, pliable stems and floating leaves. From the gazebo at the tip of a small peninsula, look through the binoculars at the lily pads, the water birds, and the ripples made by eager fish or large insects.

Stay straight (southwest) at the next two carriage path intersections. As Mohonk Path to Pinnacle Rock cuts across the carriage road and descends steeply to the left (southeast), continue straight ahead on Sky Top Carriageway. Near Odell Outlook, 2.8 miles from the start, railings stretch along the edge of the precipitous cliffs. This gazebo juts bravely over the edge, hanging several hundred feet above the valley floor, to provide an excellent view of the climbers' ledges known as the Trapps. Can you spot any climbers through the binoculars?

As it continues, the path switches right (northeast) and encircles the summit of Sky Top, quickly reaching the Smiley Memorial stone tower. The tower is named for the Smiley brothers, who bought and developed property in the area. Climb up 100 steps to the observation platform at the top, where the views of the Mohonk Preserve, Mountain House lands, and Shawangunk Mountains, Catskill Mountains, and the distant New York City skyline are unequaled. Those who elect not to climb to the top of the tower won't be disappointed: the ground views are also fabulous.

To return to your car, continue on Sky Top Road as it curls left. Pass Skytop Reservoir and a delightful picnic area, then sweep to the right below the tower. One-quarter mile from the tower, after visiting another series of gazebos, you reach a junction. Turn right, then left, at consecutive intersections, then track along the shoreline of Big Reservoir on a familiar section of Sky Top Road. Retrace your steps along the carriageways to Mountain Rest and your car.

Note: The Mohonk Mountain House charges moderate to high per-person and per-family rates on weekdays as well as weekends (weekends are more expensive). Pets are not permitted.

Hiking near the Mohonk Mountain House and Mohonk Lake

---

18. Copes Lookout and Mohonk Lake

Type: Dayhike
Difficulty: Easy for children
Distance: 2 miles, loop
Hiking time: 1.5 hours
High point/elevation gain: 1215 feet, 150 feet
Hikable: March–November
Map: NY/NJ Trail Conference Map 10A

What do a Tootsie Roll, six of the Seven Dwarfs (Grumpy's out), and the hike to Copes Lookout have in common? Give up? They're all short and sweet!

Try something a little different this time. Put the kids in charge of the hike. Give them the book and the compass and let them lead the way. The carriage paths are wide and smooth; the intersections—though plentiful—are clearly marked. The rustic gazebos that perch near frequent overlooks will serve as helpful landmarks. The most magnificent viewpoint is from Copes Lookout. From here, the stunning profile of the Trapps (the cliffs that lure rock climbers from all over the East Coast) will impress everyone—even little guys, normally nonchalant when it comes to views.

Now, what's the common denominator in this trio: Humpty Dumpty, Cathedral, and Giants? (Ohhh, no. . . . This one you'll have to figure out on your own.)

Follow the directions for Northeast Trail and Mohonk Preserve (Hike 20). From the parking area for the preserve's Visitor Center, drive another 0.6 mile on Mountain Rest Road to the entrance of Mohonk Mountain House at Mountain Rest on the left.

There are three ways to reach the trailhead from here.

1. On weekends only, pay a per-person day visitor's fee at the gatehouse and take the shuttle to the Day Visitor Center (picnic lodge).

2. If the Mohonk Mountain House has vacancies (most weekdays), drive to the Day Visitor Center and pay an additional $2 parking fee.

3. If you'd like to begin the hike at Mountain Rest (the Mohonk Preserve gatehouse), park and take Huguenot Drive to Whitney Road. Follow this road to North Lookout Road and join Mossy Brook Path, which brings you to the Day Visitor Center.

From the Day Visitor Center, follow the driveway to paved Barn Road and turn right (west). Head westward below the barn, passing a sign for Fiddlers Green parking. As you wind below the Mohonk Mountain House, with visitor parking on the left, Barn Road unceremoniously takes on a new name: Pine Hill Road. When Pine Hill Road twists to the left, bear right onto Copes Lookout Carriageway, cutting between the tennis courts and the tennis practice wall.

Dropping gently, the carriage road wanders alongside an athletic field, then enters evergreen woods accented with clusters of mountain laurel. Soon the road passes a bench on the right, then several gazebo lookouts. This route is popular with hiking families, and you can teach even the youngest children an important environmental lesson with a game of "What If Everyone Did It?" What if all of the families who walk on these paths left gum wrappers behind, picked the flowers alongside the path, pulled bark from the trees?

One-half mile from the start, the trail pauses at the junction of the Humpty Dumpty, Laurel Ledge, and Copes Lookout carriageways. Fork right to quickly reach Copes Lookout, with superb views of the Shawangunks and Catskills. (Note Cathedral Path diving steeply down the slope.) After you've gazed through the binoculars and admired the unique cliffs, return to the junction and head southward, now on Humpty Dumpty Carriageway. (Who remembers the words to the poem: "Humpty Dumpty sat on a wall . . ."?)

Pass another gazebo, then sweep past a rock slide on the left. Now trending southward, the Humpty Dumpty Carriageway passes Giants Path and Humpty Dumpty Path, foot trails that drop sharply off this ridge to the right. At an intersection 0.8 mile from the start, the Humpty Dumpty Carriageway ends at a junction. Turn left (east), following Short Woodland Drive as Long Woodland Drive marches straight ahead (south). Avoid Eagle Cliff Ascent diverging left and soon you arrive at another junction. Turn left onto Lake Shore Path (Short Woodland Drive bends right).

Lake Shore Path winds gently down through mixed woods and pockets of laurel and in 0.1 mile meets Undercliff Path. Turn left (north) onto

Undercliff Path as Lake Shore Path continues straight. Immediately, the trail snakes through a boulder maze dotted with pint-size caves. On a steamy day, pause here and drink in the cool dampness that settles among the rocks. Even on a brisk day in autumn, the kids will find it hard to resist stopping to explore.

As the southern edge of Mohonk Lake greets you, the trail strays near another gazebo, this one sited on a small peninsula. Open the backpacks and lay out the feast near the water's edge, for the views across the lake to the Smiley Memorial on Sky Top create the perfect setting for a picnic. Continuing, the trail hugs the shore, heading northward, then rises moderately above the lake, winding through hemlock and laurel. Here, the hillside slopes steeply from left to right. March past Lambdins Glen (a side trail that parts left) and descend on the wide path, passing more gazebos. The hike leaders will know they are on track when they come upon a ceiling of overhanging ledge that shelters a wooden bench.

As the trail sweeps tantalizingly close to the beach area reserved for hotel guests, turn left and climb a set of stairs (forty in all), nearing the hotel. Head northwestward, passing under a wooden footbridge, to reach Eagle Cliff Carriageway near the tennis courts. Turn right onto the carriageway, hike past the courts, and quickly return to Barn Road. Retrace your initial route to return to the Day Visitor Center.

19. The Labyrinth

Type:	Dayhike
Difficulty:	Challenging for children
Distance:	1 mile, loop
Hiking time:	2.5 hours
High point/elevation gain:	1500 feet, 250 feet
Hikable:	April–November
Map:	NY/NJ Trail Conference Map 10A

Gimme an "L"! Gimme an "A"! Gimme a "B"! Gimme . . . oh, never mind. Just take our word for it—you'll have something to cheer about when you finally emerge from the Labyrinth onto Sky Top's summit. The incredible Labyrinth will test everyone's agility and stamina as it makes hikers climb ladders up cliff walls and squeeze under, scramble over, and snake through a series of fantastic rock formations, gaining 250 feet along the way.

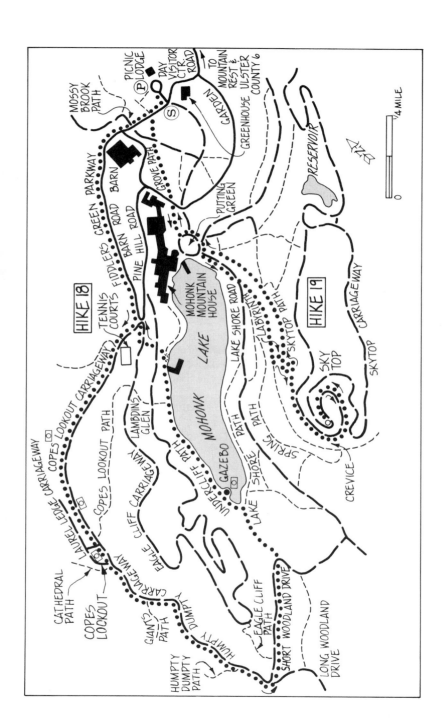

Assembling an appropriate group of hikers may be as challenging as the hike itself. Children should be at least ten years old and all members of the hiking party must be in good physical condition and quite nimble. If you're not sure your gang qualifies, give it a try. You'll know within the first 100 feet whether or not you'll make it. You have the option of turning around and taking the kinder, gentler Sky Top Path, which brings you to the summit near the Labyrinth's outlet.

 Follow the driving directions for Copes Lookout and Mohonk Lake (Hike 18).

From the Day Visitor Center, bear right on the paved road. Shortly, after passing a cabin on the left, bear left onto a paved section of Grove Path, heading for the Mohonk Mountain House. Before you reach it, go straight across paved Garden Road. Guided by a sign for day visitors, "TO SKY TOP AND THE LAKE," follow a path that swerves left to encircle a putting green. Join Lake Shore Road on the opposite side of the green and follow it along the southern shore of Mohonk Lake. Two-tenths mile from the start, a rustic gazebo rests high on a ledge overlook on the right; on the left, a sign points toward the Labyrinth.

Turn left onto the red-blazed Labyrinth Trail, passing a sign describing trail difficulties and another warning of upcoming rock scrambling. Follow blaze and arrow markings carefully. Don't attempt any shortcuts. (The kids can take turns being hike leader, quite a responsibility on this trip.) Inch through a tight boulder maze and twist right, approaching Lake Shore Road. Curl left just above the road and climb a set of wooden stairs.

Follow the trail as it struggles through a series of interconnecting crevices, curling to the right and descending. The kids can help watch for the red arrows that point left (before the end of the crevice) into a cave. Drop on all fours to crawl through the cave. Soon you'll be able to stand upright—the cave opens into a deep cavern. Climb a wooden ladder secured against the chasm's far wall to return to daylight. (Had enough? You can retrace your steps to the putting green and follow Sky Top Path to the summit instead.)

Make your way up another ladder that clings to the side of a cliff (with one adult in front and one in the rear). Head across several foot-bridges that span deep fissures in the rock. Tracking southwestward, the trail leads over more footbridges, drops through a river of boulders, then curls left, squeezing into another narrow passageway. (Be sure that your group stays together in case any little people—or big people—need assistance.)

Twisting back to the right, the trail crosses more bridges and tracks across massive rock slabs. Snaking below steep ledge on the left, the path

Visiting Smiley Memorial on Sky Top

disappears into another tunnel (these tunnels have been given nick-names such as "Fat Man's Misery"), exiting through a narrow channel. Help the kids leap over a cleft in the rock, taking time out to offer some well-deserved praise. Beyond the cleft, a handrail helps you pull yourself up a steep slope.

Crawl through a tunnel formed by two leaning boulders. When you emerge, tell the kids that they have a short reprieve from the Indiana Jones–type maneuvering. After an easy walk along the base of some cliffs, drop to the floor of a chasm and wind between the steep walls, eventually exiting to the left. As you emerge, look to the right of a hunk of ledge resembling a ship's hull. Can you spot another ladder? Climb down and follow the trail to a junction at 0.25 mile where a shortcut out of the Labyrinth exits left.

This shortcut trail climbs stiffly up a rocky, root-choked slope, bring-ing hikers to a set of steps that leads to the top of the cliffs and Sky Top Path. We recommend that families follow the steps, turning right on Sky Top Path to hike the remaining 0.25 mile to the summit along relatively gentle terrain. (The continuation of the Labyrinth Trail leads in 0.15 mile to the Crevice, a separation of ledge 50 feet deep and 100 feet long. Its width barely accommodates a solitary, slim hiker. Although the Labyrinth Trail theoretically leads through the Crevice to the Sky Top summit, this is not a manageable route for families.)

The wide, gravel Sky Top Path passes gazebos as it winds through hemlock forest and thickets of laurel, climbing moderately toward Sky Top. Although the path flirts with the cliff's edge, wooden railings protect little wanderers. Follow a side trail on the right that leads to a gazebo perched atop Thurston's Rock. From here, take in a delightful view of the Mohonk Mountain House and Mohonk Lake. The main trail concludes in another 0.15 mile at the summit; climb the tower to look down on the Trapps, the Mohonk Mountain House, and Mohonk Lake. Distant northerly views take in the entire Catskill Range.

To return to your car, follow Sky Top Path to the putting green, then retrace your earlier route to the Day Visitor Center and the parking area.

20. Northeast Trail and Mohonk Preserve

Type: Dayhike
Difficulty: Easy to moderate for children
Distance: 3.1 miles, loop
Hiking time: 2.5 hours
High point/elevation gain: 1194 feet, 300 feet
Hikable: April–November
Map: NY/NJ Trail Conference Map 10A

"Rats," you say, glancing at our description of Bonticou Crag (Hike 21). "I'd love to see that part of the Mohonk Preserve, but my family just isn't ready for a hike that tough."

For you, and the many others like you, we offer this tamer route to splendid Bonticou Crag, which avoids the difficult climb up the boulder slide, the section of Hike 21 that led to its "challenging" rating. Remember, though, that while Bonticou Crag is more accessible for young children via this route, the precipitous escarpment itself is the same. Parents must exercise caution and keep young children in sight, if not within reach.

Children will also enjoy following the self-guided nature trail around the petite pond that we've included in this Mohonk route; don't forget to stop in at the Mohonk Preserve Visitor Center to pick up a brochure describing the numbered stations.

From New York City, take the Thruway North to Exit 18 in New Paltz. Drive 2 miles west on NY 299 and turn right onto Ulster County 7 (Springtown Road) at a sign for "MOHONK MOUNTAIN HOUSE, 4." Shortly, turn left (northeast) onto Ulster County 6 (Mountain Rest Road). Drive approximately 3.5 miles on Ulster County 6 to a parking area on the left, across the road from the Mohonk Preserve Visitor Center.

From the parking area, head eastward, crossing Ulster County 6 by way of the crosswalk. Hike to the Mohonk Preserve Visitor Center and pick up a trail map and information sheet describing the self-guided Pond Loop Nature Trail. Head westward from the visitor center, climbing easily along the yellow-blazed Link Trail. Shortly, this wide path intersects with the blue-blazed Northeast Trail; turn right to follow the blue blazes northeastward toward Bonticou Crag. As former ski trails cross the path, gaze at the pretty views to the south and east over a bucolic valley. Kids, imagine what it was like to plummet down this snowy hill on skis!

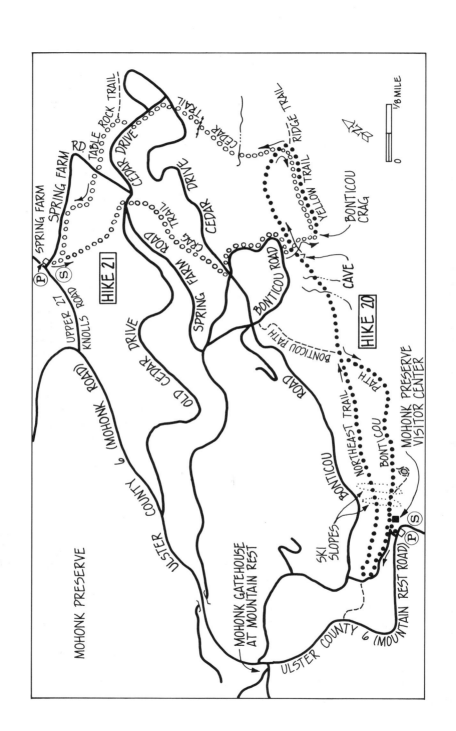

MOHONK PRESERVE

SPRING FARM

SPRING FARM RD.

TABLE ROCK TRAIL

CEDAR DRIVE

CEDAR TRAIL

CEDAR DRIVE

CEDAR

RIDGE TRAIL

YELLOW TRAIL

BONTICOU CRAG

CAVE

P SPRING FARM

S

HIKE 21

UPPER 27 KNOLLS ROAD

ULSTER COUNTY 6 (MOHONK ROAD)

CRAG TRAIL

SPRING FARM ROAD

OLD CEDAR DRIVE

BONTICOU ROAD

HIKE 20

BONTICOU PATH

BONTICOU PATH

NORTHEAST TRAIL

BONTICOU

MOHONK PRESERVE VISITOR CENTER

SKI SLOPES

ROAD

MOHONK GATEHOUSE AT MOUNTAIN REST

P S

ULSTER COUNTY 6 (MOUNTAIN REST ROAD)

0   1/8 MILE

Over the next 0.25 mile, the trail drops in and out of a series of gullies that drain spring runoff. As the red-blazed Bonticou Path cuts across the trail at the 0.6-mile mark, continue to follow the Northeast Trail's blue blazes. Descending gradually, the trail hops over two more gullies, then crosses an active brook. The blue blazes lead across an occasional stream, then direct hikers up a moderate hill through stands of oak and pine. In autumn, watch squirrels collecting acorns and toadstools in anticipation of winter. If you are hiking in the spring, you may catch a squirrel in the act of stealing a bird's egg for its supper.

At 0.9 mile, the trail climbs past boulders and ledge at the base of Bonticou Crag. On a hot day, you'll welcome the sudden "air-conditioning." To find the source of the cool air, look to the right through a rock crevice where previous hikers have worn a side trail. This unofficial path leads to a cave that sweeps around to the left, with an outlet farther up the trail. Who is daring enough to try the cave route? (We recommend the detour for very hot hikers: when the temperature on the trail is 90 degrees, the temperature inside the cave is closer to 65 degrees.)

Continue straight on the Northeast Trail as a yellow trail cuts through on its way (eastward) to the boulder slide below Bonticou Crag. One and two-tenths miles from the start, bear right with the blue trail at an intersection with the Cedar Trail, marked in red. Look to the right (east) at imposing ledges, the relatively meager tail of Bonticou Crag. Follow the blue trail to the base of the cliffs, then scale the steep (but manageable) slope to the top.

Curling right, the trail meets the blue-blazed Ridge Trail and a yellow-blazed trail. Turn right (south) onto the yellow-blazed trail, which soon sweeps southwestward on a moderate ascent. As the path snakes up through pitch pine and hemlock and across exposed ledge, the kids can count toadstools to ward off complaining. How many different varieties can you find? What purpose do you think these rather unique plants serve? (In essence, they are the forest housekeepers. By taking in dead material through their slender, hairlike roots, toadstools ensure that the forest will not be buried under layers of dead leaves and branches. They also fertilize the soil while they are tidying up.)

After 0.25 mile, the yellow trail arrives atop the lofty escarpment known as Bonticou Crag. From here, the panoramas extend across the Shawangunks and into the Catskills. (This is definitely one of those "climb-repaying" crests.) You can wander along the barren ridge of the crag for about 0.1 mile. Stop for a picnic along the cliffs and absorb the sun and the view. To keep kids from wandering close to the edge while you're eating, suggest that they touch various objects nearby and compare surface temperatures. Does a rock feel warmer than a pine cone? Is the top of your head as warm as your backpack? What do you think affects the amount of warmth an object retains?

Retrace your steps to the intersection of the Northeast Trail and Bonticou Path. Turn left (southeast) onto the red-blazed Bonticou Path and hike 0.2 mile to a side trail that splits left (east) onto the Pond Loop Trail. If you picked up a self-guided nature trail brochure at the visitor center, you'll feel as if you have your own personal naturalist leading your hike. Follow the numbered stations back to the visitor center or circle the pond to return to Bonticou Path, where you turn left, skirt the edge of a field, and return to the visitor center 0.1 mile from the pond.

Bonticou Crag

21. Bonticou Crag

Type:	Dayhike
Difficulty:	Difficult for children
Distance:	2 miles, loop
Hiking time:	2.5 hours
High point/elevation gain:	1194 feet, 550 feet
Hikable:	March–November
Map:	NY/NJ Trail Conference Map 10A

Recipe for a great hike: blend a spectacular Mohonk escarpment known as Bonticou Crag with one dramatic boulder slide, several lovely pastures and enduring stone walls, and twelve well-marked trail junctions. Garnish with clusters of mountain laurel and blueberry bushes. Mold into a manageable distance of 2 miles. *Voila!* A perfect day trip for experienced hikers!

Follow the directions for Northeast Trail and Mohonk Preserve (Hike 20). From the Nature Center parking area, follow Ulster County 6 approximately 1.5 miles and turn right onto Upper 27 Knolls Road. In 0.2 mile, turn right into a gravel parking area large enough for a dozen cars. (Don't turn onto gravel Spring Farm Road, which veers right just before the parking area.)

From the parking area, follow blue blazes south across gravel Spring Farm Road. At the edge of a field, head straight (south) on the red-blazed Bonticou Crag Trail as the blue-blazed Table Rock Trail veers left, wandering eastward. The red trail sweeps along the left side of a field, then winds up a gentle wooded hillside, trending southeastward.

As you hike through stands of imposing oaks, tell the kids to look for squirrels. Unlike many of their nocturnal neighbors, squirrels are active during the day. Can you see one darting toward its haphazard nest high above the ground or peering from its home in a hollow tree? Ask the kids how squirrels help spread oak forests like the one you are in now. (They bury acorns in the fall to retrieve in the winter, but sometimes their memory or sense of smell fails them and they miss some of their caches. With the warm spring weather, the forgotten acorns begin to grow into oak trees!)

At 0.3 mile, cross Old Cedar Drive and Spring Farm Road (both carriage paths) in quick succession, continuing to head southward. For the next 0.3 mile, wind on an easy ascent through oak groves and clusters of mountain laurel. What does the forest sound like? Do you hear a woodpecker drilling into a branch in search of grubs? The piping of birds? The drone of an airplane overhead?

Six-tenths mile from the start, the trail reaches an intricate junction with Bonticou Road and Cedar Drive. Turn to the left about 90 degrees to join the carriage path second from the left. Now heading northeast on Bonticou Road, sweep through airy woods, gradually drifting toward the south.

Bonticou Road meets a yellow-blazed trail 0.2 mile beyond the busy intersection. Leave the road to follow the yellow foot trail left (east), plunging toward a junction with the blue-blazed Northeast Trail. Follow the yellow trail straight, cutting across the Northeast Trail, to quickly encounter the base of a tremendous boulder slide.

Above and to the right are the dramatic cliffs of Bonticou Crag. The yellow trail forges ahead, angling to the left as it struggles to find the easiest route up the rugged boulder slide. Kids will need loads of encouragement (and possibly some adult assistance) on this challenging ascent. You'll have to drop to all fours at times and negotiate one hairy pass through a tight crevice.

Thankfully, after just 0.1 mile of climbing, you crest Bonticou Crag. At nearly 1200 feet, this ridge looms over the surrounding area, offering far-reaching westward views over the Shawangunk Mountains. Walk southwest along the ridge top for up to 0.1 mile, keeping young children close. Do you feel a persistent breeze on this open escarpment? Look for something the wind blew down. Have the kids blow on things. Can you make anything move with your kid-size breeze?

From the overlook above the boulder slide, follow the yellow trail northeastward. The leisurely trail drops gradually in and out of woods, leading through stands of red pine, pitch pine, hemlock, and oak, with mountain laurel and blueberry bushes crowding from either side.

One-quarter mile from the top of Bonticou Crag, the yellow trail ends at a junction with the blue-blazed Ridge Trail (heading eastward) and the Northeast Trail. Bear left (north) onto the Northeast Trail, quickly curling to the left and dropping sharply along the right side of the relatively meager tail of the Bonticou Crag. The kids may want to pause here to explore the wee caves and practice their "rock climbing" on the miniature ledges and sofa-size boulders.

Below the ledges, in the midst of a jumble of boulders, bear right (north) onto the red-blazed Cedar Trail as the blue-blazed Northeast Trail departs left (west). The Cedar Trail initially descends, sweeping over a tumbled-down stone wall. The blazes lead across a seasonal stream and up a gentle, wooded hillside. Cut through another stone wall, reaching the red-blazed Cedar Drive carriage road 0.25 mile from the last intersection. Bear right (north) onto Cedar Drive and turn left (west) to remain on Cedar Drive at the next intersection. As another carriage road joins from the right, stay straight (west) and quickly turn right onto a red side trail. Almost immediately turn left (west) onto Table Rock Trail, marked in blue, and pass through a weary rock wall.

Who can find the biggest pine cone? How about the smallest one?

Table Rock Trail falls through the woods and levels as it leads across the right side of a field. Look for signs of white-tailed deer; they tend to gather near the edges of meadows like this one. In the spring, you might find tracks in the mud; in autumn, look for marks on slender trees where bucks have rubbed the protective covering off their mature antlers. Year-round, you'll see twigs that have been chewed by hungry deer.

After an easy climb through the woods, the Table Rock Trail crosses Spring Farm Road and meets another field. As you climb along the right side of this pasture, the kids can race with the wind as it ripples the tall grass. Turn right as you join the blue-blazed Bonticou Crag Trail, cross Spring Farm Road, and return to your car.

Note: Hunting for small game and deer is permitted in this area after November 1.

The bridge at Vernooy Kill Falls

22. Vernooy Kill Falls

Type: Dayhike
Difficulty: Moderate for children
Distance: 3.6 miles, round trip
Hiking time: 3 hours
High point/elevation gain: 1750 feet, 700 feet
Hikable: May–October
Map: USGS Kerhonkson

Attention, nervous parents! Put your nail-biting, hand-wringing, and hair-pulling habits on hold and take your family on a hike to Vernooy Kill Falls. This route has no cliffs that require parents to restrain kids, no deep water to tempt little guys, no network of adjoining trails for them to mistakenly follow. So what *is* there? Just a nice, safe path that follows a steady but manageable grade to Vernooy Kill Falls. And even the waterfall is safe by waterfall standards: a series of child-friendly cascades tumbling within a shallow river. In late spring and early summer, hikers are treated to lengthy stretches of blossoming mountain laurel bushes. Summer hikers can bring extra shoes for wading, or even bathing suits and towels.

The creek and falls were named for Corn
earliest settlers in the Rondout Valley. About 2
first gristmill in the region, with equipment he ha
You can examine the remains of one such gri

From New York City, take the Thruway Nort
Follow NY 299 west for approximately 7.5 miles
intersection with US 44 West and NY 55. Turn r
44 and NY 55, and drive about 10.5 miles to the int
209. Turn right onto US 209 North and drive 1.5 miles; turn left (north)
onto Ulster County 3 (Pataukunk Road) in Pine Bush. Drive 3.5 miles
north on Ulster County 3 and turn left onto Lower Cherrytown Road (a
sign may say "CHERRYTOWN ROAD"). In 1.2 miles, bear right onto Upper
Cherrytown Road. (Notice the aqua paint blazes of the Long Path on
trees and telephone poles along this road.) Drive 3 miles on Upper
Cherrytown Road and watch for a sign pointing to a snowmobile/foot trail
on the left. Turn right here, onto a gravel road, and park in the substantial area on the left.

Cross Upper Cherrytown Road, guided by a sign that points toward
Vernooy Kill Falls, 1.8 miles away. Sidestep a gate and head northwestward,
following a woods road marked with orange snowmobile blazes and the
blue Department of Environmental Conservation hiking disks of the Long
Path. Spruce trees and mountain laurels line the way. Are these red or
white spruce trees? (Red spruces have needles that are shiny and dark
green; white spruces have whitish-green needles that smell "skunky" when
crushed.) Collect sample spruce cones to compare to the cones of other
evergreens you'll encounter farther up the trail. Descend gently for the
first 0.1 mile, then embark on a 1-mile-long ascent after crossing a sturdy
footbridge over Mombaccus Creek. Leading through stands of hemlocks,
the trail curves left (west) in 0.1 mile, away from the water on a moderate pitch. Trailside laurel returns at the 0.4-mile mark, flourishing in
a hardwood forest.

As the trail snakes steadily upward, trending to the northwest, distract
the kids from their weary legs by counting mushrooms or tree stumps
or moss-covered rocks. Play "Animal Charades." Who does the best frog,
tiger, elephant, or snake imitation? Play "Follow the Leader," changing
leaders frequently and encouraging each one to be creative! The trail
finally crests 1.4 miles from its start. Here, ferns thrive in damp conditions. Under giant hemlocks, the trail tracks westward on a gentle descent.
(Can you find hemlock cones to compare with the spruce cones you
collected earlier?) In July, search for low-bush blueberries.

At 1.8 miles, the trail opens onto a clearing at the base of Vernooy
Kill Falls. From the clearing, paths radiate in all directions; mark your
trail to avoid confusion on the return trip. Follow the Vernooy Kill upstream
for about 0.1 mile to enjoy the series of splashing cascades known as
Vernooy Kill Falls. Let the kids choose a riverside boulder to serve as

table and relax to the endless sound of water spilling down riverbed. From the footbridge at the base of the falls, the kids ay "Pooh Sticks" (from A. A. Milne's classic Winnie-the-Pooh sto-). Drop sticks into the water from one side of the bridge and peer over the other side to see whose stick appears first! Let the kids explore the riverbanks and wade in the pools that collect along the cascade. Accompany them on their investigation of the crumbling rock walls—ruins of a long-ago gristmill—that frame the river.

Return the way you came, taking care to follow your "marked" trail.

23. Hudson River at Mills Memorial State Park

Type: Dayhike
Difficulty: Easy for children
Distance: 2.7 miles, round trip
Hiking time: 2 hours
High point/elevation gain: 60 feet, 60 feet
Hikable: Year-round
Map: USGS Hyde Park

Money can't buy happiness, but it can buy lots of other neat stuff. Two hundred years ago, it bought Morgan Lewis 1600 acres in the central Hudson Valley, including the lovely riverfront property where the Mills Mansion now stands.

From the mansion, set back from the Hudson River on a manicured hillside, gently curving paths extend in all directions. Grand beech, spruce, and oak trees line the paths and roadways, the remains of an extensive greenhouse complex cover the area south of the palatial house, and elegant statues decorate the grounds. Visitors will have no trouble imagining how the estate must have looked a hundred years ago, with butlers hustling to heed orders and elegant ladies floating across the formal gardens twirling parasols with gloved fingers.

But this hike through the estate property and along the Hudson River offers more than the chance to enjoy a glimpse at the life-style of turn-of-the-century tycoons such as Ogden Mills and his wife, Ruth Livingston Mills. The kids will have a ball romping on the vast lawns, running ahead on the level paths, and counting the motorboats and sailboats bobbing far down the river. The hike offers constant water views, plus several opportunities for wading, splashing, and exploring when the trail swings close to the river's edge.

And unless you are buddies with the Vanderbilts or Rockefellers, this is one of the only ways to see a spread like this.

From New York City, take the Thruway North to Exit 10 in Tarrytown. Follow US 9 North for approximately 65 miles. Drive 0.5 mile beyond the Dinsmore Golf Club and Restaurant on the left and turn left onto Old Post Road. Drive about 0.5 mile, following signs to Mills Mansion State Historic Site. Turn right into the park; in another 0.3 mile, park in the lot near the mansion.

Stop at the mansion for a park map and, if you like, a tour. The view from the verandah across the manicured grounds to the Hudson River and across the water to the Catskills is delightful.

Run (you can't help running) down the right side of the expansive, sloping lawn toward the river. (One hundred years ago, this lawn was

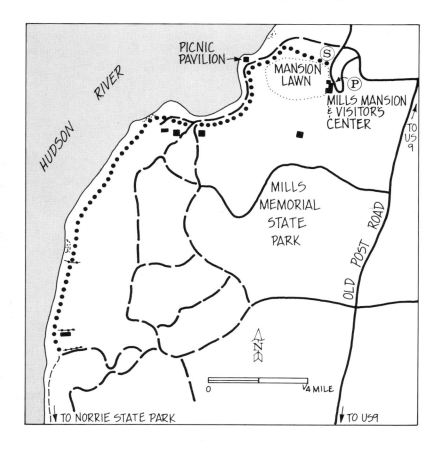

a cornfield.) Just before you reach the river, you'll meet a paved path that skirts the eastern bank. If stomachs are rumbling, continue to a sandy strip of beach and a picnic pavilion perched near the water. If you would rather postpone your picnic, turn left onto the paved path, heading southward.

Track along the ridge that follows the river, bordered on the left by the sweeping estate grounds. Does this trail service athletes other than hikers? Look for a sign that provides a clue. (The 5K marker indicates that this is a cross-country ski trail in the winter.) At a sign for a private residence 0.4 mile from the start, turn right onto another paved path that hugs the bank of the Hudson. With the residence on your left, head westward, passing a small sandy beach. One-half mile from the start, look for a Taconic Region trail marker at an intersection. Turn right here, onto a foot trail that borders the shoreline, as the now gravel road continues straight.

Seven-tenths mile from the start, the trail reaches a pebbly beach. Across the river, the Catskills loom over the nearby hills; to the south, the impressive Hudson rolls toward New York City. Tell the kids to sniff the air. Does the ceaseless westerly breeze carry an ocean scent? The Hudson is an estuary, meaning that the mouth of the Hudson meets the

Hiking brothers study the cattail marsh between Thompson Pond and Stissing Lake.

sea, is influenced by tides, and contains a mixture of fresh and salt water.

By 0.8 mile, the trail has tracked uphill and crested; the wooded slope that falls into the waters of the Hudson is steep here. Follow the path along rolling terrain through mixed woods, sweeping past a stiff drop-off guarded by a row of hemlocks. Soon, landscaped timber steps lead hikers down an embankment, closer to the water's edge.

Just under 1 mile from the start, the trail opens onto a coarse pebble beach. Drag sticks in the water to "fish," skip stones, look for water bugs darting close to shore. At the end of the beach, hop over a stone wall and mount a set of stairs to return to the elevated trail. As the path weaves through a lofty stand of white pines, look left to see an old pump house bordered by an enduring stone wall. At the 1.3-mile mark, as a trail defined by a stone wall leads left, continue straight toward a grassy knoll shaded by pine trees. An abutment supports the river's edge here, creating a sheer drop to the water. Enjoy a peaceful picnic under the pines or save your lunch for the lawn of the mansion, where you'll have lots of company.

Return to the mansion and your car the way you came.

Note: Dogs must be leashed.

---

24. Thompson Pond

Type:	Dayhike
Difficulty:	Easy for children
Distance:	2.4 miles, loop
Hiking time:	2 hours
High point/elevation gain:	410 feet, 70 feet
Hikable:	May–October
Map:	USGS Pine Plains

Thompson Pond, settled in a yawning valley west of the Taconic Range, is no ordinary wilderness lake. A national natural landmark, this 44-acre glacial kettle was created nearly 15,000 years ago when massive blocks of ice melted to create a deep hole (which eventually pinched off in two places to form nearby Stissing and Twin Island lakes in addition to Thompson Pond). Today, this circumneutral bog attracts the attention of naturalists and nature lovers due to the abundance of wildlife it supports and and its unusual combination of both bog and marsh qualities.

Kids may yawn at the background information ("Circumneutral bog?"), but they won't be bored on the hike. We met three local boys at the trailhead—brothers, aged twelve, ten, and five—who offered to act as our guides. They had just finished walking around the pond, but effortlessly repeated the route with us. They reinforced our belief that this easy trail with gentle ups and downs is appropriate for just about anyone in just about any physical condition. Although the trail circles the pond from a distance, frequent water views punctuate the route. Farms and footbridges, cattails and boardwalks combine to make this Nature Conservancy property a delight.

From New York City, take the Thruway North to the Taconic State Parkway (north). About 100 miles from the city, take the Lafayetteville exit onto NY 199 East. Follow NY 199 East for 6.8 miles to Pine Plains and the junction with NY 82. Drive 0.3 mile south on NY 82 and turn right onto Lake Road, immediately passing a fire station on the left. One and a half miles from NY 82, pull off the left side of the road into the parking area for Thompson Pond (as Lake Road bends right).

Follow the wide path southward through mixed deciduous woods, glimpsing Thompson Pond in about 100 yards. As you pass a registration box and information board 0.15 mile from the start, a blue-blazed trail veers right to make a longer loop around the pond while another blue trail splits left to sweep close to the water and quickly rejoin the main trail. Avoid the blue side trails and continue straight on the grassy, level woods road. Kids can lead the way, equipped with only the knowledge that the pond will always be on their left. Shortly after the short pond loop trail rejoins the woods road, another blue-blazed trail branches right as you head straight.

Soon, the pond dominates the landscape. Choked with white and yellow pond lilies and rimmed with marshy banks, this body of water serves the needs of frogs and turtles, not human bathers. At a junction 0.6 mile from the start, the dwindling woods road you've been following continues straight as you bear left (southeast) onto a foot trail up a slight grade. Here, hemlocks mingle with birches and maples. Hug trees to determine the age of the forest. Do your arms reach all the way around these trees? Is this a young or an old forest? The trail winds through the woods, following the curve of the shoreline but rarely approaching the pond's mucky edge.

At 0.7 mile, pause atop a bluff near a granite bench memorial to Elting Arnold, who helped preserve the pond and surrounding land. Enjoy the pleasant water views and pass around the binoculars. Golden eagles have been spotted here. Can you identify any of the birds you see? Are any woodland creatures stopping for a drink? (If it's not your turn for the binoculars, focus on the natural beauty nearby. Look for wildflowers like Dutchman's-breeches, lady's slipper, and wild geranium.)

As you approach the southern end of the pond, cross a footbridge and follow sporadic yellow arrows along rolling terrain. Follow the trail

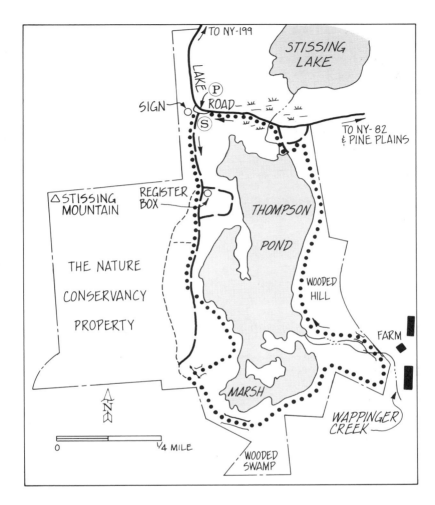

through a break in an ancient stone wall, to an intersection. As a blue-blazed trail heads right (northeast), follow the left-hand (southeast) path along a fence that marks the edge of a field.

The path veers away from the field, dips into a sag, and then scrambles out to a northerly view over the pond. The trail rejoins the edge of the field beyond the overlook and sweeps left away from the fence, plunging down a steep slope. Nearly 1 mile from the start, let the kids lead the way across a lengthy stretch of boardwalk cutting though a red maple swamp. Who can point out the skunk cabbage? If no one can identify it by sight, use your sense of smell. Break off a leaf and take a whiff to discover how this malodorous plant got its name.

Soon, the trail opens onto the swampy water's edge. Send the kids on a "hunt" for frogs: they can follow the croaking until it stops, pause until the voices resume, then close in on their prey. (Always encourage children to return any creature they capture to its original spot after examination.) Wrapping around the southern end of the pond, the trail runs along a section of raised gravel that may have been an old retaining wall. The numerous white birches seem to illuminate the woods.

As you sweep northwestward, the fire tower that crowns 1430-foot Stissing Mountain looms over the treetops. Some geologists belive that this mountain is actually a gigantic fault block—like a mountain island—that was either pushed or slid here millions of years ago. Ask the kids to guess how scientists came to that conclusion. (They compared the age and composition of the shales of the surrounding valley with the mountain's bedrock and discovered that the Precambrian mass of the mountain is significantly older.)

As you weave along a tangled fence that marks a farmer's boundary, turn your binoculars away from the deer to focus on the Holsteins grazing in the pasture. Pass outbuildings and barns on the right, and embark on another extended section of boardwalks and footbridges, 1.5 miles into the hike. Here, at the property's lowest elevation, Thompson Pond empties into this swamp and funnels into Wappinger Creek. Here the creek begins its 30-mile journey to the Hudson River. Do you see any snapping turtles?

Curling left (west), the trail winds around the southern base of a wooded hill before curling back to the right up a slight grade. As the trail follows the edge of another field, yellow arrows guide you along a path choked with seasonal undergrowth.

Notice that the hemlocks you saw on the opposite shore are absent here. Ask older kids why this is so. What are the differences between the two sides of the pond? Does the hemlock have more competition in this sunnier location from red maples, ash, and other hardwoods?

At the pond's northern end, the path meets a woods road where an arrow indicates a left turn. Within 100 feet, turn left at a second arrow, descending through a gravel gully to reach the northern shore. From here, you have the best views of the trip across the pond to Stissing Mountain. Take turns looking through your binoculars at the fire tower while the kids hug more trees. Is this forest older or younger than the one across the pond? Turn right to weave along the shoreline as the trail widens to become a woods road. You'll reach Lake Road after 2.1 miles of hiking; turn left and walk 0.25 mile to your car, crossing the causeway (beside a cattail marsh) that separates Thompson Pond from Stissing Lake.

Note: Camping and fires are not allowed.

Berry picking near Wappinger Creek

25. Rudd Pond

Type: Dayhike or overnight
Difficulty: Easy for children
Distance: 2.4 miles, loop
Hiking time: 2 hours
High point/elevation gain: 1050 feet, 340 feet
Hikable: May–October
Map: NY/NJ Trail Conference Map 14

Rudd Pond is proof that all ponds were not created equal. This clear, shallow pond, easily accessed from NY 62, is a delightful combination of natural features and man-made conveniences. The expanse of manicured lawn, dotted with picnic tables and shaded by grand trees, ushers visitors toward the beach, where they can sunbathe, swim, or rent boats for fishing or exploring. Nearby, the Rudd Pond Campground provides tent sites and platforms, a recreation hall, a playground, and shower and bath houses for families interested in staying overnight.

A gentle path leads along the eastern shore of Rudd Pond to the smaller and more rugged Iron Mine Pond, then winds along the brook that feeds the ponds, looping back through pleasant woodlands to return to the swimming beach and campground.

Wear long pants; the trail is overgrown in places.

From New York City, take the Taconic State Parkway North about 90 miles to US 44. Follow US 44 East for approximately 15 miles to Amenia and continue on combined US 44 and NY 22 for another 7 miles to Millerton. In Millerton, follow US 44 as it splits right from NY 22, then turn left (north) onto NY 62. In 1 mile, you pass a sign for "RUDD POND, TACONIC STATE PARK." Two and two-tenths miles from US 44, turn right into Taconic State Park, Rudd Pond. Drive past the caretaker's booth (pay a moderate admission fee in season) and, 0.4 mile from the entrance, turn left (before the camping area) into a parking area for hikers and park visitors.

Follow the paved park road southeastward along the shore, cutting through the campground. As the road ends in a turnaround, follow an unblazed, though well-worn, foot trail into mixed woods, still heading southward. Soon the level trail skirts the marshy outlet to the pond, giving kids a great opportunity to poke around for frogs and newts, dragonflies and water striders. Look for a water boatman, with its characteristic set of legs that act like oars propelling it through the water.

Just over 0.5 mile into the hike, the trail struggles through an

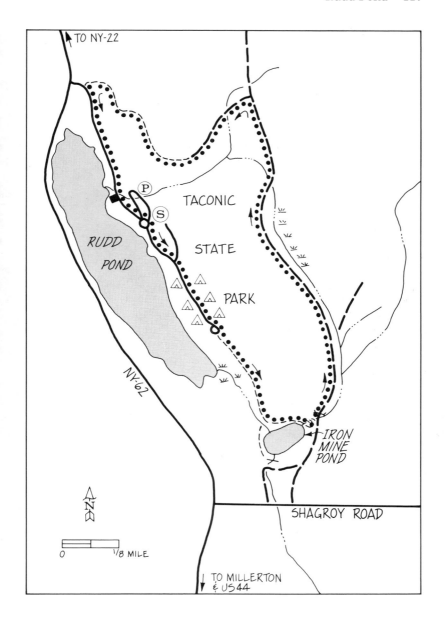

overgrown meadow. A sign nailed to a tree on the left warns that you are approaching "DEEP WATER." Indeed, you quickly arrive at the bank of Iron Mine Pond, its wild shores contrasting with the tended lawns of its

Father and son survey the still waters of Rudd Pond.

larger neighbor. And the contrast is more than just a surface one: this 5-acre pond is almost 80 feet deep, whereas Rudd Pond covers 64 acres and reaches a maximum depth of only 10 feet.

At the pond's edge, the trail divides. A right turn brings you in 100 yards to a small beach and the pond outlet. (Advise the kids to save the swimming for Rudd Pond.) Return to the junction and wind eastward along the shore. Let the kids lead the group to the boisterous waterfall at Iron Mine Pond's eastern tip. Here, an unnamed brook that originates in the Connecticut hills hurls itself down a rocky embankment to end in a final rush at the pond's edge. Rest here; the kids can tip stones on edge to see what creatures might be hiding underneath.

Cross the mouth of the stream as it joins the pond and follow a steep foot trail along the right side of the 15-foot falls. At the crest, the trail opens onto a gravel road. Turn left and immediately cross over the brook on a bridge, pass through a metal gate, and follow the road as it sweeps right to track along the brook's western bank. Initially heading northward, the trail climbs gradually over the next mile on a gravel road. The cascading stream provides soothing background noise and pleasant company. Which makes a better boat: an acorn or a twig? The banks of the brook steepen; 0.1 mile from the gate, you pass a crumbling dam. In another 0.1 mile, as the brook splits, stay on the gravel road following the left branch of what is now a stream. Shortly, at a fork, the gravel road bears right to cross the stream but you continue straight, following a woods road with frequent grassy patches. As the stream narrows to a trickling ribbon, the grade levels amidst patches of ferns and skunk cabbage. What other wetland vegetation can you identify?

The trail wanders across a small clearing, 1.4 miles from the start, rimmed with stands of tall white birches. As the footpath leaves the clearing it bends right (northeast), hops over the stream in two steps, then bends back to head northward. As the path narrows and underbrush crowds from both sides, the hike leader must watch more carefully for state park markers and for signs of previous hikers.

As the trail gently crests and passes through a wet area, look for an indistinct side trail that splits left. A state park sign marks a tree at the intersection. If you miss the side trail, you will drop down a slight slope to a small stream; retrace your steps approximately 100 feet. Follow the side trail westward and cross a raucous stream. (Here we startled a ruffed grouse from the underbrush.) Beyond the stream, the trail curls left (southwest) and begins a modest descent. Can you find any garter snakes?

The trail becomes more difficult to follow as it winds northwestward toward NY 62. Who will be the first to spot Rudd Pond through the trees on the left? Though your distant views are limited by the thick woods, you can catch glimpses into the lovely Harlem Valley.

Point out to kids the moss underfoot. What can they determine about the conditions under which moss grows? Does this plant prefer sun or shade? Damp or dry conditions? Is all moss the same? Still sweeping right, the trail avoids a steep descent and cuts into the ridge to drop gently to the valley floor. As the trail bottoms out, it becomes less distinct: watch for a faint path on the left that leads to Rudd Pond's picnic and beach area. You may need to bushwhack for 100 yards or so in a westerly direction (guided by your compass and the sound of vehicles on NY 62). Once you reach the manicured park grounds, turn left (south) on the paved park road. Pass Rudd Pond on the right and soon arrive at your car.

Note: Dogs are not permitted. The park is closed from 9 P.M. to 8 A.M.

26. South Brace Mountain

Type: Dayhike
Difficulty: Challenging for children
Distance: 4.0 miles, loop
Hiking time: 4.5 hours
High point/elevation gain: 2304 feet, 1500 feet
Hikable: May–October
Map: NY/NJ Trail Conference Map 15

Two want to visit waterfalls and three beg for a mountain climb. How can you satisfy everyone in your group? Hike to South Brace Mountain, passing a lovely waterfall as well as several overlooks along the way.

South Brace Mountain is situated in an area known as the Southern Taconic Highland or South Taconic Mountains, which extend from Mount Greylock in the north to the Catskill Mountains in the west, reaching southwest to the Hudson Highlands. Created 450 million years ago, the Taconic Range slid to its current location down a lower slope of the Green Mountains. This type of formation is referred to as a "klippe." The wild, remote land surrounding the mountain supports bobcats, coyotes, snowshoe hares, and black bears.

We recommend a fall hike due to soggy sections along the yellow trail. At other times of the year, you'll want to put everyone in waterproof footgear.

 From New York City, follow the Taconic State Parkway North for about 90 miles to US 44. Drive on US 44 East for approximately 15 miles to Amenia and continue on combined US 44 and NY 22 for another 7 miles to Millerton. As US 44 splits right (east), continue straight (north) on NY 22 for another 5.5 miles. Turn right onto Whitehouse Crossing Road; in 0.7 mile turn left (north) onto Whitehouse Road. Drive 0.2 mile to Deer Run Road; turn right. Follow Deer Run Road for 0.5 mile, then turn left onto Quarry Hill Road. In 0.4 mile, park on the left shoulder at the South Taconic trailhead.

Locate the trailhead near a wooden "TACONIC STATE PARK" sign and a tree marked with the triple white blazes of the South Taconic Trail. The trampled path skirts the right side of a privately owned field, rising gradually. As it nears the end of the field, the trail ducks into mixed deciduous woods on the right, near a trail sign. Red and white oaks, red maples, and bigtooth aspens flourish here. Once in the woods, the slope

Mount Frissell, part of the Southern Taconic Highland

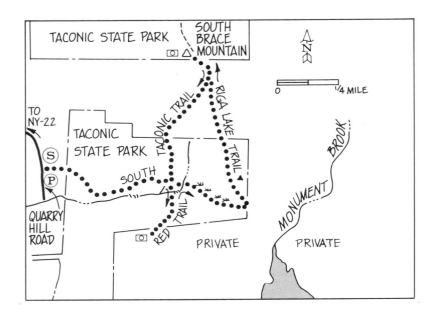

steepens dramatically as the trail climbs the Southern Taconic Highland's western escarpment. The path leads uphill toward the sound of rushing water.

One-quarter mile from the start, join a rocky ravine that cradles a galloping brook. Deep ravines such as this one, crowded with hemlock, paper birch, and striped maple, are common along the escarpment. Can the kids guess some of the items Native Americans made from the bark of the paper birch? (Waterproof household containers, parts of fish nets, canoes, moose calls, games, toys, and wigwam shingles.) Notice that most of the paper birches and shade-loving hemlocks are growing on the opposite side of the ravine, where the slope faces the northwest. (This could also be the result of selective logging.)

Climb along the left side of the creek, squeezing between two ledge outcroppings. Point out to the kids the wavy streaks of bluish-green metamorphic rock that snake across the exposed boulders on the slope. As you embark on a very steep, rugged ascent, the path trudges beside a breathtaking waterfall, diverting your attention from your tiring legs. The kids will need a lot of encouragement along this stretch—take turns telling knock-knock jokes.

Near the top of the falls, the trail switches left (north) and tracks across bedrock outcrops near the top of the Taconic ridge escarpment. Here, an outstanding westward view of the bucolic Harlem Valley—a preview of coming attractions—emerges. Quickly, the trail cuts right (southeast) as the view expands to include the Catskill Mountains. Wild blueberry bushes flourish on the slope. Stop and pick for a while—tell the kids that the tough climbing (0.25 mile in all) is over.

Approaching the top of the ridge, the trail darts into the woods, crosses a tributary of the brook, and quickly comes upon an intersection (0.6 mile from the start). To the right (south), a red-blazed side trail leads in 0.2 mile to an overlook. Follow the red side trail across the brook, where a final surge up a rocky path brings you to a spot with delightful valley views. Do you see any turkey vultures or red-tailed hawks floating on the thermals below?

Retrace your steps along the red trail to within 30 feet of the intersection with the white trail. Cross the brook just south of the junction and look right (east). Tucked under some hemlocks is a miniature waterfall and a wading pool carpeted with moss. Does the moss all look and feel the same or are there several different species here? (Have the kids describe the conditions under which moss grows. Have they ever noticed moss growing in a dry, sunny spot?)

To the left of the falls, a yellow-blazed trail begins a 0.4-mile ramble over the ridge toward Riga Lake Trail. A mountaintop marsh makes for soggy going for the first 0.25 mile, though kids never seem to mind an excuse to splash. (And everyone will appreciate the fact that the terrain is level.) The trail dries out and begins to descend, meeting the blue-blazed Riga Lake Trail amidst thickets of mountain laurel, 1.6 miles from the start.

After a rest, turn left to follow the Riga Lake Trail on a gradual ascent, heading northwestward toward Brace Mountain through a forest of slender, young trees—this area was logged in the 1800s to provide charcoal for the local iron industry. Have the kids hug some trees. Do their arms reach all the way around?

As the trail works its way back to the top of the ridge, following blue markers and an occasional cairn, feel the breezes pushing in from the west. At 2.0 miles, kids can look forward to scaling the man-size boulder on the right. In another 0.3 mile, you meet the white-blazed South Taconic Trail; turn right (north).

A brief, easy climb brings you to the rocky, rounded, and child-friendly summit of South Brace Mountain, 2304 feet above sea level. Adults can enjoy the far-reaching views to the Hudson Highlands and the Catskill and Taconic ranges (look for Riga Lake, South Pond, and Grass Pond to the southeast) while the kids pick from the abundant blueberry bushes. The tiny wild berries are sweeter than large, cultivated berries, although it takes some determined picking to fill a bucket. Grassy patches offer comfortable resting spots to those who are too pooped to either pick or gaze. Relax while the kids explore the open mountaintop.

(If your group feels particularly energetic, you can hike another 0.5 mile northwestward to the summit of Brace Mountain, marked by a large stone cairn that gives it the local name of Monument Mountain. At 2311 feet, Brace Mountain has the highest elevation of the western Taconic range, with views that take in the peaks in three states, including Connecticut's Bear Mountain and Massachusetts's Mount Greylock. Hang gliders often soar from its summit.)

Return along the white-blazed South Taconic Trail, which flirts with the western edge of the Taconic escarpment for about 0.8 mile, avoiding the Riga Lake Trail. The kids may need assistance on a couple of tricky descents. Don't miss the brief westerly views into the Harlem Valley as the trail leads every so often onto bald face.

At the intersection with the red trail, turn right (west) still following the white markings of the South Taconic Trail. Now on familiar turf, retrace the final 0.7 mile to your car, exercising caution on the steep descent.

27. Cruger Island and the Hudson River

Type: Dayhike
Difficulty: Easy to moderate for children
Distance: 2.7 miles, round trip
Hiking time: 2.5 hours
High point/elevation gain: 50 feet, 50 feet
Hikable: March–December
Map: USGS Saugerties

Buy or borrow a bird-watching guidebook and binoculars, check the tide schedule (in the newspaper, or with the local police), and then head for Cruger Island, part of the Hudson River Estuarine Sanctuary at Tivoli Bays. We recommend that you visit in the spring or fall, when the undergrowth is less intrusive and when migrating birds will be stopping here to rest.

Kids who are more interested in snapping turtles and ducks than in viewing distant peaks from a mountain summit will list this hike among

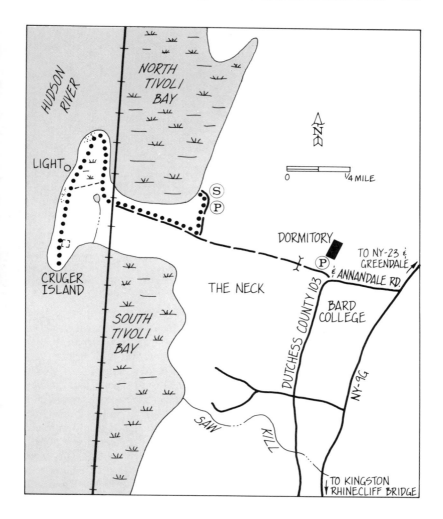

their favorites. And adults will emerge from this sanctuary relaxed and refreshed.

From New York City, take the Taconic State Parkway North to the junction with NY 199 in Lafayetteville. Drive west on NY 199 approximately 10 miles to NY 9G, west of Redhook. Follow NY 9G north for 1.9 miles and turn left onto Dutchess County 103 (Annandale Road). Enter the Bard College campus. In 0.3 mile, continue straight, now on Cruger Lane, as Annandale Road bends left. Park in the dormitory parking area on the right, 100 yards beyond the intersection, or continue on rough, narrow Cruger Lane. In 0.1 mile, pass a sign at a metal gate for the Tivoli

North Tivoli Bay, with the Catskills in the distance

Bays Wildlife Management Area. In another 0.4 mile, the road divides. Turn right and drive 0.1 mile to the parking area for Tivoli's North Bay.

From the edge of North Bay, at the tidal boat launch, survey the cattail marsh that stretches to the distant railroad tracks separating it from the Hudson River. (Together, South and North bays encompass 1400 acres.) Amidst the dense cattails, purple loosestrife, pickerelweed, and arrowhead, look for marsh-loving birds such as ducks, long-billed marsh wrens, and herons. The least bittern, a relatively tiny species of heron, is a master of camouflage, and extremely difficult to spot. Listen for its song, especially in early summer, a soft "coo-coo-coo." Peer into the water: a great many snapping turtles live in the bay, in addition to bass, perch, and minnows. What do you see?

Poll the kids: do they think the water in this marsh is fresh or salt water? Now dip in a finger and taste. Even though the tides affect the level of the marsh by as much as 4 feet, the salt front from the ocean is usually pushed back by the force of the Hudson River near Poughkeepsie. This is a freshwater tidal marsh.

Head south to return to the intersection with Cruger Lane, 0.15 mile from where you parked. At the junction, turn right (west) and walk down muddy Cruger Lane, which bisects Tivoli's North and South bays. The bays connect at high tide, so time your hike according to the tide schedule. Dense vegetation crowds the causeway as you track through a red maple, red ash, and black ash swamp. Look into the water for schools of banded killifish, common in both freshwater and saltwater habitats. Ask the kids a true or false question: swamps have trees and marshes don't. (True. Swamps are overwhelmingly wooded, while marshes are covered with a variety of grasses.)

Three-tenths mile down Cruger Lane, the road opens onto a clearing bisected by railroad tracks. This is an active line, so take care as you approach the tracks. (When we hiked here, a train passed through every five minutes or so.) Solo hikers might resent the intrusion of noisy locomotives, but families might want to linger near the tracks, treating the kids to a close-up look at a speeding train.

Head over the tracks and angle slightly right to enter dense woods on a faint, narrow foot trail. The daylilies and vinca (periwinkles) that cluster near the initial section of trail are reminders of the 1835 estate of John Cruger that once crowned Cruger Island. The overgrown foot trail climbs a minor ridge and crosses onto the island. As you duck under a fallen tree, look left to see a tiny pond. Beyond the pond, continue straight, avoiding a side trail that veers left. What sounds do you hear as you sweep along the island's eastern shore? The distant buzz of speedboats on the Hudson? The belching of frogs on the shore of the pond?

Tracking northward, the trail soon reaches higher (and drier) ground. As it leads through a gully, the trail is surrounded by airy woods, primarily oak. (Watch out for poison ivy.) Less than 1 mile from the start, the route arrives at a pebble beach on the northwest shore of Cruger Island. The Catskill Mountains rise prominently to the west. Look across the river to the cluster of buildings that make up the tiny town of Glasco; Overlook (Hike 28) and Plattekill mountains loom behind. From here, the trail curls left to run along the western edge of the island.

As they witness the flocks of birds that stop at this sanctuary on their way to a warmer climate, the kids might wonder how birds know when it is time to migrate. Because birds time their departures so precisely, ornithologists believe the length of the days influences the start of their journey. As the days get shorter with the approach of winter, birds sense that it is time to begin the trip south. Many birds could withstand the frigid temperatures in the Northeast; the lack of food during the winter is what makes migration necessary.

As it climbs a ridge, the trail is squeezed between the Hudson River on the right and a marsh on the left. The footpath becomes fainter as it winds through hemlock stands close to the riverbank. Who will be the first to spot the navigational light that keeps boats from straying too close to the island? At 1.15 miles, a side trail splits left to cut across the island's midsection and join the trail you followed on the way in. Continue straight, following the main trail as it opens onto a shale and sandstone beach. Look downstream to see the Kingston-Rhinecliff Bridge spanning the Hudson. Head across the beach, scaling a rocky, root-choked hillside, with the river on your right. Look for woodchuck and opossum tracks.

The trail works its way southward on rolling terrain overlooking the river. To the southwest, the river seems to end at the Kingston-Rhinecliff Bridge. Although the trail is somewhat indistinct here, stay close to the riverbank. Have other folks recently hiked this path? How can you tell? Is the brush trampled; are branches broken off? Or are you brushing back cobwebs? At 1.3 miles, pass a brick foundation on the left. Take turns naming all the sounds you hear: squirrels rustling in the underbrush, birds chattering overhead, the ceaseless lapping of the waves on the shore. Just under 1.5 miles from the start, the trail ends abruptly atop a grassy bluff at the southern tip of the island. Rest on the granite seat overlooking the Hudson and South Bay. Set out your picnic lunch and enjoy the river views. Return leisurely the way you came.

28. Overlook Mountain

Type: Dayhike or overnight
Difficulty: Challenging for children
Distance: 5 miles, round trip
Hiking time: 5 hours
High point/elevation gain: 3140 feet, 1450 feet
Hikable: May–October
Map: NY/NJ Trail Conference Map 41

If the ruins of a grand hotel and views from the steps of a fire tower aren't enough to interest you in hiking up Overlook Mountain, will one of the best campsites in the Catskills area do it? Just below the summit, on the mountain's eastern side, is an open ledge with lovely, long-range views. Primitive fireplaces and level, grassy spots for tents are tucked between walls of protective ledge near an oak forest.

This isn't an easy climb, but it is easy to follow, ascending a gravel road with few trail junctions. So, if your family is in good condition but has limited hiking experience (and if an overnight sounds tempting), put Overlook Mountain on your hiking list.

 From New York City, take the Thruway North to Exit 20. Follow NY 212 West for approximately 10 miles to Woodstock. At the junction of NY 212 and Ulster County 33 in the center of town, turn right (north) onto Ulster County 33. In 0.6 mile, continue straight across a four-way intersection with Glasco Turnpike (also known as Ulster County 33), now heading north on Meads Mountain Road. In another 0.3 mile, continue straight as roads go left and right. Two and six-tenths miles from NY 212, park in the wide parking area on the right.

Explore the Overlook Mountain House ruins with caution.

From the northwestern corner of the parking area, squeeze through an opening in a chain-link fence. Turn right onto the red-blazed Overlook Spur Trail (a gravel access road) and pass a sign for Overlook Mountain (2.5 miles away). Sign in at the registration box, then follow the initially level road eastward. In 0.2 mile, the trail sweeps left (northeast) and embarks on an increasingly steep ascent that continues until you reach the ruins, 1.8 miles away.

Because you are climbing steadily along an uneventful stretch of road, use some creative strategies to keep the kids interested. Begin with a scavenger hunt. Each hiker must look for something round, something that has been chewed, something squishy, and something red. Then sing songs with animals in them. Finally, play "Big and Small": find the biggest and smallest pine cone, leaf, fern, mushroom....

About 1 mile into the hike, continue straight, avoiding the side road that veers right. Late-summer hikers will find raspberries along the way. At 1.8 miles, seasonal views emerge to the east and west. (Tell the kids that they are close to the ruins now.)

Two miles from the start, weary young hikers will be revitalized by the sight of the Overlook Mountain House ruins. In 1870, this grand hotel welcomed up to 300 guests at a time and proclaimed itself the highest of all the Catskills hotels at 2978 feet. After several popular and prosperous decades, the hotel experienced a decline in business and the buildings fell into disrepair. A restoration effort was halted because of the 1929 stock market crash. The skeletal ruins that remain—two basic

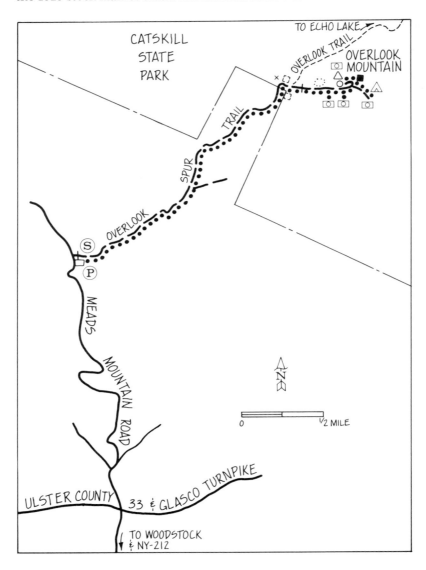

structures—are somewhat dangerous to explore, with scattered pieces of broken glass and metal, and doors that once opened onto wooden floors now leading to significant drop-offs. In fact, the state is attempting to purchase the dilapidated structure to demolish it. Parents will need to supervise any scouting expeditions.

When the kids are ready to move on, follow the gradually ascending trail past the left side of the larger structure. Before reaching some transmission equipment, turn right, passing between the two former hotel buildings. At a junction 0.1 mile beyond the ruins, the blue-blazed Overlook Trail leads left (northeast), reaching Echo Lake in 2 miles. You bear right (east) on the gravel road (still on the Overlook Spur Trail) toward the summit of Overlook Mountain, 0.5 mile away.

Who knows what "camouflage" means? (It comes from a French word that means "to disguise.") The kids can take turns running ahead and hiding just off the trail, trying to blend in with their surroundings as much as possible. How many creatures can you name that use camouflage to protect themselves from their enemies? (A polar bear's white fur blends in with the snow, the stripes on a zebra make it harder to see in tall grass, even a soldier's uniform is designed with camouflage in mind.) Can each child find a camouflaged insect?

As you pass through a metal gate, look left to see a gravel pit. On the right, a number of side trails lead to overlooks. The gravel road sweeps around the back of the mountain to approach the fire tower from the north, passing an old, rundown forest ranger's cabin just below the summit.

The fire tower is in need of repair, and parents should evaluate its condition before letting children climb the stairs. In any case, walking up just 10 or 15 steps rewards you with superb panoramic views. The Hudson Valley lies to the east; layers of mountains stretch along the western horizon. To the northeast, you can see nearby Indian Head Mountain (Hike 29). Those who have visited a number of other summits will notice the unusual vegetation here: hardwoods (especially northern red oak) cover this mountaintop.

Drop down the mountain toward the ranger's cabin. To the right of this building, follow an unmarked footpath southeastward, descending gradually for 200 feet to open ledges with superb southerly views over the Hudson Valley and the southern Catskills. Here, several campsites, well back from the ledges and protected from the strong north and west winds, welcome tents, making the arduous climb to the summit worthwhile. Blueberry bushes fringe the open area. (There are also rattlesnake dens here, but if you're careful to look where you place your hands and feet, you need not worry. As you've heard so often about everything from bears to bumblebees, they are more afraid of you than you are of them.)

When the morning sun rousts you from your sleeping bag, return to your car the way you came.

29. Indian Head Mountain

Type:	Dayhike or overnight
Difficulty:	Challenging for children
Distance:	6.6 miles, loop
Hiking time:	7 hours
High point/elevation gain:	3573 feet, 1700 feet
Hikable:	May–October
Map:	NY/NJ Trail Conference Map 41

Drumroll, please! In-n-n-troducing, the hardest hike in our book! Yes, folks, this route leads up the western side of Indian Head Mountain, traverses the thickly wooded summit ridge, and drops down the eastern slope. This is one of those mountains you hike just because it is there, or just because it is the toughest hike we've included, or just because you had three desserts yesterday and feel a need to work them off. Of course, there's more to this hike than the challenge. Along the way you'll find a sturdy shelter known as the Devil's Kitchen Lean-to, numerous streams, bridges, small caves, rocky scrambles, and several lovely overlooks.

I compare this hike to Oscar the Grouch. Even though Oscar grumbles, yells, frowns, and complains, even though he's extremely hard to like, for some reason kids do like him, perhaps because when he does say or do something nice, it's so unexpected that it is especially delightful. When the stern and formidable Indian Head relents and offers you a grand view (a brief one, mind you) or a delightful brook (just for a quick crossing) or a stand of ancient hemlocks (pass through tout de suite), you celebrate!

Now, if you prefer Big Bird and don't care for Oscar in the least . . . well, consider choosing another hike, one that offers a continuous string of pleasant rewards, commensurate with your efforts. This one is for Oscar fans.

From New York City, take the Thruway North to Exit 19 in Kingston. Follow NY 28 West for approximately 26 miles and turn right onto NY 214 in Phoenicia. Drive approximately 15 miles on NY 214 to the junction with NY 23A and turn right (east) onto NY 23A. In about 0.6 mile, turn right (south) onto Greene County 16 (also called Bloomer Road), following a sign to Platte Clove. Two miles from NY 23A, as a road splits right to Elka Park, stay left toward Platte Clove. In another 3.8 miles, turn right onto Predinger Road following a sign to Devil's Path, Devil's Kitchen

Lean-to, Indian Head Mountain, and other destinations. In 0.3 mile, park on the right (at the property owner's request) near a barn.

To locate the trailhead, look for trail signs affixed to the side of a barn. A "TRAIL ENTRANCE" placard guides you between two trees as you enter the woods. Immediately, cross a spirited stream on a footbridge. Climb easily on the wide Long Path for nearly 0.5 mile, passing a trail register and crossing several dry streambeds, to an intersection of trails marked in red and blue. Turn right onto the blue-blazed trail, a merging of the Long Path and the Jimmy Dolan Trail, heading for Jimmy Dolan Notch, 1.4 miles away.

For about a mile, you'll march up a gradual to moderate grade through mixed woods. Focus the kids' attention on their surroundings along this

Honeymooners set up camp in the Devil's Kitchen Lean-to.

lengthy uphill stretch. Who can find something sharp, something round, something squishy, and something blue? After that, look for something fuzzy, something wet, and something that doesn't belong in the woods (like a gum wrapper). Have the kids rub their cheeks against a hemlock, then an oak. Do they feel the same? Do all hemlocks feel the same? If the kids close their eyes, rub the side of a tree, step back, and open their eyes, can they identify "their" tree?

 Less than two miles from the start, the rugged footpath embarks on a stiff climb that ends 0.3 mile later at Jimmy Dolan Notch and a junction with Devil's Path. Venture into the notch for a view of the Esopus Valley and the southern Catskills.

From the trail junction, head eastward on the red-blazed Devil's Path. The red blazes lead up a rugged, moderate to steep slope for the next 0.3 mile, cresting the summit of Indian Head Mountain 2.2 miles from the start. Notice the change in vegetation as you exceed 3500 feet. The spruce/fir forest, or northern coniferous forest, reigns at this high altitude.

The trail winds eastward along the level, sheltered ridge top for nearly 0.5 mile, occasionaly pushing through groves of stunted evergreens. Why is it called Indian Head? Any guesses? (From the north or the east, the mountain is said to resemble a face looking skyward. Can you see his nose to the east?) As Devil's Path drops off the broad summit, it weaves on a moderate slope past an area with limited views to the left. One mile from the official summit, keep the kids near you as the trail opens onto a lofty rock plateau, about 10 feet wide, with excellent views into Platte Kill Clove. Look east to see the Hudson River Valley, and south to view the Shawangunk Mountains.

From the overlook, return along the trail 20 feet to an indistinct junction that you likely did not notice on the hike in. Turn left (southeast) and plunge down a steep, rocky hillside with natural stone steps. Partway down, on the left, a section of split ledge forms a small cave that kids may want to investigate. The trail levels, then embarks on a gradual ascent through spruce groves.

At 3.5 miles, the trail descends in earnest, diving down the wooded slope for 0.2 mile. Do not let the kids precede you since an upcoming overlook requires parents to exercise caution. From exposed Outlook Rock, take in northern views that encompass High Peak and, beyond, the Blackhead Mountains. Retrace your steps for a short distance and turn right (north) at an intersection. Still following red blazes, the trail swings right and descends steeply over boulders and ledge, passing another small cave on the right.

Over the next 0.5 mile, the trail descends on moderate to gradual slopes. As you pass through two stands of stately hemlocks, look high in the branches for the nests of gray squirrels. Do the kids know how to differentiate between squirrels' nests and birds' nests? (Look at what was

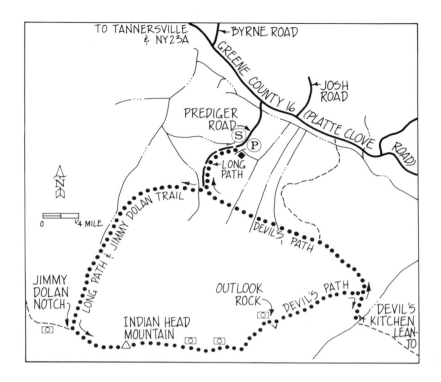

used in the construction of the nest. Squirrels use leaves as the primary building material, while owls, crows, and hawks, for instance, use sticks.) A squirrel often takes refuge in its nest during a storm, at nighttime, or when its offspring are very young.

At 4.4 miles, turn right at a junction to follow the blue blazes of the Overlook Trail on a wide, rocky path that leads uphill for 0.2 mile to the Devil's Kitchen Lean-to. This sturdy shelter tucked in the woods will accommodate eight campers. On the eastern side of the shelter, at the bottom of a hill, a dainty stream provides a dependable source of water.

Return to the junction and continue northwestward on Devil's Path. Shortly, depart the rocky path as log barricades reroute traffic. After climbing a gentle, root-crossed slope for 0.2 mile, the trail rolls downhill, crossing seasonal streams every 0.2 mile or so. One and one-half miles from the last junction, the trail completes its loop. Turn right to join the Long Path and retrace the initial 0.5 mile to your car.

Note: Since the trail initially crosses private land, please stay on the path and refrain from bushwhacking. Hunting, camping, and fishing are not allowed on private property.

30. Huckleberry Point

Type: Dayhike
Difficulty: Easy to moderate for children
Distance: 3.5 miles, round trip
Hiking time: 3 hours
High point/elevation gain: 2530 feet, 340 feet
Hikable: May–October
Map: NY/NJ Trail Conference Map 41

Looking for the kind of expansive views you have from a mountain summit without the demanding climb? Head for the overlook known as Huckleberry Point, where the breathtaking view extends west to Hunter Mountain and east to the Hudson River Valley. The 1.75-mile woods walk to the point is a cinch, but don't plan on being bored. On our hike, we saw a baby porcupine stumble along the trail, a family of deer leap over the trail, and a black bear amble away from the trail (much to our relief).

This is a good choice for a family in average physical condition without a lot of trail experience. There is little chance of getting lost, and you'll be afforded some of the best views in the Catskill area with minimal effort. (An added bonus: this trail is tucked into an out-of-the-way corner of the Catskills, so you're likely to have the woods to yourself. Well, you'll have to share with the porcupines, deer, bears. . . .)

From New York City, take the Thruway North to Exit 19 in Kingston. Follow NY 28 West for approximately 26 miles and turn right onto NY 214 in Phoenicia. Drive approximately 15 miles on NY 214 to the junction with NY 23A and turn right (east). In approximately 0.6 mile, turn right (south) onto Greene County 16 (also called Bloomer Road), following a sign to Platte Clove. Two miles from NY 23A, as a road splits right to Elka Park, stay left toward Platte Clove. Approximately 6.4 miles from NY 23A, cross over a stone bridge and park in the turnout on the right, just before a sign that indicates a very steep grade ahead.

Walk northwestward on Route 16, recrossing the bridge. Look left into the gorge to see Platte Clove. Shortly, turn right (north) onto a gravel road marked with the blue blazes of the Long Path and the orange stamps of a snowmobile trail. Climb steadily on the rutted road, where the loose rocks and deep furrows might make the going tedious for some youngsters. The frequent Platte Clove Preserve posters invite the public to explore the area during daylight hours. Pass under stands of hemlocks where a few lonely birch trees struggle for sunlight.

When your group takes its first rest stop, have the children play

From Huckleberry Point, the high Catskill peaks stretch across the horizon.

"Senses." Kids take turns closing their eyes and feeling, smelling, or listening to a forest object chosen by an adult. Who has the sharpest senses? Some ideas: kids can feel a soft patch of moss, smell "Christmas" in hemlock needles, listen to a dry leaf being crumpled.

At a junction 0.5 mile from the start, turn right (east) onto a wide path, guided by the blue-and-orange trail markers, as the unmaintained woods road continues straight (north). In another 0.1 mile, the blue-and-orange trail curls left (northeast) as you continue straight on a foot trail marked by tin can tops painted white with red centers. This trail, maintained by "Nature Friends," trends downward, passing stone piles on the left. What other signs of earlier inhabitants can the kids find? Toppled stone walls? An old foundation?

The trail drops into a damp area at 0.7 mile where hikers hop over a stream and then reach the bank of a splashing brook. Cross on stones (watch for the blazes) or use a tree that has fallen across the brook slightly upstream if the spring waters make a stone crossing too difficult.

Head across an overgrown tote road, still on the blazed trail. Rising gradually, the trail winds through the shade of another hemlock grove. Look for a large, double-trunked birch, riddled with holes from eager

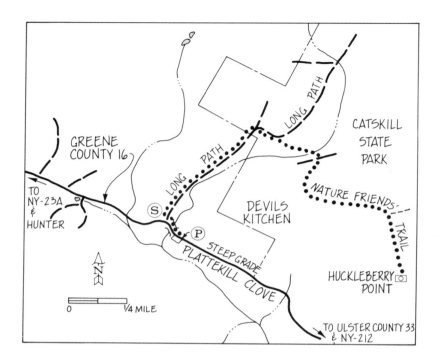

woodpeckers. Do the kids know what the woodpeckers are looking for? Who does the best woodpecker imitation?

Tucked between sections of low ledge, the trail twists up a boulder-strewn hillside. Let the kids assist as you scan the trees for blazes. Can you spot any without the red centers? As the trail crests, mountain laurel pushes persistently in from either side. In this predominantly oak forest, ask the kids to search for a double acorn, one still wearing its "hat," and one that has been chewed.

Just over 1 mile from the start, the trail drops down ledge steps, heading southwestward. As the path curls to the left (east), laurel intrudes once more, forcing hikers to push through the thick bushes. Have the kids feel the leaves on a laurel plant. How do they differ from the leaves on surrounding trees? The waxy surface of the laurel leaves protects the plant from ice and snow in the winter.

Hike another 0.3 mile to arrive at an open rocky area where pitch pines stand stalwart against the buffeting of the wind. At an intersection among the boulders, the marked trail bears right (south) on a descent; an unmarked trail heads left. Follow the markers down the slope with views from the overlook emerging before you.

Keep the kids nearby when you reach impressive Huckleberry Point, a set of tiered ledges that sits 1500 feet above Platte Clove. Here is the spot for a picnic. Can you see the transmission and fire towers crowning Overlook Mountain? Look right to see the imposing ridge that stretches from Indian Head Mountain (Hike 29) to Hunter Mountain (Hike 37). Pass around the binoculars for a closer look at the hawks that soar spring, summer, and fall above Platte Clove.

When you've finished eating and admiring, retrace your steps to the car.

Note: Camping and fires are not permitted.

31. Sunset Rock and Inspiration Point

Type:	Dayhike
Difficulty:	Challenging for children
Distance:	4.5 miles, loop
Hiking time:	5 hours
High point/elevation gain:	2430 feet, 600 feet
Hikable:	May–October
Map:	NY/NJ Trail Conference Map 40

In the nineteenth century, the trails in the North Lake region that radiated from the grand mountaintop hotels were the most popular hiking paths on the entire continent. Today, they still rank as favorites, encompassing waterfalls and mountain summits, brooks and beaches, campgrounds and cliff walks. The footpaths follow old logging roads and horse trails, routes used by long-ago hunters and surveyors, paths cut through the mountains to bring building supplies to hotel sites and to railroad operations.

This route follows a portion of the well-known Escarpment Trail, taking in two famous overlooks known as Sunset Rock and Inspiration Point, as well as several unnamed viewpoints. All of the overlooks rate as "caution points," making this trip best suited for families with older kids who have had some hiking experience. Trust us when we say that parents with little tots in tow will spend most of their time warning, lunging, gasping, grabbing, scolding, shrieking, and clinging. This is supposed to be fun, remember? So those of you with teetering toddlers or frisky preschoolers should select another hike—one that will allow all of you to relax and enjoy yourselves.

From New York City, take the Thruway North to Exit 20. Follow NY 32 north for 8 miles to Palenville and the intersection with NY 23A. Turn

Watching the sun set (what else?) from Sunset Rock

left (west) onto NY 23A and drive 7 miles to Haines Falls. At the junction of NY 23A and Greene County 18 in Haines Falls, turn right onto Greene County 18, heading east. Drive 2.1 miles and, just before the gatehouse and the entrance for the North and South Lake state campground, turn right onto Schutt Road at a sign for "FOREST PRESERVE ACCESS." In less than 0.1 mile, turn right into a substantial gravel parking area.

Cross Schutt Road and enter the woods on the blue-blazed Escarpment Trail, heading eastward. In less than 0.1 mile, the trail veers right (south) to parallel Schutt Road. Though rocks poke through the trampled soil underfoot, the terrain is not overly rugged, and will not be difficult for children to manage.

At 0.2 mile, wander through patches of ferns illuminated by spindly birch trees. In another 0.1 mile, hop over a crumbling stone wall. Look at the large pines that border the trail for the characteristic cavities left by woodpeckers drilling for insects. When you hear the hollow drumming of a woodpecker, follow the sound to its source and you'll see a bird climbing up the side of a tree using its claws to grip the bark and its tail feathers for balance.

Continue to follow blue blazes as a path leading to Schutt Road departs right. Cross a seasonal creek on a sturdy footbridge (with a handrail) and then cross Spruce Creek on a second footbridge. As you track through a mostly coniferous forest, ask the kids what all of these conifers have in common. Who said "cones"? You win the role of hike leader for the next 0.25 mile! Each cone is made up of scales that house seeds. If you are hiking on a sunny day, the cones will be open to allow the seeds to flutter to the ground. On wet days, the cones stay closed.

Six-tenths mile from the start, you meet a gravel road where several paths and trails intersect. A sign points right (west) toward Layman's Monument (0.5 mile away) and Inspiration Point (1.2 miles) via the blue-blazed Escarpment Trail. To the left (east), a yellow-blazed horse trail departs. Straight ahead a red-blazed trail (Schutt Road Trail or "Old Road") leads in 0.9 mile to Sunset Rock and in 1 mile to Inspiration Point. You will return by way of this wide path and complete your hiking loop here.

Head westward, still on the blue-blazed Escarpment Trail (now a broad and rutted road). Sidestep a gate where a sign advises that "THIS AREA TO NORTH LAKE IS CLOSED TO PICNICKING AND CAMPING." As you pass through a hemlock forest, pause to let the kids hug trees. Do their arms reach all the way around? Hemlocks grow slowly, although they often become very large. Is this a grove of young or mature trees? Ask the youngest child to find the smallest hemlock and the oldest child to find the largest one.

One-tenth mile from the gate, cross a footbridge and wind through a birch grove. As you approach the trail register, look for a well-worn, unblazed side trail dividing right, which descends 0.1 mile to the top of Kaaterskill Falls (Hike 32). Continue to follow the Escarpment Trail, passing the register on a gradual ascent. Rimmed with lush ferns and an occasional mountain laurel bush, the trail falls down a moderate slope before leveling near Layman's Monument.

This stone memorial commemorates Frank D. Layman, who lost his life here on August 10, 1900, while helping to battle a forest fire that threatened to destroy nearby homes and businesses. The views from the monument extend across Kaaterskill Clove and southeastward toward Indian Head Mountain (Hike 29). Can you hear the distant highway sounds?

From the monument, the trail hooks left (southeast) and soon splits. Turn left, squeezing between two trees marked in blue, as a side trail heads straight. Climbing over rough ledge, the Escarpment Trail displays its wilder side. Count moss-covered rocks along the trail. Keep the kids in sight for the next mile as you visit a number of overlooks and sweep close to the steep slope on the right.

About 0.1 mile from the monument, the path leads to the first overlook. From this barren rock, the view takes in the heart of the valley and reaches to the central Catskills, including Kaaterskill High Peak. Can you point out Hunter Mountain (Hike 37) to the west?

As the trail tracks farther inland, struggle up an eroded section of trail, squeezing through split ledge 0.1 mile beyond the overlook. On the right, more slices of ledge are in the process of separating from the escarpment. (Do not let the kids run ahead here: families must hike together.) One-quarter mile from the monument (1.5 miles from the start) is a second exposed ledge that falls away sheer to the valley floor. Keep the children near you as you enjoy vistas even more dramatic than those from the first overlook.

The trail rolls over loose stones for 0.1 mile to an intersection with the yellow-blazed trail. Continue to follow the blue blazes eastward toward Sunset Rock and Inspiration Point, 0.27 mile away. Stay together as the trail drops toward Sunset Rock. Once again, you are treated to lovely local and distant views. (Watching the sun sink into the hills from this ledge would certainly be a treat, but I wouldn't want to hike the return leg in the dark, especially with kids along.) Who can spot the dwelling that clings to the adjoining ridge?

Proceed with caution to nearby Inspiration Point, a sliver of ledge that juts out over the valley, offering superb southeasterly views down Kaaterskill Clove to the Hudson River. Take an energy break a comfortable distance from the edge. Talk about what the forest creatures might be snacking on right now. (Gray squirrels like acorns, fungi, seeds, and berries; porcupines prefer the inner bark of trees and sweet corn; deer munch on twigs, grass, bark, apples, and acorns.)

Beyond Inspiration Point, the trail tempers and parents can relax.

At 2.2 miles, the path wanders away from the edge of the escarpment in a cloud of mountain laurel. The kids can run ahead to the Goliath erratic boulder on the left. Six-tenths of a mile from Inspiration Point, the wide, grassy Sleepy Hollow Horse Trail joins from the left. Bear right here, still guided by blue trail markers. In 0.1 mile (0.75 mile from Inspiration Point), the blue trail and Long Path intersect. (A sign indicates that the blue-blazed Escarpment Trail leads to Boulder Rock in 1.3 miles.) As the horse trail and Long Path head east, turn left (northwest), following the combined Long Path and Escarpment Trail on a gradual ascent. In woods ruled by spruce trees, show the kids spider webs hanging from the spruce's barren lower branches. Webs are especially easy to find after a rain shower or in the morning when they are covered with dew.

The grassy footpath levels 0.2 mile along this combined path. If little hikers are looking weary, take turns thinking of an animal while the others guess what animal you have in mind. Give clues such as "My animal has a tail" or "My animal has poor eyesight" or "My animal can swim." At the next trail junction, 2.6 miles from the start, the combined trails depart right (east) to Boulder Rock (0.9 mile away) as you head left (northwest), following a sign and red blazes to "SCHUTT ROAD VIA OLD ROAD" (Schutt Road Trail), 1.2 miles away. Within 50 feet, the red trail

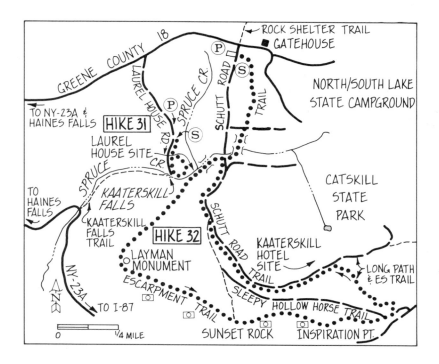

intersects Schutt Road Trail. Here, turn left (west) on the red trail, dropping gently on a grass-covered woods road.

At the 3.3-mile mark, a yellow-blazed side trail leading to Sunset Rock and Inspiration Point joins from the left. (Tell the kids that from here, your car is just 0.8 mile away.)

Pass a trail register with a broad, seasonal streambed on the right. Complete your descent on the woods road at the familiar intersection of the Schutt Road Trail and the Escarpment Trail. Head straight (north) across the intersection to rejoin the Escarpment Trail, returning to your car in 0.6 mile.

32. Kaaterskill Falls

Type: Dayhike
Difficulty: Easy for children
Distance: 0.6 mile, round trip
Hiking time: 40 minutes
High point/elevation gain: 2050 feet, 100 feet
Hikable: May–October
Map: NY/NJ Trail Conference Map 40

Here is today's final Jeopardy question. (You've bet it all. Let's see if you'll win loads of cash and return as tomorrow's champion or leave a loser with a year's supply of licorice.)

The answer is "These falls in the Catskills are higher than Niagara Falls."

After that cute little "Jeopardy" song runs its course, you guess, anxiously, "What are the Kaaterskill Falls?" You're right! The emcee shakes your hand! You will return as tomorrow's champion, sending your rivals, the part-time farmhand and the nuclear physicist, home with armfuls of licorice.

OK, OK, it's not a likely scenario. But even if knowing about the Kaaterskill Falls never makes you famous and wealthy, you'll be glad you made the trip. A wide, level path leads 0.25 mile to the top of this spectacular waterfall. Here, surefooted kids and adults can sit on the rocks and watch the water disappear over the escarpment in a pair of dramatic falls. Although children can wade and splash in the shallow pools of Spruce Creek well above the waterfall, they must take care not to venture too close to the sheer cliff over which the water spills.

The Kaaterskill Falls is considered one of the Catskills' most spectacular sites . . . and you never know when a few little facts about a waterfall in upstate New York will come in handy.

From New York City, take the Thruway North to Exit 20. Follow NY 32 north approximately 8 miles to Palenville and NY 23A. Turn left (west) onto NY 23A and drive 7 miles to Haines Falls. At the junction of NY 23A and Greene County 18 in Haines Falls, turn right onto Greene County 18, heading east. Drive 1.7 miles and turn right (south) onto Laurel House Road. In 0.4 mile, park at the end of the road. (Please do not block the gate.)

From the parking area, sidestep the metal gate and head southeastward along a wide gravel road. In 0.1 mile, near a large white pine, bear right, continuing along the more substantial path as a narrow foot trail heads straight. One-quarter mile from the car, a fence guards the ravine carved by Spruce Creek. Follow the northern bank of the creek to the top of Kaaterskill Falls, holding the hands of little children or inexperienced young hikers as you near your destination.

From the top of the falls, enjoy the magnificent view into Kaaterskill Clove. (Henry David Thoreau enjoyed these same views many years ago.) Watch the water disappear over the edge of the cliff and hear it thunder down the mountainside. (You won't be able to see the falls since the drop

Youngsters wade in Spruce Creek above Kaaterskill Falls.

is so steep.) Kaaterskill Falls actually consists of two separate falls: the first drops 175 feet into a pool, from which the second spills 85 feet, totaling 260 feet—almost 100 feet higher than Niagara Falls.

Fifty feet back from the falls, the kids can wade and splash in the shallow pools of the creek (assuming the water level is low). Never allow children to approach the falls by way of the creek—the risk of injury is too great. (There have been fatalities here.)

You cannot reach the base of the falls from the top. Years ago, during the era of the grand hotels, a staircase did lead to the bottom. Now the only access is from NY 23A along a trail of less than 1 mile. Even though parking is approximately 0.2 mile from the trailhead—necessitating some rather unpleasant highway walking—this is a popular route.

From the fence above the falls, follow the wide gravel path back to your car. Or, for a change, follow the northern bank of the brook upstream, on a narrow foot trail with frequent side trails branching right to the water. About 0.25 mile from the falls, the trail leads left, crossing the site of the Laurel House. Although modest in comparison to some of the other Catskills hotels, the Laurel House was a popular retreat in its day due to its unusual location. The owner of the hotel built a dam to impede the flow of water in the creek; for a fee, he would release the water and "create" the falls.

Soon the trail arrives at an intersection with the gravel road, near the large white pine. Continue 0.1 mile on the wide path to your car.

33. Boulder Rock

Type: Dayhike
Difficulty: Easy for children
Distance: 1.3 miles, round trip
Hiking time: 1.5 hours
High point/elevation gain: 2420 feet, 280 feet
Hikable: May–October
Map: NY/NJ Trail Conference Map 40

If Robin Leach had been tracking down rich and famous folks back in the nineteenth century, he undoubtedly would have spent lots of time at the Catskill Mountain House. Considered *the* place to vacation in the northeastern Catskills during the era of the grand hotels, this Greek Revival-style resort lorded over the Hudson Valley from atop the escarpment that runs from Kaaterskill Falls to Windham High Peak.

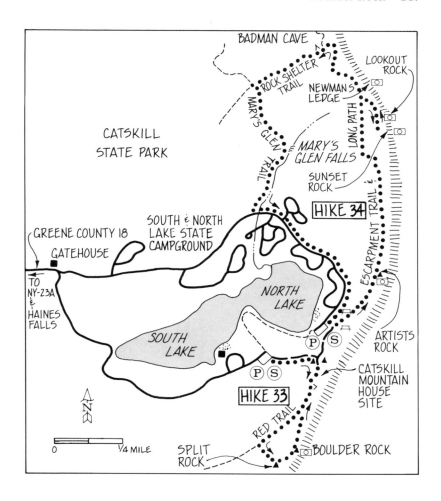

The resort site (with dizzying views over the valley) is one of the more spectacular spots along the 24-mile-long Escarpment Trail, which connects the North Lake area with the majestic Blackhead Range. The 0.6-mile-long section of the trail described here leaves the site of the hotel and travels south, passing a kid-size cave, several overlooks, Split Rock (an impressive crevice), and, finally, Boulder Rock. This monstrous glacial erratic rests near the edge of a sheer cliff and deserves a more spectacular and less redundant name than (ho-hum) Boulder Rock.

See if your family can come up with a better one.

From New York City, take Thruway North to Exit 20. Follow NY 32 north for 8 miles to Palenville and the intersection with NY 23A. Turn left (west) onto NY 23A and drive 7 miles to Haines Falls. At the junction

A view from the 24-mile Escarpment Trail

of NY 23A and Greene County 18 in Haines Falls, turn right onto Greene County 18, heading east. Drive 2.2 miles to a gatehouse and the entrance for the North and South Lake state campground. Beyond the gatehouse, the road splits; turn right and follow the park road for 1.3 miles to its conclusion at a large parking area on the right (0.1 mile beyond the South Lake parking lot on the left).

From the parking area, head eastward on a wide gravel road with power lines strung along the right side. Avoid the gravel, blue-blazed Escarpment Trail that departs left (north). At 0.1 mile, walk between a pair of stone pillars that once guarded the driveway leading to the Catskill Mountain House. Bear right to reach the site of the hotel, now an open, grassy plateau on the edge of the escarpment overlooking the Hudson Valley. As you survey the valley from an elevation of 3000 feet, you are seeing the plains and distant hills from the same spot where General Sherman, and presidents Grant, Cleveland, and Theodore Roosevelt once stood.

In the early nineteenth century, vacationers flocked to the Catskills by steamboat, stagecoach, and railroad, lured by the lovely views and "healthful mountain air." The Catskill Mountain House, an imposing hotel built in 1824, quickly garnered a reputation as the most prestigious place to stay in the region. Wealthy guests journeyed up the Hudson River and then took a stagecoach or carriage from the Catskill Landing up the winding mountain road to the hotel. Later, the Catskill Mountain Railroad delivered visitors as far as Palenville; eventually, the Otis Elevating Railway carried folks up the mountainside to the hotel (the railway remains are near the hotel site).

Other resorts were built nearby to attract vacationers, but the Catskill Mountain House remained the finest and most popular mountaintop hotel. In the late 1800s, the hiking trails that radiated from many of the Catskills hostelries were walked more than any other footpaths in the entire country. Sadly, with the advent of more modern means of transportation and the Great Depression, the grand hotels experienced a significant decline in business and most fell into disrepair. And as the plaque overlooking the valley so eloquently states, "Only the commanding view of this historic resort now remains."

On the right (west) side of the clearing is an information board (describing the Catskill Mountain House) and a trail sign that points the way to Boulder Rock, 0.46 mile along the blue-blazed Escarpment Trail. Follow the blue blazes into the woods, heading southwestward. Soon, the trail begins a moderate to steep ascent up a densely wooded hillside, snaking around chunks of ledge. Amidst thick groves of hemlock and spruce and pockets of mountain laurel, the trail crests, 0.1 mile from the trail sign. After a brief respite, the Escarpment Trail resumes its stiff ascent, sweeping around obtrusive ledge on the right. Overhanging ledge on the left forms a kid-size cave. Revive the children's interest by pausing to let them investigate it.

 As you crest shortly beyond the overhang, keep youngsters in sight; the trail runs close to the precipitous edge of the escarpment. While the adults admire the fine views southeast into the Hudson Valley, the kids are likely to be more interested in the leaning, cigar-shaped boulder on the right. Soon you return to the safety of the woods, treading on a rugged, worn path well marked with frequent blue blazes. The sedimentary rock underfoot seems to wash across the trail in waves, and clusters of mountain laurel add splashes of green even in early spring and late autumn.

At a junction with a red-blazed trail at 0.45 mile, the blue Escarpment Trail turns left (south) to reach Boulder Rock in 0.1 mile. You continue right (southwest) on the red side trail (which rejoins the Escarpment Trail in 0.2 mile). In June, when the mountain laurel that pushes in from both sides of the trail is in bloom, this short trip along the red trail is delightful. Mountain laurel leaves are poisonous to many animals, so even during the winter when food is scarce, these bushes do not tempt deer and other wildlife. Christmas tree-size spruces, moss-covered boulders, and clusters of ferns add to the lovely scents and sights along this path. After a gentle descent, the red trail ends at an intersection with the Escarpment Trail. Turn left (southeast) onto the blue Escarpment Trail (avoid the straight branch of the blue trail), guided by a sign to Boulder Rock, 0.2 mile away.

This delightful slice of the Escarpment Trail drops gradually through a sea of mountain laurel. One-tenth mile from the intersection with the red side trail, you encounter Split Rock, a formidable crevice in the ledge bordering the trail. Notice that additional sections of ledge are beginning to separate, due in large part to the forceful freezing and thawing cycles.

One-tenth mile beyond Split Rock, the trail sidesteps Boulder Rock, an elephant-size glacial erratic that perches on the edge of the escarpment. From here, the panoramas stretch across the Hudson Valley to the Hudson River and the Taconic Range, fading at the distant Berkshires. From Boulder Rock (did you come up with a new name?), the trail ducks back into the woods, trending north. A short walk returns you to the intersection with the red-blazed trail. Turn right, still following the blue blazes of the Escarpment Trail, and return to the site of the Catskill Mountain House the way you came.

34. The Escarpment

Type: Day or overnight
Difficulty: Challenging for children
Distance: 3.3 miles, loop
Hiking time: 4 hours
High point/elevation gain: 2650 feet, 750 feet
Hikable: May–October
Map: NY/NJ Trail Conference Map 40

Step right up, folks! You won't want to miss this hike—it's as close to a carnival as Mother Nature gets! With a multitude of attractions—from overlooks that will give you more butterflies than a Ferris wheel to scrambles through narrow crevices that will get your heart pounding harder than a trip through the fun house—the Escarpment has a never-ending lineup of neat natural features. Hide in Badman Cave. Take photos

Mountain laurel in bloom

of the kids near Mary's Glen Falls. Point out peaks in Connecticut and Massachusetts from Sunset Rock. Explore a mucky trailside swamp. You might even catch a wild animal act or two! But you won't have to stand in endless lines, push through sweaty crowds, fish around in your pocket for tickets, or remind your kids 301 times that cotton candy always makes them sick. (This "carnival" is most appropriate for preteens with some hiking experience, since the overlooks require you to exercise extreme caution.)

So . . . step right up!

From New York City, take the Thruway North to Exit 20. Follow NY 32 north for 8 miles to Palenville and the intersection with NY 23A. Turn left (west) onto NY 23A and drive 7 miles to Haines Falls. At the junction of NY 23A and Greene County 18 in Haines Falls, turn right onto Greene County 18, heading east. Drive 2.2 miles to a gatehouse and the entrance for the North and South Lake state campground. Beyond the gatehouse, the road splits; stay straight, proceeding to North Lake. (The road to the right leads to South Lake.) Drive 1.7 miles to parking for North Lake beach.

Looking eastward from Newman's Ledge to the Hudson River

From the North Lake parking area, walk northward on the park road to the trailhead on the right. The North Mountain trails sign provides distances to points of interest: Artist Rock, 0.3 mile; Newman's Ledge, 0.8 mile; Mary's Glen, 2.4 miles; North Point, 2.6 miles. Follow the wide path into the woods, heading eastward, and cut through a picnic and camping area. A number of paths radiate from the area, so be sure to head east, toward the edge of the ridge known as the Escarpment.

One-tenth mile from the trailhead, turn left (north) onto the blue-blazed Escarpment Trail. Track along level ground through hemlocks and mountain laurel. To the right are cropped views over the Hudson Valley. Examine the frequent ledge outcroppings. Does the pattern on the rock's surface remind you of anything? Waves lapping on the beach, perhaps?

Shortly, the trail scales a steep, rugged slope, threading through a boulder maze as it crawls upward. Crest after the brief ascent, soon leaving the North and South lakes camping and picnic areas. As you pass a trail register, a side trail leads right to Artist Rock, with a pretty view of the Hudson Valley. Can you spot any pink lady's slippers? (The flower, that is!)

Trending northeastward, the main trail squeezes through more intrusive ledge. As you weave between a pair of boulders, ask the kids if they need an energy break or want to rest on these rocks. Treading on ledge, the path levels as it cuts through a pitch pine forest. Eastern views continue to expand, now taking in the distant Taconic Range.

One-half mile from the start, the trail opens onto the Escarpment at Prospect Rock, a barren ribbon of ledge that travels along the edge of sheer cliffs. Fortunately, the path is about 12 feet wide, allowing parents to keep kids a safe distance from the edge. After a hairy (but breath-taking) 100 yards, the blazes lead back into the woods through a striking colony of mountain laurel. Heading northwestward, climb a steep, rocky hillside, urging kids on by promising them a rest stop inside the cave near the top. Let the youngsters catch their breath under the overhang, while the adults pant nearby. Continue up and over the ledge above the cave.

Guarantee the kids some really neat stuff within the next 0.5 mile: they won't be disappointed. Beyond the cave, on level ground, follow a side trail that bears left and leads to a dramatic overlook of North and South lakes. Return to the main trail and turn left (north). Soon you scale Sunrise Rock, a mound of exposed ledge with limited views. This substantial rock owes its name and reputation to Thomas Cole, who was associated with the Hudson River School of landscape painting.

Two-tenths mile from Sunrise Rock, look right to the top of Sunset Rock. Notice the unusual rock configuration, more similar in appearance to man-made cement than natural stone. (Tarzan types will want to follow the side trail that leads right up Jacob's Ladder, squeezing through the steep, tight crevice to emerge atop Sunset Rock. Although this is a very tricky ascent, it cuts 0.35 mile from the total hiking distance. We followed two preteens who had no trouble with the scramble, although the folks behind us didn't fare as well and had to turn back. Let the kids decide: if they think they can make it, give it a try.)

If you prefer the longer, kinder route, continue northward on the Escarpment Trail for 0.15 mile to an intersection where you turn right onto a yellow-blazed side trail. A nearby sign marks your progress: you have come 0.9 mile from the North Lake camping area. As you near Sunset Rock, 0.2 mile from the junction, you march along an exposed ridge with a pitch pine forest on the right and superb views over the Hudson to the left. From the top of this broad, barren rock, you'll savor the views of the Hudson and the Taconic Range to the east and North and South lakes as well as the Catskills Range to the west.

Return to the blue-blazed Escarpment Trail and turn right (north), following a sign to Newman's Ledge. Under an evergreen canopy, climb a rugged hillside, inching upward through a labyrinth of boulders. As it levels, the trail swings right (northeast) and ducks beneath moss-covered ledges. Approaching exposed Newman's Ledge, you track along the eastern edge of the escarpment, with only a thin ribbon of trees protecting you from the steep drop-off. Keep children away from that side of the trail by challenging them to find a mini-cave on the left, tucked under the roots of an ancient hemlock tree. (Do not let them precede you on this section of trail, however.) Is any creature living here now? If there aren't any cobwebs covering the opening, if the leaves in front of the hole are matted down, and if there are bits of fur nearby, this is probably the home of a woodland creature. Beyond the cave, push through thickets of laurel with ledge underfoot.

One and four-tenths miles from the start, step onto dramatic Newman's Ledge for a brief encounter of the breathtaking kind. The eastern views envelope you as the ground falls away sheer at your feet, plunging 1000 feet through Rip Van Winkle Hollow to the valley floor. You can see into Massachusetts and Connecticut from this spot. Are any hawks soaring on the thermals below?

From the lookout, the trail darts back into the woods, heading westward. This tree-lined path seems safe and secure after your adventure on the Escarpment. Make your way on rugged terrain to the base of another hill. As it climbs, the trail dodges a small cave on the right. Cresting, the footpath weaves gingerly through a soggy spot, then embarks on another short, steep ascent with the blazes leading up stratified ledge "steps."

The trail returns to the edge of the Escarpment just briefly, offering more commanding views over the Hudson River. Back in the woods, go past a series of interesting rock outcroppings on the left as the trail sweeps from north to southwest. Track through lush mountain laurel colonies, especially lovely in June when the blossoms are on display.

The Catskills region is teeming with creatures of all kinds, from hurrying hares to sluggish turtles.

Beyond a swampy area is an intersection: the blue-blazed Escarpment Trail turns right (west) and the yellow-blazed Rock Shelter Trail heads straight (southwest). For now, take the blue-blazed path for about 150 feet to Badman Cave, actually a great overhanging ledge. You can invent your own stories to explain the name, although legend has it that the cave sheltered bands of outlaws during the eighteenth century.

Return to the junction with the Rock Shelter Trail and turn right (southwest). Drop down a gentle slope; the kids can run ahead to a sitting rock 0.15 mile from the intersection. Wander through a hemlock forest before tumbling down a rather tame rock slide. At the bottom, the Rock Shelter Trail meets the Mary's Glen Trail. (A trail also heads straight, southwest, to Haines Falls Road/Greene County 18.)

Turn left (south) onto the Mary's Glen Trail and follow the red blazes down a gentle hill, sweeping through a birch forest 0.2 mile from the junction. Soon, you cross a splashing brook on a row of flat stones. Can you hear a waterfall? Drop down a steep slope to an intersection and turn left (northeast) onto a side trail that leads to the base of Mary's Glen Falls. The water drops about 30 feet in two tiers and collects in a pool at the bottom. (The falls may disappoint you if you visit during a dry spell.) Wade, splash, and relax.

Return to the Mary's Glen Trail and turn left (south), winding along the western bank of Mary's Glen Brook. Less than 0.5 mile from the waterfall, after tripping over roots and rocks and hopping over damp spots, pass a trail register and reach the paved park road for North Lake. Turn left and walk 0.7 mile back to the North Lake parking area and your car.

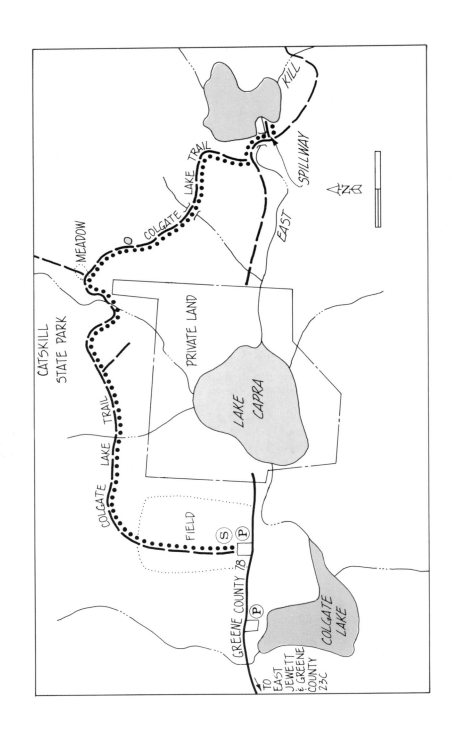

35. Colgate Lake Trail

Type: Dayhike
Difficulty: Easy to moderate for children
Distance: 4 miles, round trip
Hiking time: 3 hours
High point/elevation gain: 2280 feet, 220 feet
Hikable: June–October
Map: NY/NJ Trail Conference Map 41

The remote, unnamed pond along the Colgate Lake Trail is not for swimmers or sunbathers, but it is for kids. The wild banks beckon all types of creatures; what you don't see first-hand you'll likely find evidence of in tracks or droppings. Parents will appreciate the mosaic of small, shallow pools near the pond outlet that allows kids to explore safely. Bring everything your youngsters will need for a pond adventure, including nets, high rubber boots or wading shoes, buckets, and binoculars. (Don't forget insect repellent.)

After the hike, drive 0.2 mile westward on Greene County 78 and turn left into a parking area. Here, a more civilized lake with a small beach area will please the swimmers in the family (explorers can still find loads of frogs and other critters). This is the place to spread out your picnic lunch.

From New York City, take the Thruway North to Exit 19 in Kingston. Follow NY 28 West for approximately 26 miles and turn right onto NY 214 in Phoenicia. Drive about 15 miles to the junction with NY 23A and turn right (east) onto NY 23A. Drive 2.5 miles to the traffic light in Tannersville and turn left (north) onto Greene County 23C (also called Hill Street). In 3.1 miles from Tannersville, turn right onto Greene County 78 in East Jewett. Drive another 1.7 miles, passing a parking area for Colgate Lake, to substantial parking on the left at a sign for "FOREST PRESERVE ACCESS."

Head northward on a woods road, sidestepping a metal gate and soon passing a trail register. Follow the yellow blazes of the Colgate Lake Trail along the left side of a seemingly endless meadow lined with birch trees. In 0.2 mile, journey into mixed woods on level ground. This grassy trail is child-friendly: easy to follow and kind to little feet. What evidence can you find that this land was once farmed? Look for piles of stones and old fences. At one time, there was more open than wooded land in the Northeast.

At 0.3 mile, pass a row of perfectly shaped "Christmas" trees (spruce). As the trail sweeps right (east), it becomes rockier, much like an old streambed. Trending eastward, the trail runs over soggy spots. Who can find a slug? Look for them by turning over logs, leaves, or mushrooms. If you gently touch one, it will move, leaving behind its telltale shiny trail. One-half mile from the start, after a mild ascent, the trail crests. Hop over a seasonal brook, then veer left (northeast) at 0.8 mile, guided by an arrow and a log blockade. (Apparently, the trail used to continue straight but was rerouted to avoid crossing private property.)

The trail descends on increasingly rugged terrain, crossing an active stream on stones at 1.1 miles. (This crossing may be difficult in the spring.) Head straight across an old logging road, and climb an embankment to meet another woods road. Here, a sign guides you left (northeast). Take a vote: who thinks that the trail markers look like smiling faces?

At the edge of a clearing, another trail sign directs you right (southeast), as the woods road continues straight and then fades into the meadow. Can you find a twig that has been chewed? By examining it closely, you may be able to determine what type of animal browsed here. Because deer do not have upper incisors, they tear the tips off twigs. Hares, with their sharp upper and lower teeth, leave a cleanly clipped twig behind. Does the branch look torn or neatly bitten?

Beyond the clearing, at 1.3 miles, the trail sweeps right (south) to skirt a frog pond on the left. How many different frog voices do you hear? Do you hear any ducks? Soon the trail cuts left to head southwestward. As you cross a stream on a sturdy footbridge, toss leaves and twigs into the splashing water and watch the inevitable "shipwrecks." March through a damp area where hemlocks flourish. What other types of plants prefer these cool, shady conditions? As the trail slices right, peer left through the trees for a glimpse of a wild, anonymous pond. What would you name this pond?

Tracking well away from the pond's edge, the spongy trail cuts through an immature evergreen forest. Balance on a lineup of logs that spans the wettest terrain. At 1.8 miles, turn left (east) onto a woods road. Cross a bridge that spans East Kill and soon reach the western bank of a real wilderness pond. This is a wonderful spot for kids to explore, with water collecting in small, shallow pools along the edge of the pond near the outlet stream. For better access to the true shoreline, bear left just before the main trail leads away from the pond, crossing an old spillway that leads to the water's edge.

What will the kids find today? Look for an eastern spotted newt in its red eft phase. After spending a summer in the water, the newt moves onto land as a brightly colored red eft. This salamander is poisonous when eaten by a predator; kids, what purpose do you think its color serves? After a few years on land, the newt turns from red orange to green and resumes its life in the water.

Do you see any dragonflies? They can be hard to catch, even with

A remote pond greets hikers near route's end.

a butterfly net, since they move as fast as 30 miles per hour and are able to spot predators 40 yards away. (Dragonflies have the largest eyes of any insect.) Stir the bottom of the muddy pond with a stick to see what might surface.

After you're done exploring, return to your car the way you came. (Do not follow the shorter route along the road skirting Lake Capra. The owners of the property surrounding this lake do not want hikers trespassing on their land, and will not welcome you, to say the least.)

36. Acra Point

Type: Dayhike or overnight
Difficulty: Moderate for children
Distance: 4.9 miles, loop
Hiking time: 4.5 hours
High point/elevation gain: 3100 feet, 1100 feet
Hikable: June–October
Map: NY/NJ Trail Conference Map 41

River crossings, a series of lovely overlooks, and a shelter for overnight camping make this a super hike for families in good shape with older children. We nicknamed this one "Son of Indian Head" because it has many of the same features as its "dad" (Hike 29—the toughest hike in the book). This hike to Acra Point, thankfully, covers a shorter distance with a smaller elevation gain, making it "moderate" rather than "challenging" for children. (Windham's Clarence D. Lane Park and the Batavia Kill Recreation Area are located 2 miles west of the trailhead; parents can relax while sticky little hikers enjoy a dip in the pond under lifeguard supervision. I know, parents never *really* relax. . . .)

From New York City, take the Thruway North to Exit 21. Follow NY 23 West for approximately 22 miles to NY 296 in Windham. Turn left (south) onto NY 296 and drive 1 mile to Hensonville. Here, turn left onto Greene County 40. Drive 1.9 miles and turn left onto Greene County 56 (also known as Big Hollow Road) in Maplecrest. Greene County 56 turns to gravel in 4 miles (where a sign indicates that the road is closed from November 1 through April 1). Drive another 0.2 mile and park in the lot on the right.

Continue on the gravel road southeastward to a trailhead sign: 1.3 miles to the Batavia Kill Lean-to; 3.25 miles to Acra Point. As the gravel road veers left over a bridge, head straight on a wide path marked with the red blazes of the Black Dome Range Trail. Hop over a seasonal stream, then cross Batavia Kill ("Kill" is from the Dutch *kil*, meaning "creek") on a sturdy footbridge. How many of the trailside trees can the kids identify by sight? How about by feel (eyes closed, of course)?

At 0.35 mile, rocks intrude underfoot and you recross Batavia Kill, this time on stones. The red-blazed Black Dome Range Trail and the yellow-blazed Batavia Kill Trail meet 0.4 mile from the hike's start. As the red trail leads right (south) to Blackhead Mountain, follow the yellow markers straight (southeast) toward the lean-to, 0.68 mile away. (From this junction, Acra Point is 2.73 miles away.) How many colors can the

Crossing the Batavia Kill

children find in the forest? At first, greens and browns seem to prevail, but look closer and you'll notice red berries, white mushrooms, yellow flowers, blue pebbles.

The yellow trail, now narrow and rugged, crosses Batavia Kill once more, flirting periodically with the bank as it heads southeastward. Cross several seasonal streams that swell in the spring. What types of animal tracks can you find along the muddy banks? The deep impressions of deer hooves? Or the fainter tracks of a raccoon, shaped like tiny hands?

Soon, the trail snakes past the Batavia Kill Lean-to, with the creek (a seasonal water source) a short distance through the woods on the right. Talk about surviving in the woods. If you had to build a shelter here, how would you do it? What materials would you use? Where would you put it? What lessons can we learn from the creatures who make their homes in the forest?

Beyond the lean-to, the trail embarks on a moderate to steep ascent, first slipping on loose stones, then struggling over the bony roots of birch trees. The trail curls eastward and levels, ending 0.25 mile from the lean-to at the junction with the combined Long Path and Escarpment Trail. Turn left, following blue blazes into a sag, 1.6 miles from Acra Point.

After working its way out of the gully, the trail rolls easily through stands of birch, spruce, and hemlock. At the 1.9-mile mark, offer a few words of encouragement to the kids as you trudge up a brief but steep incline wedged between boulders and ledge. (Some blazes may be a lighter blue here.)

Two miles from the start, the trail sweeps close to the edge of the Escarpment along level ground, reaching a sheltered lookout with grand views to the east toward the Albany area and the Taconic Mountains.

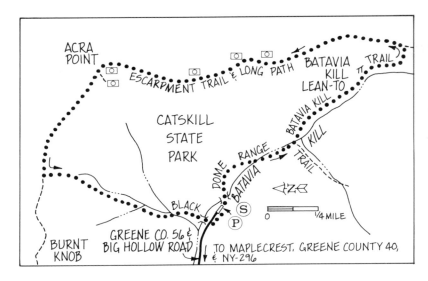

A 0.2-mile jaunt through the woods leads to a second lookout. At 2.8 miles, the trail passes another spot offering limited northeasterly views.

After more than 3 miles of hiking, you reach Acra Point, a ridge-top meadow overlooking the Black Dome Range. Although thickening foliage threatens to intrude on the view, the panoramas from this 3,100-foot viewpoint are still worth a pause and a picture.

Tumble down a grassy trail, watching for blueberry bushes as you descend. These miniature, wild berries are sweeter than their larger, cultivated cousins and make a delightful snack. Soon, a side trail branches left, leading to an open ledge where commanding views take in the nearby Black Dome peaks (with Black Dome and Thomas Cole mountains to the left) and stretch over the nameless rolling hills to Hunter Mountain (Hike 37) in the central Catskills. At the western end of the valley are Van Loan Hill and Round Hill, drumlins created during the Ice Age. (I know, the kids don't care about the far-off mountains. What kinds of animal shapes can they find in the puffy clouds overhead?) Spread out your picnic lunch and enjoy the vistas (and the animal parade in the sky).

Back on the main trail, follow the blue markers on a moderate descent, passing overhanging ledge and indistinct side trails leading right to limited views. At a trail junction 3.8 miles from the start, leave the blue trail (it continues to Burnt Knob) and turn left (south) onto the red-blazed Black Dome Range Trail. (Let the kids know that they have just a little more than 1 mile to go!) Drop gently through hemlock, birch, and deciduous woods, crossing a hasty stream 0.7 mile from the Escarpment Trail. Recross the stream 0.3 mile later, arriving at a hikers' registration box. Shortly, cross Batavia Kill on a footbridge. When you reach Big Hollow Road, turn left and walk 100 yards to your car.

37. Hunter Mountain

Type:	Dayhike or overnight
Difficulty:	Moderate for children
Distance:	4.2 miles, round trip
Hiking time:	3.5 hours
High point/elevation gain:	4040 feet, 820 feet
Hikable:	June–October
Map:	NY/NJ Trail Conference Map 41

Surprise! You thought Hunter Mountain was just for skiing, right? Well, when the slopes are green and the skiers are sailing, come to Hunter to explore the extensive, well-maintained trail system. Take the thrilling Hunter Mountain Skyride to the top of the ski slope (the longest and highest such ride in the Catskill Mountains). Enjoy immediate views from Colonel's Chair before tracking southward for 2 miles to the summit fire tower. It's not an easy walk, but it's within the capabilities of most young kids.

Once you've enjoyed the extensive views from the child-safe mountaintop, you will return the way you came, anticipating the hike's finale on the heart-thumping Skyride. This one's a sure winner in the "hike-with-the-funnest-finish" category.

From New York City, take the Thruway North to Exit 19 in Kingston. Follow NY 28 West for approximately 26 miles. Turn right onto NY 214 in Phoenicia. Drive about 15 miles on NY 214 to the junction with NY 23A and turn left (west). In 2 miles, in the town of Hunter, turn left following signs for "HUNTER MOUNTAIN SKI AREA" and "FESTIVALS." Cross the metal bridge over Schoharie Creek and drive 0.25 mile on the access road to the ski-area parking. Purchase your Skyride tickets at the ski lodge.

Take the Hunter Mountain Skyride (the skiers' chair lift in the wintertime) to the top of the mountain. (I'll bet that's the easiest 1500 vertical feet you've ever put behind you!) As you exit the lift, bear left (south) on a gravel road and walk past the outlet to another chair lift that feeds in from the left.

This shoulder of Hunter Mountain is known as Colonel's Chair, named after Colonel William Edwards. The town of Edwardsville (now known as Hunter) also bore the name of this early "tanlord." Leave the road to head east (left) toward a red-and-blue cable fence strung along the edge of a cliff. From behind the fence (where you'll find benches and picnic tables), you can see the Hunter summit. Look to the southeast along the ridge—at the highest point, a fire tower looms over stunted trees. (Pass around the binoculars.) If you scan right along the gently sloping ridge, you'll be previewing your hiking route to the tower. You'll also see North Mountain, High Peak and Roundtop, and the Blackhead and East Jewett ranges from this lovely spot.

Return to the road and turn left to head southward, passing another chair lift that unloads on the right. Soon, bear left onto a grassy road (marked with yellow circles and an arrow) as the gravel road veers right toward the Annapurna ski slope. The route you are following, known as Colonel's Chair Trail, services cross-country skiers and mountain bikers as well as hikers.

Although the yellow blazes of the hiking trail are sporadic, the markings of the cross-country ski trail with which it coincides are more frequent. Follow Trail 1 (indicated by red paint on wooden signs), avoiding ski trails 3, 4, and 3A, which split left and right. Four-tenths mile from the Skyride, turn left (southeast) onto cross-country ski trail 2 (still merged with the yellow hiking trail), following a sign for the Hunter Mountain summit, as Trail 1 departs right. Who does the best cross-country skier imitation? You are 1.6 miles from the fire tower.

Within 0.1 mile, Trail 2 ends abruptly and Trail 4 veers left. Continue straight (sidestepping a cable gate), passing signs that warn skiers and cyclists that the terrain ahead is "EXTREMELY DIFFICULT." Ignore more signs ("DO NOT ENTER," "OFF AREA") that are not intended for folks on foot and embark on a steep ascent. The unmarked, grassy path tracks uphill through the woods, soon curling westward and leveling.

Are the smaller kids getting bored with nothing but trees to look at on either side of the trail? Walking through the woods is more fun if you pretend to be a stalking tiger, bouncy bear cub, or wild horse.

At a grassy plateau 0.7 mile from the start, turn left off this wide path to head into the woods on a hard-packed foot trail. For the next 0.4 mile, the trail climbs gently through groves of spruce and birch. Count the different varieties of wildflowers. The rocks that border the trail are smothered in lichens and moss in varying shades of green.

Are the kids familiar with lichens? These pioneers are often the first plants to establish themselves on a rock's barren surface. They initiate the lengthy process of converting rocks into soil. An alga and a fungus, the two plants that make up a lichen, cooperate to ensure the lichen's survival under its harsh living conditions: the alga shares food with the fungus, which provides a moist environment for the alga. Count lichen-covered rocks along this stretch.

Who will spot the wooden marker that indicates you've reached an elevation of 3500 feet? (Camping is not permitted above this point.) At a T-intersection with a woods roads, turn left (southeast) on the blue-blazed Spruceton Trail. (A right turn will bring you in 0.3 mile to the John Robb Lean-to.) Let the youngsters know that you are more than halfway there: the fire tower is 1 mile away and Colonel's Chair is 1.1 miles behind you.

The woods road winds pleasantly through groves of spruce and birch, encountering only a few brief ascents along the way. Who can make the prettiest bracelet from the curls of birch bark that are strewn alongside the trail? Sections of the road may be seasonally muddy, but stones and small logs span the wettest terrain. Can you recognize any animal tracks in the mud? Look for signs of raccoons, deer, wild turkeys, and bears.

As the road curls right (south), you'll glimpse the fire tower reaching above the treetops. Beginning with the youngest hiker, take turns estimating the distance to the tower. The one who guessed 0.6 mile (or came closest) wins a granola bar.

A little more than 1.5 miles from the start, a side trail departs left, leading in 50 feet to a rock overlooking the Colonel's Chair area and the impressive northern Catskills, including Windham High Peak and Black Dome Mountain. Back on the main trail, continue 0.2 mile to a side trail on the left, marked "SPRING." Follow this yellow-blazed trail as it tumbles to the base of some intricate overhanging ledges. (The water source is seasonal.)

Return to the Spruceton Trail and turn left. A final uphill surge leads to the summit, an expansive, circular field rimmed with spruce trees. Let the kids run free; the summit is sheltered on all sides so parents need

Scanning the nearby slope of Hunter Mountain from Colonel's Chair

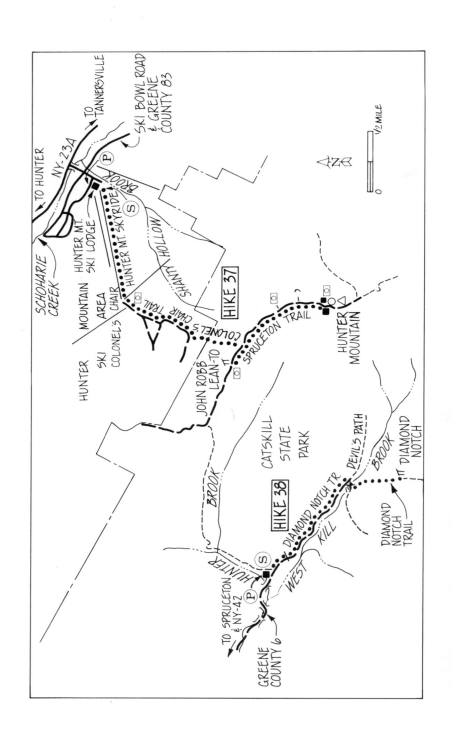

not worry about steep drop-offs. Pass the fire warden's cabins to reach the sturdy fire tower. Stop at any of the tower's landings—you'll get panoramic views after climbing as few as 25 steps. You can climb all 81, although the room atop the tower is closed. Be sure that the kids look northward toward the ski area to appreciate the distance they've covered. Rest, relax, lie on your backs, and find animals in the lazy parade of clouds overhead.

Return to your car the way you came, stopping for an overnight at the spacious John Robb Lean-to (on the blue trail) if you're equipped for it. The shelter is tucked to the right of the blue trail just below the 3500-foot marker. Below the lean-to and to the left of the trail is an overlook offering delightful southerly views into the central Catskills.

Note: The Skyride operates daily (weather permitting) during July and August and on weekends from Memorial Day into foliage season. Normal operating hours are 11 A.M. to 4:30 P.M. (The hours may be extended during festival season.) Currently, a Skyride pass costs $7 for an adult, $3.50 for a child between the ages of six and twelve, and $1 for a child under six.

38. Diamond Notch Falls

Type:	Dayhike or overnight
Difficulty:	Easy for children
Distance:	2.9 miles, round trip
Hiking time:	2.5 hours
High point/elevation gain:	2620 feet, 500 feet
Hikable:	May–October
Map:	NY/NJ Trail Conference Map 41

A waterfall is always a favorite destination for hikers, and one that is scaled down to kid-size is more appealing to families than a formidable one with limited access and dangerous drop-offs. An easy 1-mile walk along the entertaining West Kill (Brook) leads to Diamond Notch Falls, where kids can wade, splash, or just sit (do kids ever do that?) on the moss-covered slopes.

If you've been contemplating a family camp-out, consider hiking another 0.5 mile to the spacious Diamond Notch Lean-to. (An added bonus if you spend the night: you can visit the falls again in the morning!)

From New York City, take the Thruway North to Exit 19 in Kingston.

Follow NY 28 West for approximately 35 miles to Shandaken and turn right (north) onto NY 42. In about 12 miles, turn right onto Greene County 6 in Lexington, following signs to Spruceton. Greene County 6 turns to gravel in 6 miles and crosses a 4-ton-rated bridge in another 0.3 mile. Turn left into a large parking area at a sign for "FOREST PRESERVE ACCESS," 6.5 miles from NY 42.

Return to the gravel road and turn left (southeast), passing a trail sign that gives the distance to Diamond Notch Falls, 1 mile, and to the Diamond Notch Lean-to, 1.46 miles. Following the blue blazes of the Diamond Notch Trail, hike along the road for 0.3 mile to another parking area with, strangely, a "NO PARKING" sign. Sidestep a metal gate and continue southeastward on an unmaintained section of the road.

Ducking into the woods, the trail meets the West Kill (Brook) and climbs easily along the left bank. As you wind along the creek toward the falls, the kids can race stick and leaf boats. One-half mile from the

Diamond Notch Falls

start, the brook cascades into cool pools. Conduct a few water experiments. Will an acorn float? How about a pine cone?

Ask your kids to consider this question as they hike along the riverbank: do brooks have a beginning? When they turn to you for an answer, tell them that rivers and brooks begin as rainwater falling on the mountains and trickling downhill, seeking the easiest route. As a number of these tiny streams choose the same path, they join, forming a brook.

At 1 mile, you reach Diamond Notch Falls. Relax, parents: no sheer cliffs rim this waterfall. The West Kill Brook slides down a granite slab to dive 10 feet into a rocky pool. The shaded ravine is carpeted with multicolored mosses. Cross the footbridge over the falls or step down the footpath that splits right before the bridge, which leads to the base of the falls. Take off your boots to wade in the (*brrr!*) water or toss stones in and listen to the differently pitched *kerplunks*.

At the falls, the Diamond Notch Trail meets the red-blazed Devil's Path Trail. (The left branch of the Devil's Path Trail leads to the summit of Hunter Mountain; across the footbridge, the right branch leads to West Kill Mountain.) If you intend to spend the night or if you want to extend the hike, cross the footbridge and continue to follow the blue markings of the Diamond Notch Trail, bearing left (south) toward the Diamond Notch Lean-to.

Climb moderately on the rugged trail, hopping over frequent rocks placed to divert spring runoff. If the steady uphill march threatens to turn little hikers into big whiners, play a memory game. Try to name the Ten Essentials (from our introduction), the Seven Dwarfs, the Ninja Turtles characters, or the residents of Sesame Street.

Just under 0.5 mile from the falls, you'll see the eight-person shelter to the left of the path, resting on a knoll. (There is an outhouse below the lean-to.) Beyond the shelter, a path leads to a 25-foot-deep ravine lined with hemlocks. Little people can explore this shady canyon while the big people set up camp.

In the morning, return to your car the way you came—passing the pretty falls once more.

39. Reconnoiter Rock

Type:	Dayhike
Difficulty:	Difficult for children
Distance:	5 miles, round trip
Hiking time:	5 hours
High point/elevation gain:	3000 feet, 1350 feet
Hikable:	June–October
Map:	NY/NJ Trail Conference Map 43

Are you a rock fan? I don't mean rock as in the Rolling Stones, big diamonds, Mr. Hudson, or swaying back and forth. I'm talking about rock as in any relatively hard, naturally formed mass of mineral or petrified matter. If you're into that kind of rock, then this is your hike. Not only is your destination a rock, but all along the way you'll encounter rocks of varying sizes and shapes: rocks for resting on, rocks for climbing and jumping off, rocks that lean against one another to form little caves. The trip is long—6 miles—and, yes, the path is rock-strewn and rugged, but most kids in good shape will be able to make the trip. (Be sure to allow enough time for frequent rest stops.)

After the hike, you may want to drive on Peekamoose Road (also called Ulster County 42) due east for about 1 mile to a small parking lot on the left. Head northward from the parking area and hike a short distance to the base of breathtaking Buttermilk Falls.

From New York City, take the Thruway North to Exit 19 in Kingston. Follow NY 28 West for about 17 miles and turn left onto Ulster County 28A in Boiceville. Drive 3 miles on Ulster County 28A to West Shokenden and turn right onto Peekamoose Road (Ulster County 42). In 9.8 miles, pull into a small parking area on the right for the Peekamoose trailhead.

From the western side of the parking area, follow an unmarked path that climbs northward up a wooded slope to intersect in 50 yards with the combined Peekamoose-Table (PT) Trail and Long Path. (The actual trailhead is 100 yards farther west on Ulster County 42.) Turn right (northeast) onto this unmaintained woods road marked with the blue blazes of the PT Trail and Long Path. Climb steadily along the road, passing a trail register at 0.1 mile. As the road curls northeastward through open woods, a weary stone wall crawls beside you.

Within 0.6 mile, the woods road you've been following bears left (northwest) as you bear right (northeast) onto a footpath, following the blazes. As you march through a stand of red pines, pause to let the kids examine the needles. Are they long or short? How many needles are in

Splashing in the pool beneath Buttermilk Falls

each bunch? Climb through more clusters of pines before dodging ledge outcroppings. At 0.8 mile, you arrive atop a wooded plateau. Be sure to point out anything that interests you—a brightly colored berry, a puffy mushroom, an unusual insect—to the kids, whether or not you know its name. If the children bombard you with questions, suggest that all of you take a trip to the library after the hike to do some research.

One mile from the start, the trail snakes among erratic boulders and around exposed ledge. If the kids seem to be tiring, look ahead and point out good "resting rocks," then take turns selecting the next resting rock farther ahead. After weaving through rugged woods, the trail embarks on a twisting ascent that steepens at 1.4 miles. On level ground at last, squeeze between ledge outcroppings to reach a plateau littered with more boulders. Stop here for an energy break and to let the kids play on this natural jungle gym.

The rugged trail continues, picking its way through groves of mature oaks. How did these trees escape loggers' saws? (Perhaps the rugged

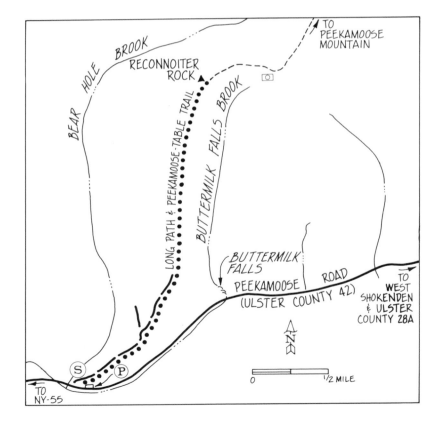

terrain made the trees inaccessible.) At 1.7 miles, another steep ascent leads to the base of some minor cliffs. The trail cuts to the left, switches back to the right, and crests. In another 0.1 mile, cross a river of rocks and boulders.

After a steady 0.2-mile climb through mixed woods, the trail mounts another hill overrun with boulders, 2 miles from the start. How does this rocky hillside differ from the ones you scaled within the last mile? Quickly, the trail reaches an area crowded with large rocks and ledge outcroppings. You won't have any trouble spotting Reconnoiter Rock, perched on top of a slab of ledge. Who can climb to the top of this massive boulder? (Those who meet the challenge will be treated to grand seasonal views to the south, west, and east. Look southward to see Samson Mountain in the foreground and the Shawangunk Mountains stretching along the horizon.) How do you think Reconnoiter Rock landed in its present position?

Explore the small caves and overhangs that punctuate the area surrounding the rock before returning to your car the way you came.

40. Slide Mountain

Type: Dayhike
Difficulty: Challenging for children
Distance: 6.3 miles, loop
Hiking time: 7 hours
High point/elevation gain: 4180 feet, 1800 feet
Hikable: May–October
Map: NY/NJ Trail Conference Map 43

This is the second toughest hike in the book (Indian Head Mountain, Hike 29, is the toughest). It's also the second longest in our book: 6.3 miles. Tricky river crossings (in the spring or after a rainstorm) mean that wet feet may be unavoidable. But before you flip to the next hike, you should know that the trails leading up formidable Slide Mountain are the most popular in the Catskills. Why? Perhaps folks like to brag that they've climbed to the highest peak in the Catskills. Perhaps they like to wander through one of the area's largest tracts of wilderness. Or maybe it's the views from the mountaintop—views that seem to stretch to the ends of the earth. Whatever the reason, we've included it because, hey, how could all of those other hikers be wrong?

From New York City, take the Thruway North to Exit 19 in Kingston.

Comparing notes with other hikers along the Curtis-Ormsbee Trail

Follow NY 28 West for about 32 miles to the junction with NY 42 in Shadaken. From this junction, continue on NY 28 West for 3.8 miles. Turn left onto Ulster County 47 (also known as Slide Mountain Road), following a sign to Oliverea. Just over 9 miles from NY 28, turn left into a driveway, directed by a sign for "SLIDE MOUNTAIN TRAILHEAD PARKING." (The parking area can accommodate at least two dozen cars.)

From the eastern side of the parking area, head into the woods on the yellow-blazed Phoenicia–East Branch (PE) Trail, passing a sign that indicates the Slide Mountain summit is 2.7 miles away (you'll be taking a longer route than this—yes, *longer*). Cross the wide, shallow Neversink River on stones and quickly hop over two more seasonal streams that feed the river. Who can find a leaf that's been chewed? At 0.15 mile, the blazes lead across a fourth minor stream. Remind the kids to conserve their energy; you have 6 miles to go.

The PE Trail tracks eastward, plodding uphill on rugged terrain. Rock steps give a boost along the steeper slopes. To distract the little ones from the climb, look for faces in tree trunks (we always seem to find Jimmy Durante). At 0.3 mile, the trampled path dodges right around protruding ledge. Just under 0.5 mile from the start, the trail meets an old woods road; turn right onto the road, now heading southward.

Let the kids run ahead, with instructions to wait for you at the spring. After the 0.5-mile mark, a pipe spews clear, chilly water across the trail. Revive yourselves with a drink before resuming the gradual climb. Continue straight on the PE Trail (now a narrowing woods road) as the Wittenberg-Cornell-Slide (WCS) Trail heads left (east).

The PE Trail climbs easily over the next 0.8 mile, leading over a number of streams that may present a challenge in the spring or after heavy rains. One mile from the start, the trail crosses a footbridge. Toss sticks off one side of the bridge and look to the other side to see whose stick appears first. The side trails that split right near the bridge lead to campsites that are not authorized by the New York Department of Environmental Conservation (due to their proximity to water and to the trail). At 1.2 miles, a second spring floods the trail, making wet feet hard to avoid.

Soon you reach a sign posted at an intersection that confirms that you have journeyed 1.5 miles from the Slide Mountain parking area. Here, depart the PE Trail (it continues straight to the Denning Lean-to) and turn left (east) onto the blue-blazed Curtis-Ormsbee (CO) Trail toward Slide Mountain, 2.25 miles away. Notice the small granite monument on the left is dedicated to "purveyors of the Curtis-Ormsbee Trail" who were killed nearly a century ago in a sudden summer snowstorm on Mount Washington, New Hampshire. The Fresh Air Club of New York cut the trail and maintained it for many years.

One-tenth mile from the monument, the steep trail picks its way through a canyon rimmed with boulders and child-size caves. Stop here for a rest and an energy break before mounting the arduous assault on Slide Mountain.

As the trail switches above the canyon, glance back for a look into the ravine. Climb moderately through coniferous woods. Who can find the tiniest pinecone? Who can find the biggest one? At 2.2 miles (0.7 mile from the last intersection), head up a stiff slope past more sedimentary rock ledge. As you crest this section, look to the left for cropped western views; Doubletop is the most prominent peak. With a final uphill surge, you reach the 3500-foot elevation marker; camping is prohibited above this point. (Did the kids make it up the hill without a complaint? Give them all pats on the back.)

Just under 2.5 miles from the start, a yellow-blazed side trail splits right (southeast), leading to an overlook with expansive views across the Neversink Valley to Peekamoose Mountain. Can you spot the characteristic flat top of Table Mountain? Rest here before returning to the CO Trail. Tracking northeastward on fairly level terrain, the trail encounters spongy ground with halved logs laid across the wettest sections. Aspiring acrobats will love inching across these narrow bridges.

For the next 0.5 mile, the trail rolls through mostly coniferous woods, trending uphill. What do the kids notice about the size of the trees at this elevation? Pause for a moment to listen to the forceful wind pounding the upper reaches of the mountain.

At a junction with the red-blazed WCS Trail (3 miles from the start), turn right (east). (The left-hand path leads back to the PE Trail—you'll

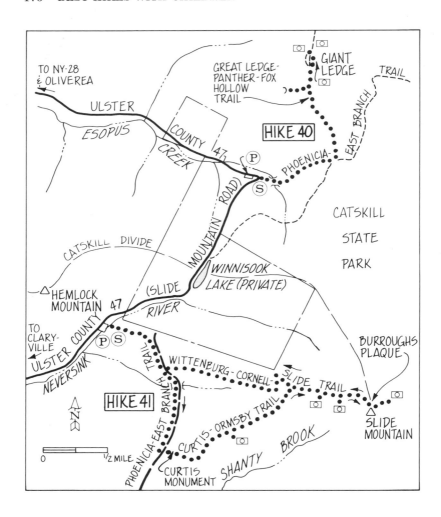

take this route on your return.) From here, the summit of Slide Mountain is 0.6 mile away. As you continue the modest climb, warn kids about the cost of whining, grumbling, or complaining: offenders must tell three riddles or two knock-knock jokes.

From the well-traveled WCS Trail, side trails branch right, leading to the edge of the ridge. From these spots, lovely southerly views encompass Ashokan Reservoir and the Hudson River. The WCS Trail sweeps along nearly level ground for 0.4 mile, where a final steep climb crests near the summit. To the left, a safe ledge offers dizzying views to the north, taking in nearby Panther Mountain and Giant Ledge (Hike 41) and the distant Hunter Mountain (Hike 37) as well as local hills.

Just beyond the overlook, the trail trudges uphi
balsam fir and opens onto the true summit, a clear
views. At one time, a pair of lean-tos provided shel
here. Continue to follow the trail eastward for anotl
wide rock ledge. From this spot below the 4180-foot
if not forever, at least to the Hudson River eastwa.u. _
Jersey and Pennsylvania. This is the hike's choice picnic spot. The snue
north of the summit, for which the mountain is named, is the result of
an avalanche in 1820, and has since been buried in plant growth.

Who can find the Burroughs plaque? It claims that poet and naturalist John Burroughs "introduced Slide Mountain to the world." Indeed,
this writer-naturalist brought notoriety to the southern Catskills area
through his essays, causing anxiety among the owners of the grand hotels
in the northern Catskills.

To return to your car, reverse direction and follow the red-blazed
WCS Trail to the intersection with the blue CO Trail, 0.6 mile from the
summit. Continue to follow the red trail westward, descending easily for
1.2 miles to the yellow-blazed PE Trail. Turn right here and trudge the
final 0.6 mile on the familiar PE Trail to your car. If you can muster the
strength to lick, find an ice cream stand!

41. Giant Ledge

Type:	Dayhike or overnight
Difficulty:	Moderate for children
Distance:	3.4 miles, round trip
Hiking time:	3.5 hours
High point/elevation gain:	3400 feet, 1200 feet
Hikable:	April–October
Map:	NY/NJ Trail Conference Map 43

Whoever said that the best things come in small packages has never
hiked to Giant Ledge, part of the long ridge of Panther Mountain. While
the superb views from the ledge are for the big folks, the shallow caves
and overlooks you pass on the way up will appeal to the kids.

Designated a wilderness area by the New York Department of
Environmental Conservation (DEC), this remote section of the central
Catskills is rich in legend and folklore. One popular tale discloses the
details of the relationship between an Indian named Winnisook and a
farmer's daughter. His mysterious death several years into their love affair

much speculation, and intriguing stories have survived to this day.
nearby town of Big Indian—Winnisook was more than 7 feet tall—
as named after him.

From New York City, take the Thruway North to Exit 19 in Kingston.
Follow NY 28 West for about 32 miles to the junction with NY 42 in
Shadaken. From this junction, continue on NY 28 West for 3.8 miles. Turn
left onto Ulster County 47, following a sign to Oliverea. Seven and two-
tenths miles from NY 28, just before the road curves sharply right, pull
into a substantial shoulder parking area at a sign for the "GIANT LEDGE
TRAILHEAD PARKING AREA."

Walk eastward on the paved road to the bend; here, cross the road
and enter the woods. Immediately, the Phoenicia–East Branch (PE) Trail
crosses a footbridge over a dry gully. On the left, a trail sign announces
that Giant Ledge is 1.6 miles away. Follow yellow blazes along a wide,
worn path with rocks intruding underfoot, soon passing a registration box
on the left. (Teach the kids how to sign in and out: it helps park officials
keep track of trail usage and also lets them know if any hikers are still
out on the trails.)

The kids will have fun balancing on logs that span a sometimes-soggy
area. As you hike through this deciduous forest, find a maple tree to
examine. Ask the kids whether the leaves on a given tree are all the same
size and shape. (No. Their size and shape vary with their age and position

Signing in at the trail register before hiking to Giant Ledge

on the tree.) Who knows what we make with the sap from the sugar maple tree? (Maple syrup!) If you're hiking in autumn, you'll notice that the red or swamp maple tree is among the first to change color; its leaves contain a significant amount of red pigment called anthocyanin.

Just 0.15 mile from the start, cross a creek over a solid footbridge. In another 0.1 mile, the trail sweeps northeastward and begins a moderate ascent on ledge with roots occasionally spreading across the path.

Following a rock slide, pick your way up convenient stepping stones. Play "Follow the Leader," with the first in line charged with choosing the best footing. For the next 0.25 mile, the trail frequently leads over rocky tracts: let the kids take turns being the leader. Seven-tenths mile from the start, the trail confronts a ledge outcropping and switches right to climb to the top of the ledge and arrive at a trail junction.

Bear left (the right branch leads onto private land), quickly reaching another junction. Again turn left (northeast) toward Giant Ledge, 0.85 mile away, as the PE Trail continues straight to Woodland Valley. Now following the Giant Ledge–Panther Fox Hollow Trail (marked in blue), track along the ridge on fairly level ground. (Let the kids know that the significant climbing is over for awhile.)

One mile from the start, a row of flat rocks forms a bridge over a wet spot. The trail gains more altitude over the next 0.2 mile and passes more frequent ledge outcroppings. At 1.4 miles, watch for a wooden sign that indicates a left-hand side trail. Follow the trail for less than 0.1 mile to a pipe that sends icy springwater splashing across the trail. Rest in this area after your drink. The kids can play on the natural jungle gym created by the ledges on the uphill side of the trail.

Back on the main trail, look carefully for a child-size cave on the left as you begin another stiff ascent on rock steps. Because this climb will be demanding on little legs, allow the kids frequent stops to explore the curious overhangs and the tiny caves that hide among the rocks. The ancient Romans believed that nymphs and sibyls lived in caves like these. The kids can probably make some more accurate guesses as to what kinds of creatures call these caves home.

Soon the trail crests, arriving at crisscrossing unmarked trails atop the ridge. From here you can choose a route to nearby Giant Ledge. Avoid the main trail that heads down the center of the ridge and offers limited views. Instead, follow the side trails that lead left and right to the protruding rocks along the long ridge known collectively as Giant Ledge. The long-range views from both sides are spectacular.

The right-hand trail leads to the ridge's eastern edge, with the first overlook at 1.5 miles. Here, the ledges are tiered, so while you won't need to restrain the kids completely, do keep them from wandering to the lower tier, which ends in a sheer drop-off. From the relatively safe upper ledge, the views are spectacular, taking in the Catskills to the east and south, notably Wittenberg and Slide mountains (Hike 40).

From here, follow the unblazed path that heads westward i the center of the ridge. Soon you arrive at a lovely, but unauthor campsite protected by rock walls and sheltered under a ceiling of her locks. Continue westward to another overlook. The extensive vistas take in the western Catskills, with Big Indian dominating the horizon. Parents can relax on this overlook: there are no dangerous cliffs to detract from your enjoyment.

It's best for families to turn around at this point, because as the trail continues it inches closer to the edge of the cliffs, especially on the eastern side. From the campsite, pick up the blue-blazed trail that leads southward down the center of the ridge, returning to your car the way you came.

42. Dry Brook

Type: Day or overnight
Difficulty: Moderate for children
Distance: 4.2 miles, round trip
Hiking time: 3.5 hours
High point/elevation gain: 2400 feet, 350 feet
Hikable: June–October
Map: NY/NJ Trail Conference Map 42

Whenever we ask kids what features they appreciate most on a hike, "Water" is what we hear time and again. And why not? It's pretty to look at, fun to play in, and home to a great many interesting creatures. On this hike, you and the kids follow two delightful brooks, crossing over and back several times, tracking on fairly level terrain. About 2 miles from the start is a well-constructed lean-to on the northern bank of Shandaken Brook (just inside the Catskills State Park boundary). You can spend the night—or perhaps just relax—before heading back along the riverbank.

For younger kids who prefer hands-on hikes to trips featuring long-distance views, this one is a winner. Don't forget to bring whatever your youngsters need for river exploration: wading shoes, nets, jars, towels.

 From New York City, take the Thruway North to Exit 19 in Kingston. Follow NY 28 West for about 36 miles. Turn left onto Ulster County 49A, following signs to the Highmount and Belleayre ski areas, and drive 5.2 miles. At a stop sign, turn left onto Ulster County 49. In 1.4 miles, at

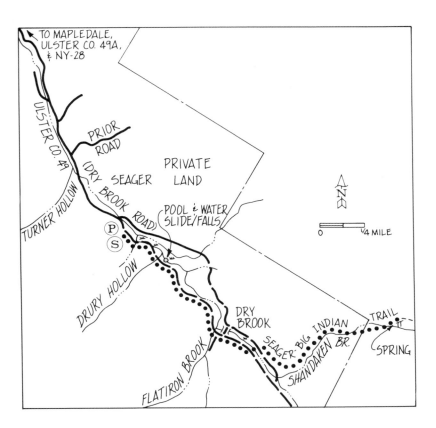

an intersection of gravel roads known as "Stuarts Turn," near a wooden building, bear right, following a sign for "SEAGER PARKING AREA, 2.9 MILES." (The mileage on the sign is slightly off.) Drive another 2.5 miles, passing a covered bridge on the left, and soon arrive at the Seager trailhead parking area.

Sidestep a red metal gate and head southeastward, following the yellow-blazed Seager–Big Indian (SE) Trail. (Signs indicate that only hikers are permitted to trespass on this private property.) Track along the southern bank of Dry Brook under high hemlocks on a wide path. At 0.15 mile, the blazes lead over a broad, seasonal tributary and return to the bank of Dry Brook. Look for tracks beside the brook: deer, raccoon, mink, otter, even coyote. (Coyotes are common in the Catskills, although it is not known whether any inhabited the area before the mid-1900s. In the 1950s and 1960s, researchers tracked their movement across Canada, into upper New York State and New England. Today, traveling in small packs, these predators help to control the deer population. You likely will not encounter a coyote on a dayhike; like most wild animals, they avoid contact with humans. The bobcat is another Catskills creature—less common than the coyote—that you'll probably never meet. You may spot tracks, or droppings on exposed ledges, but you won't come face-to-face with one.)

Before long, cross a section of the brook on stones to reach a belt of land running down the middle of the brook. After a brief walk on this "island," recross the brook to return to the southern bank. Let the youngsters take turns leading the way on these crossings: the leader chooses the stones that the rest of you will step on to get across. Whether your leader picks the easiest route or the toughest is up to her! At the 0.4-mile mark, the trail divides a marshy area. What varieties of plants prefer these damp conditions?

One-half mile from the start, the trail crosses a seasonal stream (called Drury Hollow) and reaches Dry Brook's most appealing segment, where water pours down a chute and plunges into a moss-lined pool. The kids can toss twigs into the water above the miniature falls and watch the inevitable shipwrecks below. If you plan to take an extended rest here, play a game with the kids. Ask them to close their eyes, then lead each one in turn to a tree, rock, patch of moss, or flower. Have the child feel the object, then help him return to his original spot. After he opens his eyes, can he point to the object he was just touching?

Beyond the falls, the trail snakes along the riverbank, soon joined by a gravel road that merges from the right. A sign at this junction reminds you that you have come 0.9 mile and that you have 1.1 miles to go to reach the Shandaken Brook Lean-to. Immediately, the gravel road departs left, crossing Dry Brook on a bridge, as you follow the yellow-blazed woods road straight, continuing to wind along the brook's southern bank. In 0.2 mile, the woods road you've been following also departs left to cross the brook; follow the yellow foot trail straight. You cross the brook soon, too, but at an easier point, marked with a yellow arrow and a trail sign (count on wet feet).

Once you're across, another trail sign updates your progress: you are just 0.85 mile from the lean-to. Head eastward, away from the brook, cutting across a woods road and climbing an embankment. As the SE Trail, still marked in yellow, rises and begins to track southeastward, it resembles an overgrown woods road. Look carefully at the trailside ferns. Are they all the same color? Are they all of the same variety? To the right, through the dense hemlock forest, catch your first glimpse of Shandaken Brook as it hurries through a dark, narrow chasm. The trail becomes increasingly soggy; wet feet are unavoidable at 1.6 miles.

At 1.8 miles, the trail drops toward Shandaken Brook and crosses on stones. As the blazes lead hikers along the wide, nearly dry streambed, the path begins to fade. Just under 2 miles from the start, cross onto state-owned land near a hiker registration box. After a final stone-to-stone crossing of Shandaken Brook at 2.05 miles, you can spot the lean-to atop a grassy knoll. Nearby, a pipe gushes cold springwater. One last uphill effort brings you to the remote cabin, solid and relatively new, with room for eight and a hearth for cooking. Unpack your overnight gear or return to your car by way of the Seager–Big Indian Trail.

Note: This trail is primarily on private land. (Refer to the map for boundaries.) The owner has permitted trail markings for the benefit of hikers. Hunting, fishing, and camping are not permitted. The Shandaken Brook Lean-to is on public land, in the Catskills State Park.

Stop for a rest near Dry Brook's pristine pool.

43. Rider Hollow

Type: Dayhike or overnight
Difficulty: Easy for children
Distance: 0.6 mile, round trip
Hiking time: 40 minutes
High point/elevation gain: 2100 feet, 60 feet
Hikable: May–October
Map: NY/NJ Trail Conference Map 40

Campgrounds seem too civilized, but the notion of pitching a tent miles from nowhere seems too, well, uncivilized. How about a compromise? Stay in a rustic cabin just 0.3 mile from your car, with a drinking water source nearby, and a brook for wading or swimming. The setting is perfect for a first family overnight. And if the kids change their minds about staying overnight at 11:45 P.M., a flashlight will guide you along the wide woods road back to your car. (Bring bug spray, even for a dayhike.)

 From New York City, take the Thruway North to Exit 19 in Kingston. Follow NY 28 West for about 36 miles. Turn left onto Ulster County 49A, following signs to the Highmount and Belleayre ski areas, and drive 4.8 miles. Turn left (east) onto Rider Hollow Road. In 2 miles, the road ends at the parking area for the Rider Hollow trailhead.

On the eastern side of the parking area, a New York Department of Environmental Conservation (DEC) sign displays the various destinations along the red-blazed Oliverea-Mapledale (OM) Trail: Rider Hollow Lean-to, 0.3 mile; Belleayre Mountain, 2.2 miles; Balsam Mountain, 2.5 miles. The lean-to is your goal today.

Sidestep the metal gate and head southeastward on a wide, level woods road. On the left, Rider Hollow Brook babbles and chatters beside you. How do different objects sound when tossed into the brook? Does everything make a noise when it hits the water? One-tenth mile from the start, cross the brook on a sturdy footbridge. As you pass through stands of hemlock trees, pause to examine their short needles. Are they the same color on either side? Are they all the same length? These needles collect on the forest floor and create soil so acidic that few plants can survive. Thus, hemlock forests feel open and airy, free of the thick underbrush so common in other woodlands. What do you notice about hemlock root systems? Do you trip over the roots? Shallow roots allow hemlocks to grow in thin, rocky soil.

Follow the trampled path for 0.3 mile to the edge of a meadow. To the left is the cavernous Rider Hollow Lean-to, which accommodates

Grandfather and granddaughter pause for a rest.

about a dozen overnighters. To the right of the lean-to, a small dam contains enough water to create a small bathing pool. On a hot summer day, youngsters are attracted to this pool like pigs to mud puddles. If it's too cool to swim, tell the kids to watch for wildlife. Sit very still for 5 minutes and blend in with the surroundings so that the forest creatures will accept you as part of the natural environment. Soon, you may see birds landing nearby, squirrels scampering within a few feet of you, or rabbits hopping curiously in your direction.

Beyond the lean-to, the OM Trail continues southeast to a pipe that spews forth springwater, an added convenience for campers. This marks the official end of the hike, but you'll probably want to do some exploring once you've dropped off your gear at the lean-to. After passing the spring, the OM Trail meets the Mine Hollow Trail. If you turn right, still on the OM Trail, and cross Rider Hollow on a metal bridge (at the junction of Rider Hollow and Mine Hollow brooks), you can wander along the bank of the brook.

Back at the lean-to, the kids can help gather wood for the fire, put dinner on, prepare the bunks, and hang supplies out of the reach of curious raccoons or hungry black bears!

44. Long Pond

Type:	Dayhike or overnight
Difficulty:	Easy for children
Distance:	2 miles, round trip
Hiking time:	2 hours
High point/elevation gain:	2190 feet, 210 feet
Hikable:	June–October
Map:	NY/NJ Trail Conference Map 43

Long Pond is a terrific destination for a family new to hiking or camping. The 2-mile, round-trip hike covers relatively level terrain and involves few trail junctions. Whether or not you plan to spend the night, the kids will enthusiastically investigate the well-built lean-to (it sleeps six) before racing to the pond in search of critters.

For a day visit, we recommend that you bring a sheer net for skimming across the surface of the pond (or an old nylon stocking stretched over a coat hanger), a book to identify the animal tracks you'll see along the bank of Willowemoc Creek and the shoreline of the pond, extra shoes for wading, towels for overeager waders, binoculars, and a picnic lunch. If you plan to stay overnight, bring along a flashlight covered with red cellophane. You can take a midnight stroll to spot wildlife: animals won't be able to see your red light, but you'll be able to see them!

From New York City, follow the Thruway North to Exit 16 and NY 17 West. Leave NY 17 at Exit 100 and follow NY 52 West to the center of Liberty. At the intersection of NY 52 and Sullivan County 176 in Liberty, take Sullivan County 176 north approximately 4 miles to Parksville and the junction with Sullivan County 85. Head north on Sullivan County 85 (it becomes Sullivan County 84 approximately 3.5 miles from Parksville) to Willowemoc, a total of 7 miles from Parksville. Here, at the junction with Hunter Road, continue straight on Sullivan County 84 for 0.8 mile and turn sharply left (another road bears left) onto Flugertown Road. One and four-tenths miles from Sullivan County 84, pass a "ROAD CLOSED" sign (unmaintained road). In another 0.9 mile, pull off to the right near a distinct "LONG POND TRAIL PARKING AREA" sign.

From the trailhead sign, head southeast on a wide path, guided by the red blazes of the Long Pond–Beaverkill Ridge (LB) Trail and infrequent orange snowmobile markings. Cross Willowemoc Creek on a solid footbridge. (Even though the trailhead seems remote, it's obvious from the trampled path that many hikers have preceded you on this walk to Long Pond.)

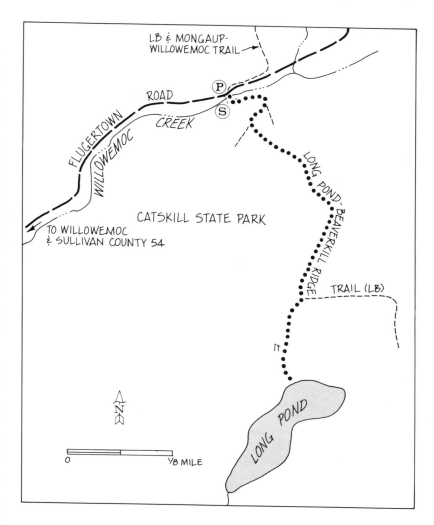

Trending northeastward, the trail flirts with the bank of the creek. Across the water, less than 0.1 mile from the start, a table waits in the shade to serve post-hike picnickers. Soon, the trail rises modestly and meets an unmarked trail that heads southeastward. Bear right, still following red blazes, to head southwest.

As you stumble over the roots of a massive hemlock, try to guess its age. Hemlocks, which can live for up to 600 years, tend to cluster in damp, shady locations, where they grow very slowly. A tree as thin as a chair leg can be a half-century old. When exposed to full sunlight,

Reflections in Long Pond

hemlocks grow much more quickly. Pause to examine these hemlocks closely. Look for white, woolly patches under the needles, an indication of woolly adelgids. These insects are invading the region and threatening to damage the hemlock population.

Hop over a seasonal stream and look to the right. Who can spot the bridge that you crossed near the start of the hike? The LB Trail has come close to making a complete circle.

At 0.25 mile, the trail sweeps left (south) on a rocky, eroded path and embarks on a moderate ascent; avoid a meager trail that leads straight. Sing songs with animals in them as you climb. (You know, "Three Blind Mice," "Old MacDonald Had a Farm," "Puff the Magic Dragon". . .) Cresting within 0.15 mile, the trail crawls under the branches of mature deciduous trees. Somehow, these giants escaped the loggers' saws.

Six-tenths mile from the start, the trail is soggy in the shade of hemlock trees; ferns press in from either side. At the 0.8-mile mark, reach an intersection near a registration box. Here, the red LB Trail heads left toward "east access and parking, 3.8 miles"; pointing behind you, the sign says "west access and parking, 0.8 mile." A third sign tells you that the Long Pond Lean-to is 0.1 mile away, accessed by the right-hand (west) path.

Follow the trail toward Long Pond until you reach a clearing where the stout shelter sits near a stone hearth. A short path leads left (south) to the edge of the tranquil pond. Rimmed with low berry bushes, the pond offers kids muddy shores with crisscrossing animal tracks to identify and clear, shallow water for frog and turtle hunting. If you want to find a salamander, carefully turn over logs near the water's edge; these amphibians have sun-sensitive skin and require damp, darkened conditions to maintain a critical level of moisture. (Be sure to replace the log after you've looked under it.)

Skim the water with your net. What will you capture? A whirligig beetle, water strider, water boatman, or dragonfly naiad? The dragonfly hatches from a small egg and lives in the pond as a naiad for two to three years. When it is large enough, the naiad makes its way out of the water onto the stem of a plant. Soon, pairs of wings split through its outer casing and the dragonfly takes flight.

Spend the night in the lean-to or explore the pond by day, and return to your car the way you came.

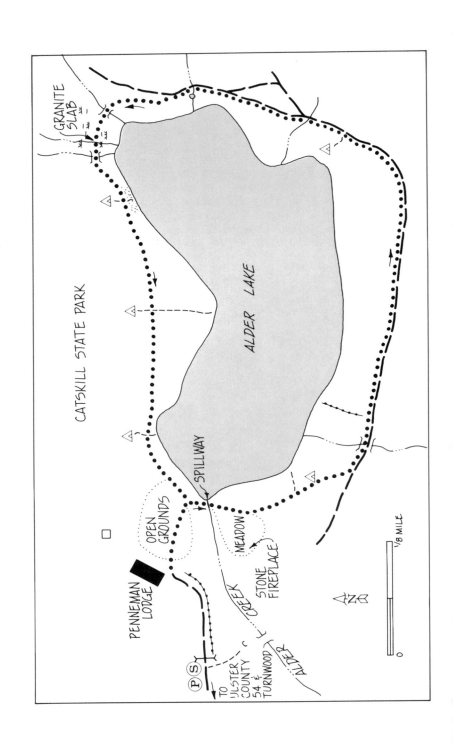

45. Alder Lake

Type: Dayhike or overnight
Difficulty: Easy for children
Distance: 1.8 miles, loop
Hiking time: 1.5 hours
High point/elevation gain: 2200 feet, 75 feet
Hikable: May–October
Map: NY/NJ Trail Conference Map 42

The toughest part of this trip is getting to the trailhead. If your car can manage the rutted, country back roads that lead to the gate near secluded Alder Lake, you can breathe a sign of relief. The hike around the lake is the easy part!

What a delightful place to spend an afternoon—or a weekend! Begin near the old, abandoned mansion that once offered lodging to visiting city folks and work your way around the lake, passing frequent campsites and access points to the water. Along the northern shore, the kids have many opportunities to visit the water and search for newts and frogs, whirligig beetles and water striders. Though the trail is somewhat indistinct in places, you won't get lost if you remember to keep the water on your left.

From New York City, take the Thruway North to Exit 16. Follow NY 17 West for approximately 50 miles to Exit 96 in Livingston Manor. Take Sullivan County 179 north, following signs to Beaverkill, Deckertown, and Lewbeach. In 1.2 miles, turn right following signs to Beaverkill onto Sullivan County 151 (also called Johnson Hill Road). In 4.1 miles Sullivan County 151 merges with Sullivan County 152 in Beaverkill; continue straight ahead. In another 4 miles, cross into Ulster County; the road becomes Ulster County 54. Seven miles from Beaverkill, pass the entrance to Little Pond Campground. Continue on Ulster County 54 (through the village of Turnwood) for another 3.7 miles to where the road turns to gravel. When the dwindling road divides, bear right onto a rough, narrow dirt road. Follow this road for 0.3 mile, to its conclusion at a substantial parking area for Alder Lake.

Follow the driveway bordered by an intricate stone wall, and pass imposing Penneman Lodge, now vacant and boarded up, a skeleton of a once-grand lakeside resort. Make up a collective story about this "haunted" house, beginning with "Once upon a time there was an old house near a lake," and ask each hiker to add a sentence in turn. With kids involved, things will get spooky and silly pretty quickly. Cut across the open grounds that spread before the lodge, dropping gently to meet the western shore of Alder Lake.

Turn right when you reach the water to follow the edge in a counterclockwise direction. Look for pond skaters and water striders scooting across the surface of the water. These and other aquatic insects are food for the fish, frogs, and birds that live in and near the lake. After passing over the spillway, you reach the edge of a meadow. Follow an unblazed path that hugs the left side of the field with the pond still in sight. The kids may want to explore the remains of a cabin that sit across the field, marked by a large fieldstone fireplace and chimney. At the pasture's southern corner, the path ducks left into the woods near a stand of birches.

At an indistinct intersection 0.25 mile from the start, bear right onto a faint path, passing through a campsite. When you reach an unmaintained woods road 100 feet above the campsite, turn left, guided eastward along the road by tin-can-top blazes painted blue. Soon you cross a footbridge

Near an Alder Lake campsite

over a seasonal brook. Watch for the ancient stone wall that dives 300 feet down the wooded hillside to meet the water.

Initially heading east, the grassy road bordered by ferns rises gently. Although you are some distance from the lake now, you can look through the trees to see the sunlight reflecting off the water. About 0.7 mile from the start, the woods road curls northward. Who will be the first to spot the tent site hidden in a pine grove on the left? Cross a wide creek on stones (likely to cause wet feet in the spring). Twenty paces beyond the creek, the trail splits; take the left (north) branch. After a brief climb, the trail crests as a woods road joins from the right.

Shortly, a stream passes under the road, forming a dainty pool between the road and the lake. Examine the pond vegetation with the kids. Where are the roots of these pond plants? (Some are floating, others are anchored in the bottom of the pond.) Some water plants grow only underwater, others grow only on the bank. Seventy-five feet beyond the pond, follow a grassy trail that splits left off the woods road. The footpath, crowded by ferns, leads quickly to the lake's breezy northeastern shore.

Cross a flimsy bridge over a stream and follow the trail as it curls left (west), passing the marshy inlet to the lake. A granite slab and a second crumbling footbridge carry hikers over two more streams that feed the pond. Beyond these crossings, side trails split right (to a camping site) and left (to a grassy beach). If kids turn left to explore, they might see spotted newts swimming in the shallow water. Look for newt eggs hidden in the grass on the shore.

As you continue on the main trail, cut through an overgrown field where more side trails lead right to oak-shaded camping spots and left to the edge of the lake. Look for signs of the white-tailed deer that frequently gather at the edge of forests such as this. Can you find twigs and buds that have been chewed off or trunks that are stripped of bark? How about deer tracks or droppings?

Push through persistent berry bushes for a view of Penneman Lodge. Your younger companions might be amazed (as ours were) to discover that they have walked all the way around the lake.

A stone wall lays buried in brush on the right side of the trail. As the trail continues to sweep left (southwest), following the curve of the lake, another side trail branches right to find the hike's final camping site.

Back at the untended lawn of the old lodge, relax, swim, or picnic before returning to your car along the familiar drive. As you come to the end of the stone wall and pass through the gate, turn left and drop down a wooded slope for about 75 feet where ice-cold springwater spills from a pipe. Fill your water jugs to quench the kids' post-hike thirst. Good luck on your drive back to civilization!

Note: Camping is prohibited except at sites designated by the New York State Department of Environmental Conservation.

Young canoeists on Little Pond

46. Little Pond and Touchmenot Mountain

Type: Dayhike or overnight
Difficulty: Moderate for children
Distance: 3.4 miles, loop
Hiking time: 3.5 hours
High point/elevation gain: 2750 feet, 800 feet
Hikable: May–October
Map: NY/NJ Trail Conference Map 44

If your gang can't agree on how tough a hike you should tackle, begin the 3.4-mile trip over Touchmenot Mountain with the knowledge that you can cut the hike short about 1 mile from the start at a lovely spot where a broad, grassy expanse allows safe exploring and offers local views that kids as well as adults can appreciate. A nearby frog pond will entice kids who like to "hunt" for water critters, and the variety of wildflowers that blanket the meadow will appeal to nonfroggers. Those who elect to complete the loop will be treated to challenging ascents, breathtaking descents, and the opportunity to take a dip at Little Pond's beach area near the end of the loop. Give it a try—you might surprise yourselves with your perseverance and stamina.

 From New York City, take the Thruway North to Exit 16. Follow NY 17 West for approximately 50 miles to Exit 96 in Livingston Manor. Drive north on Sullivan County 179 following signs to Beaverkill, Deckertown, and Lewbeach. In 1.2 miles, turn right onto Sullivan County 151 (also called Johnson Hill Road), guided by signs to Beaverkill. Drive 4.1 miles and, as Sullivan County 151 merges with Sullivan County 152 in Beaverkill, continue straight ahead. In another 4 miles, as you cross into Ulster County, the road becomes Ulster County 54. Seven miles from Beaverkill (where Sullivan County 151 and 152 met), turn left onto Barkaboom Road following a sign to "NY 30" and another for "LITTLE POND CAMPGROUND NYDEC." In 0.1 mile, turn left onto the access road signed to "LITTLE POND PUBLIC CAMPGROUND AND DAY USE AREA." Stop at the guardhouse and pay a small day-use fee. Follow the park road to campsite 37; just beyond the campsite, park at the boat launch parking area.

From the parking area and western side of Little Pond, head north-ward on a foot trail that runs beside a wooden fence, soon passing a massive stone hearth. Sharp yellow blazes lead hikers over three dainty streams on footbridges before the trail begins to curl eastward. Count the tent sites near the water that are sheltered under a hemlock canopy. Two-tenths mile from the start, just beyond some outhouses, turn left (north) onto the yellow-blazed Little Pond Trail. (This trail also contin-ues straight, east, to encircle the pond; you will return along this path.)

Embark on a steady climb, marching along a shallow ravine on the right that carries a stream. Just under 0.5 mile, pass a small beaver pond on the right and then reach the base of a large dam that holds back the water of Old Beaver Pond. The beaver is an industrious mammal: it significantly alters its surroundings to create an acceptable habitat. Beaver dams generate ponds that provide the builders with food and protection. If beavers leave an area and the dams deteriorate, a change in the water level will lead to significant changes in the types of trees and plants in and around the abandoned dam. Ask the children whether beavers are still living here. What would indicate beaver activity? Look for a lodge, piles of bare, pointed sticks near the water, teethmarks on standing trees, branches that have been gnawed, and trees that have been downed.

If you find unusually high marks on trees, urge the kids to analyze how they got there. Did a beaver climb the tree trunk? Did another animal make the marks? (The correct answer: beavers chewed the trees during the winter, when they were standing on snowbanks.) Why do you think beavers chew trees? Do they eat wood? (No, they eat the inner bark, and are especially fond of newer branches.) Why, then, do they down mature trees? (To be able to reach the young branches on top!)

At one time, when beaver fur was highly coveted for coats and hats, the animals nearly became extinct at the hands of overzealous trappers. Due to stringent trapping rules and other conservation measures, their numbers have steadily increased and they are now fairly common in the Catskills.

Three-quarters mile from the start, the trail opens onto a lovely meadow, lined by spruce trees on the left and deciduous trees on the right. As you climb across the meadow, heading northwest, you may have to fight through brambles. The trail passes briefly through a belt of spruces and tracks across another open field. If there is a breeze, the kids can race with the wind, judging its progress by watching the grass bow down in waves. At the top of the field, the trail meets an overgrown woods road. Turn right (northeast) onto the road, soon entering another meadow. Dive back into the woods, cutting through a break in a stone wall. Imagine the old farm that once occupied this land. Animals must have grazed these pastures, contained by the ancient stones walls. Who will find the

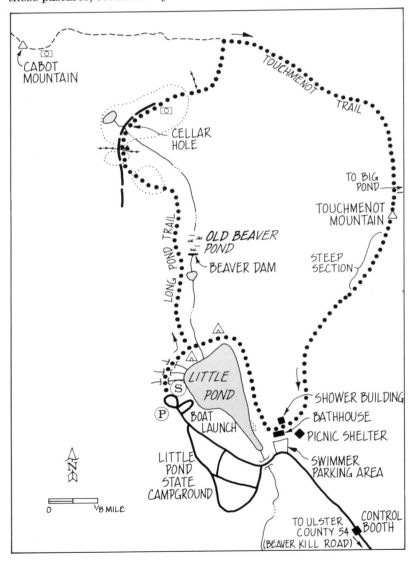

large erratic boulder just beyond the stone wall to the right? Who can climb to the top?

As the blazes lead across a vast field at about 1 mile, the kids' gaze will be diverted to the frog pond on the left as the adults take in the lovely Beaverkill Valley views to the right. Listen to the frog voices at the pond. How many different sounds can you hear? Can you distinguish the guttural quacking of the wood frog from the spring peeper's shrill voice? Do you hear the low rumble of a bullfrog? Partway across the field, avoid stepping in a cellar hole just off the path on the right. Continuing to bend eastward, the trail crests a grassy knoll. Here, the views stretch southward toward Little Pond and into Sullivan County. Depending on the mood and condition of your group, you may decide to spread out a picnic lunch and end the hike at this lovely spot.

To continue, cross the field on an easterly course. Soon, the grassy meadow surrenders to young woods. A stone wall crawls in from the left but never quite reaches the trail. After climbing a wooded hillside, the trail crests at 1.3 miles near an intersection with the red-blazed Touch-Me-Not Trail. (Energetic groups interested in adding a mile to the total distance can turn left on the seldom-traveled path to the top of Cabot Mountain. Beware of bothersome nettles along this trail, however.)

Turn right (east) onto the red-blazed trail to continue the original loop. Two-tenths mile from the intersection, the trail climbs a rugged, densely wooded slope. Give little ones a hand as you scale a slab of ledge. On the left, a narrow path leads through a crevice. Is anyone daring enough to attempt a brief side trip through this "squeezer"? Back on the main trail, climb to the top of the ridge, passing through stands of grand beech trees. American beeches are as easy to recognize by touch as by sight: their characteristic light gray bark is quite smooth.

The trail continues to snake through thick woodlands, pressing between ledge at 1.8 miles. Another winding ascent leads to a junction where a red-blazed side trail departs left toward Big Pond. You continue straight (south) toward Little Pond on the path marked in blue. As you approach the ambiguous top of Touchmenot Mountain (with views limited by the heavy woods), ledge intrudes on both sides of the trail. Two miles from the start, the trail embarks on a steep, 0.4-mile descent. The altitude that you gained gradually over 2 miles is lost in less than 0.5 mile! Did you descend fast enough to make your ears pop? As the trail levels, thick clusters of ferns crowd the path. At one time, ferns were one of the dominant plant forms on this planet.

After 0.3 mile of fairly level walking, listen for voices that grow in volume as you near Little Pond's swimming area. The trail approaches the pond's day-use area by a bathhouse. Stop for a swim or a few tricks on the playground equipment, and then find the yellow-blazed trail (initially a gravel road) that follows the shoreline. Pass picnic areas and campsites as you encircle the pond in a counterclockwise direction to return to your car.

47. Little Spring Brook

Type: Dayhike
Difficulty: Easy to moderate for children
Distance: 3 miles, round trip
Hiking time: 2.5 hours
High point/elevation gain: 2510 feet, 550 feet
Hikable: June–October
Map: NY/NJ Trail Conference Map 44

You expect to have company on Storm King, Lake Minnewaska, and Indian Ladder trails, (Hikes 9, 15, and 51). But what about when you, like Greta Garbo, "want to be alone"? Head for Little Spring Brook Trail, which winds through a remote area in the western Catskills beside a pleasant brook, passing a frog pond and leading to an overlook by way of the Pelnor Hollow Trail. This is a terrific hike for the whole family, especially if you have little guys who enjoy tracking down pond critters. Put together a "Pond Explorer's Kit" before you go, with shoes for wading, a fine-mesh net, a guidebook to pond life, a plastic container to hold a salamander or crayfish while you examine it up close, a magnifying glass, and a towel . . . just in case.

Remember, now, the best thing about this spot is its obscurity. So let's keep it just between us, OK?

From New York City, take the Thruway North to Exit 16 in Harriman. Follow NY 17 West to Exit 94 in Roscoe. Drive north on NY 206 for 6 miles and turn right onto gravel Little Spring Brook Road. In 1.1 miles, the road ends at a cul-de-sac. (If you continue straight ahead on what appears to be a driveway, you cross onto New York State Department of Environmental Conservation land.) Since parking is not permitted at the cul-de-sac, turn around and drive approximately 0.1 mile back down Little Spring Brook Road and park on the right-hand shoulder.

Head north on Little Spring Brook Road, returning to the cul-de-sac, and follow a woods road onto state property. At the official trailhead, a sign lists distances on the yellow-blazed Little Spring Brook Trail; the 0.6-mile measure to Pelnor Hollow Trail is accurate, though the other mileages are not. The yellow blazes lead hikers along the initially soggy, then washed out, woods road. As the trail trudges northward, Little Spring Brook tumbles by on the left. At 0.15 mile, the brook darts under the road in a culvert as a stone wall crawls along on the left.

One-quarter mile from the start, the road, now buried in thick grass, passes a great, shallow pond—muddy, murky, and full of frogs. Surely

A cut through an old pine plantation on the Pelnor Hollow Trail

the kids will want to stop and investigate. Can you hear the song of a spring peeper? The deep rumble of a bullfrog? Find a crayfish hiding under a rock near the shore or try to catch a dragonfly as it flutters past with its two pairs of pretty wings. Look for a water strider sweeping across the surface of the pond without making a ripple. Tiny hairs on the ends of its feet allow it to rest on top of the water without sinking. What kinds of birds gather near a pond like this? Do you see any red-winged blackbirds or swallows? Geese or cedar waxwings?

As you continue northward with the yellow blazes, Little Spring Brook now babbles along on the right, cradled within a cool ravine. Enduring stone walls bracket the trail. At 0.6 mile, the Little Spring Brook Trail ends unceremoniously at the edge of a clearing. Here, the blue-blazed Pelnor Hollow Trail veers right (east) and the Campbell Mountain Trail, combined with a wide snowmobile trail, goes straight (north). Follow the Pelnor Hollow foot trail, guided by a sign for the Mary Smith Trail, 0.8 mile away.

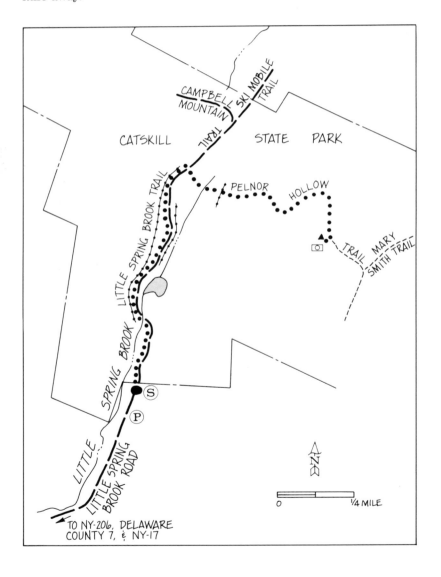

The narrow, blue-blazed trail winds through the woods for 0.1 mile, then crosses a seasonal section of Little Spring Brook on stones. (Who can hop across with the fewest steps?) Squeeze through a break in a stone wall to reach a lofty spruce and fir grove. How can you tell a spruce from a fir tree? Examine the needles: spruces have sharp, square needles and firs have flat needles that have an odor when they are rubbed. Can your little naturalists notice any other differences? (The cones on a fir tree grow upright; the cones on a spruce tree dangle from the ends of the branches.) Little ones will have to pick up their feet to avoid tripping on the roots snaking across the spongy path.

Leaving the evergreen forest, the trail climbs over loose, flat rocks that are slippery when wet. Oaks stretch into the sky and moss-covered rocks break through the soil underfoot. After 0.1 mile of climbing, the trail crests, curls right (south), and widens. Drop gently for 0.1 mile, watching for a tree with double blue blazes on the right. Beyond the double marks, turn right (southwest) onto a side trail, as the main trail begins to curl gently to the left. In 50 feet, you reach a glacial erratic boulder that perches on the edge of a cliff. If your group is agile and surefooted, walk around the left side (not the right side) of the boulder and jump over a crevice to a piece of ledge that has separated. Settle down for a picnic lunch, and enjoy the view of the distant western Catskills. We guarantee that you won't share this spot with any other hikers.

Retrace your steps to the car.

48. Trout and Mud Ponds

Type: Dayhike or overnight
Difficulty: Moderate for children
Distance: 4.5 miles, loop
Hiking time: 4.5 hours
High point/elevation gain: 2510 feet, 900 feet
Hikable: June–October
Map: NY/NJ Trail Conference Map 44

Water, water, water! We know kids love it, so we've included this hike, which encompasses one waterfall, two ponds, and more streams than you can count. Since a sinkful of tapwater will keep most kids amused on a rainy afternoon, imagine how many games your young hikers will invent on this route through the western Catskills. It is the length (4.5 miles), rather than the elevation gain, that makes this hike challenging for some little tykes. Allow plenty of time for the kids to take extended energy breaks, dawdle on stream banks, skim nets across the surfaces of the ponds, and even take a swim. If you think your gang might be better off tackling this trip in 2 days, bring overnight gear and pitch your tent near Trout Pond, taking care to follow the posted camping rules for restricted areas.

From New York City, take the Thruway North to Exit 16 in Harriman. Follow NY 17 West to Exit 93: "TO COOK'S FALLS." Drive northwest for 1 mile to Butternut Grove and turn north onto Russell Brook Road. Drive 3.8 miles to substantial shoulder parking on the left. (This is a "seasonal limited use highway," unmaintained from December 1 through April 1.)

Head southwestward on Russell Brook Road. Almost immediately, turn hard right (north) onto an access road. Dodge a metal gate and drop toward hurrying Russell Brook. After crossing the brook on a footbridge, cut through a clearing used (illegally) for camping. When the road forks at 0.1 mile, the Trout Pond Trail heads northwestward as you turn left (southwest) onto another gravel road, marked with the blue blazes of the Mud Pond Trail and the orange markings of a snowmobile trail. Just beyond the fork, the Mud Pond Trail leads over a sturdy footbridge spanning a stream and begins a moderate ascent. At 0.4 mile, cross a seasonal stream on stones.

At 0.6 mile, an attractive gorge with another seasonal stream comes into view. Shortly, hop across the stream in three or four steps and embark on a gentle climb through spruce forest, now trending westward. Who will be the first to spot a trailside spider's web? (Hint: Look closely at the barren lower branches of spruce trees.) Do the kids know why spiders don't get caught in their own webs? (In addition to the sticky thread it produces, a spider incorporates strands of "nonsticky" thread in its web so that it is able to walk across without getting stuck.)

Nearly 1 mile from the start, the trail opens onto a meadow that nurtures a few isolated pines. Tell the kids to push aside the tall grass to look for woodchuck den holes. Woodchucks, common to the Catskills, prefer to live in clearings where they can see a predator approaching. If you find a hole, you may find its inhabitant, since woodchucks never wander very far away from the safety of their homes. As it divides the field, the trail crests and begins to descend.

Beyond the field, a sign at a trail junction indicates you have come 1.1 miles from the Russell Brook parking lot; Mud Pond, it promises, is another 0.3 mile straight ahead (northwest). An indistinct trail meanders left toward the park boundary, while to the right (north) the Mud Pond Trail marches 2.1 miles to Trout Pond and completes the loop to the Russell Brook parking area in 3.5 miles. For now, continue straight toward

Water trickles over Russell Brook Falls during a dry spell.

Mud Pond. As you descend gradually through the woods, tell the kids to look for cellar holes on either side of the trail. (Warn the kids that where there are cellar holes, there may be old wells, still filled with water, but no longer covered.) Old homesites often yield treasures such as bottles, tools, or dishes. Watch through the trees for glimpses of Mud Pond.

Two-tenths mile beyond the intersection, the snowmobile trail continues straight as you turn left (south) to follow a woods road toward Mud Pond. After tracking across a soggy pasture, the trail reaches the wild bank of Mud Pond. True to its name, this pretty little pond has a very mucky bottom, although you can walk along the firm bank for a good distance in either direction. The kids can change into their wading shoes and search for water critters. Unpack the coat hangers, nylon stockings, empty peanut butter jars, and magnifying glasses. Send the kids on a "hunt" for minnows, tadpoles, water striders, and pond skaters. Ask the kids how they distinguish frogs from toads. (Toads are dry and bumpy while frogs are smooth and slick.) Observant little naturalists may have noticed that most frogs have teeth and most toads don't. Those who prefer not to wade can skip stones across the still water. The grassy area above the pond's bank is a nice area to picnic or just relax.

Return to the intersection 1.1 miles from the parking area and turn left (north), still following the blue blazes of the Mud Pond Trail (and the orange snowmobile markers). The initially grassy path rises gently and, 0.2 mile from the intersection, wanders through an overgrown field and then crosses a seasonal stream. One-half mile later, the character of the trail has changed, and you tread on rocks, pushing aside wild blackberry and raspberry bushes in an area known as Cherry Ridge. In another 0.25 mile, a faint woods road joins from the right.

Finally the road embarks on a descent, and shows signs of mild erosion. Can you spot any garter snakes slithering among the rocks? As the road arcs southeastward, it drops moderately through mixed deciduous woods. The kids will revive along this stretch since you are descending. Peer through the trees for the shimmering water of Trout Pond. The first one to spot it wins first use of the net!

Two miles from Mud Pond, you reach the northern end of Trout Pond near the site of an old cabin. Mud Pond Trail ends as Trout Pond Trail leads left (away from the pond) and right, along the shoreline. A sign posted here indicates that your car is 1.4 miles away (all gradually downhill). Turn right and follow the eastern bank of the long, thin pond. If you've decided to spend the night here, set up your tent in the woods to the left of the trail (more than 150 feet away from the trail and the pond).

At the pond's southern shore is an outhouse and a sign pointing toward the parking area, now 0.9 mile away. Explore the shoreline; sections

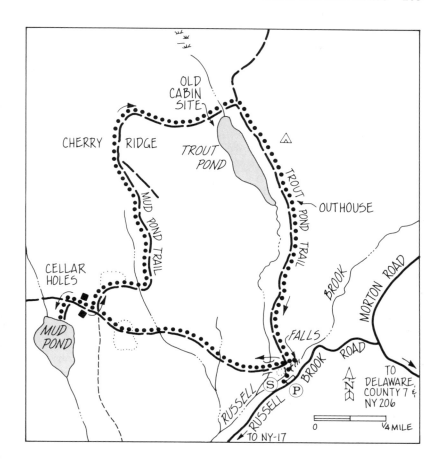

are actually sandy. Dive in if the weather's warm. Back on the main trail, begin a steady descent on the wide woods road, tracking beside a cool ravine on the right that carries a tributary to Russell Brook. Pass the intersection with the Mud Pond Trail and return to the footbridge over Russell Brook (but don't cross it). Head upstream, hugging the western bank. Less than 0.1 mile from the footbridge, you'll discover the delightful Russell Brook Falls. Stop for a rest before returning to the footbridge and retracing the final 0.1 mile to your car.

Note: Use of this area is restricted due to overuse. Camping is forbidden within 150 feet of a stream, pond, or spring. Cutting standing trees, alive or dead, is not permitted.

49. Mine Kill State Park

Type: Dayhike
Difficulty: Easy for children
Distance: 2.8 miles, round trip
Hiking time: 3 hours
High point/elevation gain: 650 feet, 200 feet
Hikable: June–November
Map: USGS Gilboa

This hike is for the birds . . . and the flowers, and the trees, and the deer. All that you need to maintain the kids' interest on this easy hiking loop are a magnifying glass, binoculars, and a nature guidebook to help with the identification of various plants, birds, and animal tracks.

Mine Kill State Park, 500 wooded acres nestled in the rolling hills of the Schoharie Valley, offers not only hiking trails, but picnic and games areas (where equipment for softball, basketball, and volleyball may be borrowed), an Olympic-size swimming pool, and a wading pool. Special family programs are offered throughout the summer.

From New York City, take the Thruway North to Exit 21. Follow NY 23 West approximately 40 miles to Grand Gorge and the junction with NY 30. Drive 5.6 miles on NY 30 North and turn right into a driveway, following the sign to Mine Kill Falls Overlook. Park in the expansive parking area.

From the sign, head northwestward on a gravel path that bisects a clipped field lined with pine trees. (You may want to spread out your post-hike picnic lunch on one of the tables near the trailhead.) Drop into the woods, avoiding (for now) the side trail that turns right. Descend the fenced-in steps that lead to a platform perched high above Mine Kill Falls. (No need to worry about the children near this waterfall.) The falls, tucked in a deep, narrow ravine well below this observation deck, are somewhat obscured by foliage—you'll have a better view shortly as you hike around to the base.

Return to the junction with the side trail and turn left. This wide path winds under stands of oak, hemlock, and pine trees on a moderate descent. Ask the kids a nature question: must plants and animals keep growing to stay alive? (Plants must continue to grow since their cells constantly die and need to be replaced, but the same is not true of animals.)

Follow the sound of the boisterous falls, leaving the path to explore the edge of the pool below the falls. (Swimming and wading are not permitted here.) From the base of the sheer cliffs, you have a good view of all three tiers of this dramatic waterfall.

Head northeastward from the falls, winding beside Mine Kill (Creek). As the trail becomes increasingly rocky, have your young hikers pick out stones shaped like triangles, diamonds, or rectangles. One-tenth mile from the falls, follow the side trail that splits left, leading to the most manageable stone-to-stone crossing of the creek. (In the spring or after substantial rains, this crossing may be quite difficult.) The bridge that once spanned the brook farther downstream has been removed.

The trail works its way up the brook's opposite bank to crest near an overgrown jeep road. Follow this grassy road northeastward under a canopy of stately pines; in 0.15 mile, a stream slips under the trail through a culvert. The trail begins a gentle rise and shortly intersects another jeep road. Turn left (north) onto the road on an ascent. Can the kids guess how Mine Kill State Park got its name? (It's not as dramatic as it sounds: "Kill" is from the Dutch word *kil*, meaning "creek," and the "Mine" came from the copper mine that was situated nearby.)

After a moderate climb, you come upon marker 10 of the Mine Kill State Park self-guided nature trail. (The pamphlet available at the park headquarters is very interesting and informative, but not helpful on the nature trail: the numbered items do not correspond to their written descriptions.)

Look right to see piles of stones, reminders of long-ago pastures. As you hike, look for other signs that this forest was once farmed land. Look for more stone walls, lengths of barbed wire fence (available by the late 1800s), and spiny plants arranged in rows, all of which contained grazing animals many years ago. Another clue to past farming activity is the apple trees that provided food and drink to the settlers. Today, they feed the white-tailed deer, squirrels, raccoons, mice, foxes, and many types of birds that inhabit the park.

Bear right (northeast) at an intersection at marker 11, as the other branch of the trail heads left (northwest). Children can close their eyes and rub tree trunks, concentrating on the feel of the bark. Notice the different types of bark: the rugged coat of the shagbark hickory tree contrasts with the American beech's smooth bark. As new bark is continuously formed, the old bark is pushed out, causing it to stretch, crack, and peel. The bark on different types of trees reacts differently to this process. Kids, can you name some things that bark protects the tree from? (Fire, heat, cold, rain, insects. . . .)

Although the trail drops off steeply to the right, parents needn't worry since the edge is well guarded by hemlocks. Can you spot stumps and felled trees in the woods? These are left over from logging operations that took place here during the last century. Bark from hemlock trees was used in tanning leather and dyeing fabric, so loggers often stripped the bark and left behind the rest of the tree. Can the kids guess what other uses people have for bark? Any child who guesses that some spices (like cinnamon), certain medicines, and commercial cork all come from bark wins a piggyback ride for 30 paces.

The trail tracks along a stone wall, passing markers 13 and 14. At an intersection 0.75 mile from the start, turn left (north), guided by an arrow, to climb a steep slope. Log steps facilitate the ascent, carrying you past signpost 15. Quickly, you arrive at an intersection with a grassy path; turn right (north).

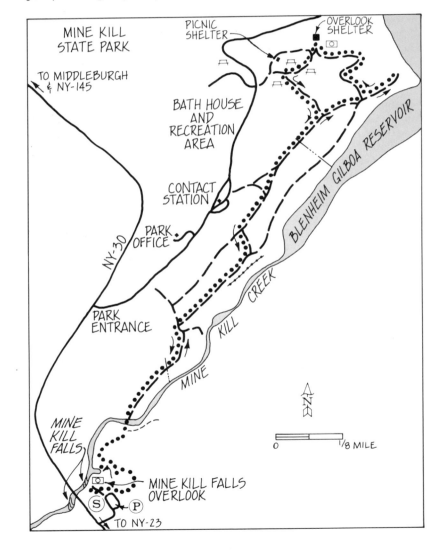

Follow this grassy path northeastward, hiking by markers 4, 3, and 2. If you spot an American beech with its characteristic pair of triangular nuts in a spiny husk, look for signs of wild turkeys—they are attracted to the nuts. Although these sizable birds roost in trees at night, they build nests of leaves on the ground under a log or bush.

From the 0.9- to the 1.3-mile mark, avoid side trails that split left and right. Continue straight toward the head of a reservoir, where Mine Kill (Creek) and the Schoharie River merge. Although swimming is not allowed here, the kids can skip stones and look in the water and along the shore for aquatic insects, frogs, salamanders, and fish. Perhaps you will spot a fox or a white-tailed deer pausing for a drink.

Backtrack and turn right onto the first side trail. The trail passes under a canopy of pines and enters an open field. Sweep northward along the meadow's left side on a clipped path. Climbing steadily, the trail cuts right into the field, then curls left, passing birdhouses (bald eagles have been spotted soaring over the park). Soon, the path crests at an overlook shelter that provides good local views. Look eastward to see the New York Power Authority's Blenheim-Gilboa Pumped Storage Project and the 430-acre lower reservoir you just visited. Behind the power plant, at the top of Brown Mountain, the trees part to reveal the upper reservoir. The water falls from the upper reservoir through a shaft inside Brown Mountain, creating a force that turns the powerhouse turbines and generates power. Water is pumped back up to the upper reservoir and the process is repeated.

From the overlook, walk westward along the paved path. Near the swings and picnic shelter, turn left off the paved path onto a mowed area that funnels into a hiking trail. Follow this path, bordered by pines on the left and a scruffy field on the right. When you reach an intersection, turn right to follow a trail from the initial leg of the hike. Return to the falls, and then your car, the way you came.

Note: If you choose to drive through the main park entrance, you must pay $3 for your car. Use of the wading, diving, and swimming pools costs $1 per adult and 50 cents per child. The main park closes at 9 P.M.; the Mine Kill Falls Overlook area closes at 8 P.M.

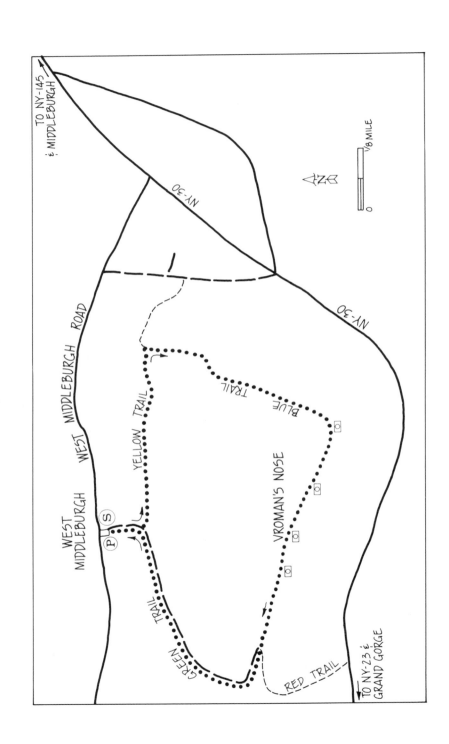

50. Vroman's Nose

Type:	Dayhike
Difficulty:	Moderate for children
Distance:	2 miles, loop
Hiking time:	2.5 hours
High point/elevation gain:	1220 feet, 480 feet
Hikable:	April–October
Map:	USGS Middleburgh

Rising abruptly to an elevation of 1220 feet, Vroman's Nose dominates the expansive lowlands, a solitary island in the grassy sea of the Schoharie Valley. Short and sweet, the hike to the tip of the nose yields dizzying views across farmland to the Catskill Mountains. The Vroman's Nose Preservation Corporation was formed in 1983 to preserve this unique natural area.

To get the nose concept, the kids will have to view the cliff from the east, with their heads tilted at an angle. (Mr. Vroman is lying on his back.) If your family had been in charge of naming this piece of land, what would you have called it?

From New York City, drive on the Thruway North to Exit 21. Follow NY 23 West for approximately 10 miles; turn right onto NY 145 in Cairo. Drive about 30 miles on NY 145 to Middleburgh. From the junction of NY 145 and NY 30 in Middleburgh, take NY 30 South. In 0.6 mile, turn right onto West Middleburgh Road and follow it for 0.6 mile to a substantial off-road parking area on the left near a sign for Vroman's Path.

Follow the jeep road along the right side of a pasture, heading southward. A barbed wire fence joins from the right as the trail, marked in green, squeezes between two fields. The Green Trail enters the woods as a wide foot trail, soon reaching an intersection with the less-traveled Yellow Trail. Turn left (east) onto the Yellow Trail as the Green Trail curves sharply right (west). (You are taking the shorter, steeper route to the summit and will return on the gentler Green Trail.)

The Yellow Trail winds easily uphill through woods. Compare the oak trees with the pines along the trail. Do the kids know the difference between deciduous and coniferous trees? (Deciduous trees lose their leaves in autumn and coniferous trees have cones and always retain some of their needles.) Curling slightly southeastward, the trail makes sporadic uphill surges along rolling terrain. As the elevation increases, the trail passes through stands of hemlock, birch, and other hardwoods. (Can your young hikers pick out the conifers in this forest?)

The Yellow Trail ends unceremoniously at an intersection with the

Blue Trail, 0.5 mile from the start. Turn right (southwest) onto the Blue Trail to climb steeply toward the summit as the eastern branch of the Blue Trail descends straight ahead. On the final 0.1 mile of the ascent, your calf muscles will feel the strain as you lean into the demanding slope. Don't let the kids lead the way on this section of trail: the sheer cliffs ahead are dangerous for unsupervised exploring. Just shy of the 1-mile mark, warn the kids to stay back from the edge as you approach the summit.

The trail flirts with the edge of the 600-foot cliffs, inching westward along the ridge top. Parents (and kids) who are uncomfortable with the proximity to the drop-off can walk through the woods, well back from the cliffs, on overgrown side trails. From the escarpment, you have spectacular views to the southwest of the Catskills, to the south over the Schoharie Creek and the surrounding hills, and to the east over the village of Middleburgh. Watch for turkey buzzards soaring on the thermals (powerful up-currents of heated air).

The escarpment continues westward for 0.35 mile. Directly below, farmers' fields connect in a patchwork pattern that stretches across the Schoharie Valley. Watch the cloud shadows sweeping across the pastureland. Many years ago, Indian villages and campsites dotted these rich flood plains.

This is how birds see the world. If the kids could take flight from here, where would they go? To the cornfields below or to the peak of a distant mountain?

At the far end of the exposed ridge is a large, flat section of Hamilton sandstone. These thin sheets of sandstone (or flagstone) have been used for sidewalks in Albany, Schenectady, and other nearby cities. Scan the rocks for scratches and chatter marks, 50,000-year-old markings left by a retreating glacier.

The crude fireplaces along the trail were built (by chance) in the vicinity of long-ago Indian campsites. The kids can look for tiny chips of chert and flint and pieces of arrowheads. What do you think the Indians ate for supper?

As you track along the escarpment, the trail markings change from blue to green. Between the flat ledge and the fire hearths, the trail leaves the exposed rock and drops moderately down a wooded hillside. As the trail curls northwestward, leaving the cliffs behind, you have final, fleeting glimpses into the valley. Count the tiny houses and the Matchbox-size cars moving along NY 30. Shortly, the trail passes through a small clearing that surrounds a fire hearth. At the junction with the Red Trail 1.5 miles into the hike, head straight (west), still on the wide Green Trail, and drop downhill toward West Middleburgh Road.

Under a ceiling of pines, the Green Trail sweeps in a clockwise arch to the north, then east. The descent is gradual, although the slope from right to left is initially steep. Remember the Indian campsites? The kids can pretend to be Indians hunting for their dinner. Can they creep through

A bird's-eye view of farmlands from Vroman's Nose

the woods without making a sound? Slowpokes can play rabbits while other kids pose as the Indians hunting them down. See how quickly the pace picks up!

Finally, as the barbed wire fence encroaches on the left side of the trail, you reach the original junction with the Yellow Trail. Turn left (north) and descend through the sloping fields for another 0.1 mile to your car.

51. Indian Ladder

Type:	Dayhike
Difficulty:	Easy for children
Distance:	1 mile, loop
Hiking time:	1 hour
High point/elevation gain:	1000 feet, 100 feet
Hikable:	April–October
Map:	USGS Altamont

It doesn't say so in the brochure, but I believe that exclamation points were invented on the Indian Ladder Trail. The path follows a ledge along the breathtaking limestone cliffs of the Helderberg Escarpment, with caves, waterfalls, bridges, and far-reaching vistas adding interest at nearly every turn. In addition, this easy walk provides the kids with some geology lessons and Native American history as you follow a former Mohawk Indian route next to one of the richest fossil-bearing formations in the world.

Along the spectacular Indian Ladder Geology Trail

Don't come expecting a solitary, wilderness hike, though—not only is this trail immensely popular, but the 2200-acre John Boyd Thatcher State Park that encompasses it caters to summertime crowds with a variety of family attractions. Visit the Olympic-size swimming pool (and the kiddie pool for toddlers); the games area with courts for paddle tennis, handball, basketball and volleyball; the two playground areas and several baseball diamonds; and the picnic sites with tables, fireplaces, and charcoal grills. Refreshment stands and toilet facilities make this family hike a little more civilized than most. The walk takes less than an hour, but you'll have no trouble spending a delightful day here—with lots of other folks who had the same great idea!

 From New York City, take the Thruway North to Albany. From Albany, drive west on NY 85 for 16 miles to the intersection with NY 157 in New Salem. Follow NY 157 West (also called Thatcher Park Road) for 3.3 miles. Turn right into the parking area for the Lagrange Bush Picnic Area and Indian Ladder Trail. (There is no charge to enter the park here on weekdays, but you must pay $3 per car on weekends. If you drive another 0.5 mile on NY 157, you'll reach the parking area for the Indian Ladder Picnic Area and Play Area. Here, you pay $3 per car every day; the fee includes the use of the swimming pools and play areas.)

From the western side of the Lagrange Bush parking area, follow the sidewalk a short distance to a junction. Here, turn right (north) onto another paved path. You quickly reach an intersection with gravel paths; continue straight, now on gravel, and descend a flight of flagstone steps between wooden fences. Continue your descent on a metal staircase (36 steps) to arrive at the Indian Ladder Geology Trail (also known as the Lower Bear Path), which runs along the tremendous Helderberg Escarpment. Parents will appreciate the fence that protects the right side of the trail whenever the drop is precipitous.

Heading northeastward, big people must crouch to scoot under the set of massive ledges that overhangs the trail (preschoolers will smugly walk upright). Drop down another metal staircase for 24 more steps, passing station 7 (you pass the stations in descending order numerically, but that doesn't make any difference). The mound at the base of the cliff, called a talus slope, is caused by the accumulation of material that fell from the face of the cliff. Look up to see the top of the escarpment, 80 feet above you. No need to worry about motivating kids on this hike— the tremendous cliffs stretching ahead of you are inspiration enough.

Follow the heavily traveled trail to Minelot Falls, marked as station 6, where the kids will delight in the broad cave that extends 25 feet into the massive cliff wall. The cliffs are composed of Manlius and Coeymans limestone formations. The dark blue Manlius limestone is more subject to erosion and has been cut back farther than the overhanging Coeymans limestone, which is thicker and more resistant to the effects of weathering. At this point, the erosion of the Manlius limestone has created a cavernous pocket that beckons little explorers. In time, the large overhanging blocks will break off from the cliff face, as evidenced by the large chunk of rock in the deep gorge beneath the falls on the right. Looking eastward from this point, you can see the Taconic Mountains in the distance.

The trail continues to snake along the ledge beside the cliffs, following the route used long ago by the Mohawk Indians on their journey from the Albany trading post to their homes in the Schoharie Valley. Soon, you reach station 5, near Outlet Falls and Outlet Creek. After a heavy rain, the falls rush with such torrential force that you walk behind them on the trail. The creek does not carry the volume of water that it once did; most of the water drains underground now with just a trickle seeping out of a broad, squat cave.

Cross a swift stream over a footbridge at station 4, where you can see evidence of a so-called sinkhole (formed when underground caves collapse to form surface depressions), common in limestone regions. Because limestone is so soluble, the water that seeps into the joints gradually dissolves the rock until caves and depressions form. Most caves in this region are still being formed—they are quite small and have water running through them.

The trail curls with the cliffs and passes a yawning cave with a curved ceiling. The kids will want to examine the inside of this cave, perhaps in search of the fossils of sea creatures (trilobites) embedded in the limestone. (Hundreds of millions of years ago, a shallow sea covered this entire area.) As you pass station 3, you can see more evidence of limestone's susceptibility to erosion. The vertical cracks and joints enlarge as more groundwater seeps through them.

Curling left (west), the trail passes along another section of Manlius

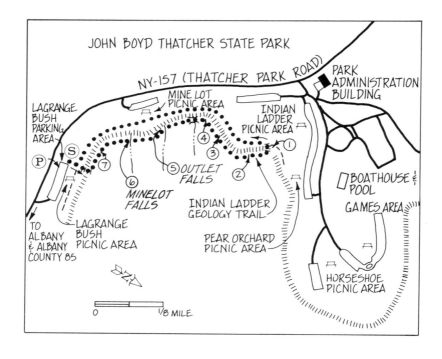

limestone formation (at station 2) with the more resistant Coeymans limestone forming another overhang. At the top of the formation, running between the two types of limestone, is the ledge known as Upper Bear Path.

Climb two sets of 30-step metal stairways to arrive near the top of the cliffs. Pause to study the Coeymans limestone along the stairway, looking for more remains of tiny sea animals. As it curves left (southwest), the trail runs through a passage between sections of 10-foot-high ledge. As you pass through this old road cut at station 1, you're hiking on a route that was once part of Indian Ladder Road (dating back to 1828), which connected Albany with the Schoharie Valley. In this area, long-ago Indians laid a notched tree trunk against the cliff wall to act as a ladder, providing this trail with its current name.

Returning to the top of the ridge on flagstone steps, turn left on a gravel path and wind along the top of the cliffs, guarded at the edge by a sturdy wooden fence. The easterly views are among the best in the state, encompassing the Adirondacks, Taconics, and peaks in Vermont's Green Mountains. Three-tenths mile from the flagstone steps, pass through a picnic area with barbecue hearths and return to your car.

Note: Pets must be leashed. The Indian Ladder Trail is open from 8 A.M. to dusk, May 1 through November 15, weather permitting.

Addresses

Appalachian Mountain Club
202 East 39th Street
New York, NY 10016
(212) 986-1430

Appalachian Trail Conference
P.O. Box 807
Harpers Ferry, WV 25425
(304) 535-6331

U.S. Geological Survey
Federal Center
Denver, CO 80225
(Distributes USGS maps)

Catskill 3500 Club
41 Morley Drive
Wyckoff, NJ 07481
(201) 447-2653

Catskill Center for Conservation
 and Development, Inc.
Arkville, NY 12406
(914) 586-2611

Delorme Publishing Company
Main Street
Box 298
Freeport, ME 04032
(Publishes *Atlas* and *Gazetteer*
 for New York State)

Friends of Mills Mansion
P.O. Box 416
Spartanburg, NY 12580

Indian Ladder/John Boyd
Thatcher State Park
(518) 872-1237

Lake Minnewaska State Park
(914) 255-0753

Little Pond Public Campground
(914) 439-5480

Manitoga
P.O. Box 350
Garrison, NY 10524
(914) 424-3812

Mills Mansion
(914) 889-4100

Mine Kill State Park
(518) 827-6111

Mohonk Preserve
1000 Mountain Rest Road
Mohonk Lake
New Paltz, NY 12561
(914) 225-0919

The Nature Conservancy
Lower Hudson Chapter
223 Katonah Avenue
Katonah, NY 10536

The Nature Conservancy
New York Field Office
1736 Western Avenue
Albany, NY 12203

New York/New Jersey Trail
 Conference
G.P.O. Box 2250
New York, NY 10116
(212) 685-9699

New York State Department of
Economic Development
Division of Tourism
One Commerce Plaza
Albany, NY 12245
(518) 474-4116 or 1-800-225-5697

New York State Department of
Transportation
Map Information Unit
State Campus Building 4
Room 105
Albany, NY 12232
(518) 457-3555

New York State–operated
campgrounds
1-800-456-CAMP

North/South Lake Public
Campground
(518) 589-5058

Office of Parks, Recreation, and
Historic Preservation
Empire State Plaza
Albany, NY 12238
(518) 474-0456

Ogden Mills and Ruth
Livingston Mills State Park
(914) 889-4646

Palisades Interstate Park
Commission
Bear Mountain, NY 10911
(914) 786-2701
(212) 562-8688
(Information on Bear Moun-
tain–Harriman state parks and
Storm King)

Pawling Nature Preserve
Quaker Lake Road

P.O. Box 599
Pawling, NY 12564

Taconic State Park, Rudd Pond
(518) 789-3059

Department of Environmental Conservation Offices

50 Wolf Road
Albany, NY 12233
(518) 457-2500
(Headquarters, camping
information)

Dutchess, Putnam, and
Westchester Counties
Box C
Millbrook, NY 12545
(914) 255-5453

Region 3 Headquarters: Ulster
and Sullivan Counties
21 South Putt Corners Road
New Paltz, NY 12561
(914) 255-5453

Region 4 District Office:
Schoharie and Delaware
Counties
Jefferson Road
Stamford, NY 12167
(607) 652-7364

Weather Information

National Weather Service:
(212) 315-2704 or 2705; 10 A.M.
to 4 P.M.
Albany (recorded):
(518) 476-1122
Kingston (recorded):
(914) 331-5555
Sullivan County (recorded):
(914) 791-9555

Index

CYNTHIA and THOMAS LEWIS are residents of East Sullivan, New Hampshire. Cynthia is a full-time mother and author of several books, including *Mother's First Year*. Tom is an environmental chemist. Avid outdoorspeople, they explored every corner of New England on a tandem bicycle and on foot to write *Best Hikes With Children in Connecticut, Massachusetts, and Rhode Island* and *Best Hikes With Children in Vermont, New Hampshire, and Maine*, also from The Mountaineers. They shared these and their recent Catskill and Hudson River Valley adventures with their two children, ages five and three.

THE MOUNTAINEERS, founded in 1906, is a non-profit outdoor activity and conservation club, whose mission is "to explore, study, preserve and enjoy the natural beauty of the outdoors...." Based in Seattle, Washington, the club is now the third largest such organization in the United States, with 15,000 members and five branches throughout Washington State.

The Mountaineers sponsors both classes and year-round outdoor activities in the Pacific Northwest, which include hiking, mountain climbing, ski-touring, snowshoeing, bicycling, camping, kayaking and canoeing, nature study, sailing, and adventure travel. The club's conservation division supports environmental causes through educational activities, sponsoring legislation, and presenting informational programs. All club activities are led by skilled, experienced volunteers, who are dedicated to promoting safe and responsible enjoyment and preservation of the outdoors.

The Mountaineers Books, an active, non-profit publishing program of the club, produces guidebooks, instructional texts, historical works, natural history guides, and works on environmental conservation. All books produced by The Mountaineers are aimed at fulfilling the club's mission.

If you would like to participate in these organized outdoor activities or the club's programs, consider a membership in The Mountaineers. For information and an application, write or call The Mountaineers, Club Headquarters, 300 Third Avenue West, Seattle, Washington 98119; (206) 284-6310.

Send or call for our catalog of over 300 outdoor books:
The Mountaineers Books
1001 SW Klickitat Way, Suite 201
Seattle, WA 98134
1-800-553-4453